Childhood Lost

Childhood Lost
How American Culture Is Failing Our Kids

EDITED BY SHARNA OLFMAN

Childhood in America

Westport, Connecticut
London

Library of Congress Cataloging-in-Publication Data

Childhood lost : how American culture is failing our kids / edited by
  Sharna Olfman.
      p. cm. — (Childhood in America)
    Includes bibliographical references and index.
    ISBN 0–275–98139–8 (alk. paper)
    1. Children—United States—Social conditions—20th century. 2. Children—
United States—Social conditions—21st century. 3. Children—Government
policy—United States. 4. Family policy—United States. 5. Children—Health
and hygiene—United States. I. Olfman, Sharna. II. Series.
HQ792.U5C41995 2005
306.85′0973—dc22   2004028036

British Library Cataloguing in Publication Data is available.

Library of Congress Catalog Card Number: 2004028036
ISBN: 0–275–98139–8

First published in 2005

Praeger Publishers, 88 Post Road West, Westport, CT 06881
An imprint of Greenwood Publishing Group, Inc.
www.praeger.com

Printed in the United States of America

The paper used in this book complies with the
Permanent Paper Standard issued by the National
Information Standards Organization (Z39.48–1984).

10 9 8 7 6 5 4 3

Copyright Acknowledgments

Every reasonable effort has been made to trace the owners of copyright materials
in this book, but in some instances this has proven impossible. The author
and publisher will be glad to receive information leading to more complete
acknowledgments in subsequent printings of the book and in the meantime
extend their apologies for any omissions.

For my husband Daniel Burston, a kindred spirit in all things

Contents

Acknowledgments

I wish to express heartfelt thanks to all of the contributors to *Childhood Lost*, each of whom have dedicated much of their working lives to the betterment of children's lives. Their chapters create a powerful narrative about children's irreducible needs and the village that we can and must create for them. The work of Stanley Greenspan and Stuart Shanker, co-chairs of the Council on Human Development, has been an invaluable source of information for this project. Raffi, founder of Child Honoring and child advocate extraordinaire, has expanded my vision and sense of hope that we can indeed "turn this world around" for future generations. Greenwood acquisitions editor Deborah Carvalko was quick to recognize the worth of this book and is a pleasure to work with. Special thanks go to Kim Bell, chair of the Department of Humanities and Human Sciences at Point Park University, for her unfailing support. Katherine Henderson, president of Point Park University, and Susan White, vice president of Institutional Advancement, have been exceptionally generous in their support of the Childhood and Society Symposium, which served as a think tank for many of the ideas that are presented here. My mother Bess Olfman is a constant source of affirmation, and my father Mitchell Olfman is a paragon of courage and of acting on the courage of one's convictions. My beloved children Adam and Gavriela are a wellspring of joy and optimism. I reserve my deepest gratitude for my husband Daniel Burston, an intellectual's intellectual with a heart to match.

Introduction

Sharna Olfman

The rich diversity of cultures created by humankind is a testament to our ability to develop and adapt in diverse ways. But however varied different cultures may be, children are not endlessly malleable: they all share basic psychological and physical needs that must be met to ensure healthy development. *Childhood Lost* examines the extent to which American culture meets children's irreducible needs. Without question, many children growing up in the United States lead privileged lives. They have been spared the ravages of war, poverty, malnourishment, sexism, and racism. However, despite our considerable resources, not all our children share these privileges. Indeed, in the current cultural climate, many children are taxed beyond their capacity for healthy adaptation, and parenting has become intolerably labor-intensive.

Although elected officials across the political spectrum profess their commitment to "family values," national policies that support family life are woefully lacking and significantly inferior to those in all other wealthy nations. As a result, American families are burdened by

- inadequate parental leave and nonexistent child sick leave;
- a healthcare system that does not provide universal coverage for children;

- a minimum wage that is not a living wage;
- "welfare to work" policies that require thousands of mothers to return to forty-hour work weeks but fail to provide them with affordable, regulated, high-quality childcare options;
- a two-tiered public education system that delivers inferior education to poor children and frequently ignores individual differences in learning styles and talents;
- entertainment and gaming industries that have been given the mandate to police themselves, exposing children to graphic depictions of sex and violence and undermining parental authority and values;
- an unregulated advertising industry that spends over $15 billion annually in direct marketing to children, shaping lifetime addictions to junk food, alcohol, and cigarettes, and contributing to a childhood obesity epidemic that is poised to become the leading cause of death in the United States;
- weak environmental protection policies that have allowed tens of thousands of toxins to erode our air, soil, and water, undermining children's physical, neurological, and endocrinological development.

Hundreds of volumes have already been written about specific stressors in children's lives, such as the impacts of media violence, marketing to children, education reform, etc. While each of these issues is of critical importance and must be understood and analyzed in its own right, this anthology demonstrates how all of these seemingly disparate stressors are intimately interconnected. Consider the following example:

Sam—a child living in poverty—is exposed to toxins such as mold and cockroach droppings, both of which are known triggers for asthma in his decrepit apartment. He lives in a high crime area, so his mother encourages him to spend more time indoors watching TV, increasing his exposure to the relentless efforts of advertisers and an endless stream of violent and sexual programming. Although she wishes that she could afford better fare, his mom buys mainly junk food because it is cheap and filling. Sam's sedentary, junk food lifestyle explains his obesity. At his school, leaded paint is peeling from the walls, the heating system works intermittently, and the playground is a small patch of concrete. His 40 classmates use dated textbooks and science equipment. Art, music, and physical education have been eliminated from the curriculum in order to make time to prep for standardized tests. Sam misses several weeks of school because his family has no health insurance to treat his asthma. When he does attend, he fares poorly because lack of exercise, poor diet, and hours of daily television viewing—an established risk factor for Attention Deficit Hyperactivity Disorder—have undermined his ability to concentrate. Sam's school, which serves predominantly poor, high-need kids, has just lost its Title One funding due to low standardized test scores.

In Sam's story, we see some of the links between poverty and exposure to environmental toxins, media deregulation, and school "reform," and their synergistic impact upon children's physical, psychological, and academic functioning.

In addition to their intricate interconnections, childhood stressors are linked in a more fundamental way. They all speak to the fact that despite claims to the contrary, America has not given children's welfare high priority. We stand virtually alone among wealthy nations in our failure to create national policies that ensure the health, safety, and integrity of families and children.

Why have we not created such policies? Part of the answer lies in the beliefs and values that undergird our culture. First, Americans have a deep faith in and fascination with technologies that remove us farther and farther from the natural world and the constraints of our bodies—even as they destroy our ecosystems and undermine our physical and mental health. So enamored are we of our machines that the information-processing model of thinking, with the computer as its guiding metaphor, has become the backbone of American educational philosophy. Second, Americans give primacy to individual rights and freedoms even when those rights and freedoms undermine humane consideration of our collective responsibilities to children, families, and communities. Our uncritical embrace of technologies and our relentless defense and pursuit of individual goals and pleasures explains

- why we are not deeply alarmed that our kids are interacting with unregulated screen technologies for more hours every day than any other activity but sleep;
- why we don't demand that our government ensure that all children have access to healthcare and childcare;
- why we confuse the ability to download and process facts with real education;
- why we are so out of touch with children's bedrock human needs for close physical and emotional attachments, fashioned by millions of years of evolution;
- why we feel so few qualms about destroying our ecosystem.

Our runaway pursuit of individualism leads us to defend the rights of corporate CEOs to pay their workers slave wages, the rights of pornographers to make their Websites available to anyone who can turn on a computer, the rights of moviemakers to expose children to graphic acts of violence, and the rights of alcohol and tobacco companies to spawn the next generation of addicts. Tragically, in the process, we have trampled upon our children's fundamental right to grow up in a wholesome environment that supports physical, emotional, and intellectual well-being. Record levels of childhood obesity, asthma, high school failure, psychiatric disturbance, youth suicide, and preteen sex speak to the fact that we are failing our children. The time has come to acknowledge that ensuring a healthy generation of children is not a private matter but a national priority. It is time to temper our pursuit and protection of individual rights when those rights undermine the needs of our youngest citizens.

Childhood Lost has pooled the talents of scholars and writers from the fields of anthropology, economics, education, environmental studies, journalism, psychology, and religion. The book is divided into two parts. Part 1, "Children's Irreducible Needs," explores the bedrock elements of healthy child development, giving us a yardstick with which to gauge the extent to which American Culture is measuring up where kids are concerned. Part 2, "How American Culture Is Failing Our Kids," examines a multitude of interwoven stressors in children's lives, and a rich array of solutions. Each chapter can be read on its own or as part of a narrative that describes children's irreducible needs, how we are failing them, and what we must do to address this cultural crisis and become a "village for our children."

Part I

Children's Irreducible Needs

1

The Natural History of Children

MEREDITH F. SMALL

Humans belong to the taxonomic order of primates. This order is distinguished by many characteristics, one of which is giving birth to dependent young. Humans are extremists in this particular characteristic—we give birth to the most dependent infants and care for them for more years than does any other animal on earth.[1] As such, infancy and childhood are major life cycle stages for humans, stages that deeply influence the development of the individual as well as the formation of family and community.[2] Yet, we still have much to learn about the physical, emotional, psychological, and social development of infants and children.

In this chapter, I present an anthropological view of infancy and childhood. Although there has been some ethnographic work on children, few anthropologists have studied infants, and even fewer have been interested in explaining how biological development and cultural experience shape parenting practices, or how childhood experience forms adults.[3]

The anthropological perspective is both deep in time (evolutionary) and broad in scope (cross-cultural). This is of critical importance because it helps us to evaluate which features of the parent-child relationship amid the rich cultural mosaic of parenting styles are essential for healthy child development. This perspective is particularly relevant at this juncture because western culture seems to have lost its ability to understand children. The West now has the lowest birthrate in the world, and as such, many new parents have little or no experience with babies. Also, most parents in the West—out of choice or necessity—spend much of their day in the workplace, where children are not usually welcome, which in turn limits family interactions to after work and weekends. As a consequence, adults with children have limited time with them. Extended families are also more disconnected these days, and so there are fewer adult relatives to help care for children or advise parents.

Pediatricians and parenting books have made a concerted effort to fill the gap in parenting support. Since 1900, about 2,000 parenting advice books have been published in the United States.[4] Although these books continue to experience brisk sales, most are not based on research of any kind. More to the point, I believe that caregivers need, instead of advice, a deeper understanding of both the biological and cultural influences that shape the lives of infants and children. With this knowledge, parents, caregivers, and members of the wider community will be better equipped to make their own wise choices about childcare.

EVOLVED HUMAN INFANCY

Humans are animals with a rich evolutionary history. We are part of the animal order of primates, which includes lemurs, lorises, monkeys, and apes. Primates began to evolve 65 million years ago when the dinosaurs became extinct and left room for small mammals to occupy various habitats and then proliferate.[5] Humans are a very young species among the primates: human-like creatures appeared only about 5 million years ago. These early ancestors, called australopithecines, were small-brained, chimpanzee-like creatures, but they were distinguished from the other apes because they stood up and walked on two legs. Real humans, ones whom we would recognize if they walked down the street, appeared about 200,000 years ago.

In order to glean a historical perspective of the parent-child relationship, it is not sufficient to hearken back to the 1950s, the turn of the century, or even to our first appearance as a species 200,000 years ago. Rather, we must turn to our evolutionary primate history, which began 65 million years ago.[6] By turning to the behavior of nonhuman primates and to our fossil record, we can obtain clues that help us understand the evolved relationships between parents and offspring.

LESSONS FROM OUR PRIMATE COUSINS

Social Butterflies

Humans share broad patterns of behavior with nonhuman primates that are integral to parenting. Whereas most mammals are solitary, primates depend on each other for survival. As a result, primate babies are designed by evolution to understand and participate in an intense social milieu.[7] Our complex interpersonal interactions weave a network of attachment, especially among kin, but also among non-kin as we form friendships and alliances.[8]

Intense Mother-Infant Primate Relationships

Unlike most other mammals, primate mothers carry their infants constantly, defend them against others, and teach them social tasks and what is appropriate to eat. The most striking difference between primate mother-child relationships and those of all other animals on earth is that the former is *long-lasting*. Among chimpanzees, for example, males do not leave their mothers until they are sexually mature. Humans, like all primates, are designed to be involved with the upbringing of their offspring for many years, but as we will see, particular evolutionary pressures have rendered the human caregiver-child relationship especially intense and long-lasting.

LESSONS FROM THE PRIMATE AND HUMAN FOSSIL RECORDS ON THE ORIGINS OF ATTACHMENT RELATIONSHIPS

The study of ancient primate and human fossils provides another source of information about our evolutionary history. From this work, we have learned about a rather surprising but very significant chapter from our evolutionary past that had a major impact on the relationship between parents and infants. About 4 million years ago our ancestors stood up on two legs and began walking upright, and that change in locomotion completely altered the architecture of the human pelvis.[9] The pelvis of a quadruped such as the chimpanzee is long and thin because in those animals there is no need to have an extensive network of strong muscles for walking. But when early humans stood up and started to walk on two legs, that type of locomotion required an enlargement of the gluteus maximus and minimus muscles, which in turn pushed for a short and broad bony pelvic shape. As a result, the pelvic opening, or birth canal, also changed; the opening became essentially ovoid instead of round, with the sacrum tilted inward and forming a bowl.[10] This change in pelvic architecture was not a problem at first because our earliest ancestors still had small brains—comparable in size to the brains of modern chimpanzees—and infants could easily navigate the birth canal. The real crisis came about 1.5 million years ago when there was intense pressure for brain growth in the human lineage and suddenly babies had much bigger heads relative to the size of their mothers' pelvic openings.

At this point, evolution had to make a compromise because there was only so far one could push the width of the pelvis to accommodate infant head size; if the human pelvis were any wider, women would not be able to walk. Instead, natural selection opted for another route: now human infants are born too soon—neurologically unfinished, compared to other primates. As a result, they are physically and emotionally very dependent.[11] But this level of dependence could not have appeared if there hadn't been some corresponding evolutionary shift in parental behavior that facilitated the capacity to respond to infant needs. So, there must have been a "co-evolution" of dependent infants and responding adults for human infants to have survived. *A human newborn, therefore, is designed by evolution to be "entwined" with an adult of its species.* In other words, human infants have evolved to be "attached" both emotionally and physically to their caregivers, and when that attachment is denied, the infant is at risk.

The idea of "attachment" has a controversial history in American culture. Our current cultural ideology of independence and self-reliance for children is based on the puritan work ethic and our capitalistic economic system, in which individual achievement is favored.[12] For most of American history, parents have embraced that ideology and modeled their parenting styles in ways they thought would promote independence in children. Those who were more connected to their children were considered "lenient" in their parenting.

In the 1960s, John Bowlby published his classic work *Attachment and Loss*, which suggested that the American way of parenting might not be the best for infants.[13] Bowlby was trained as a psychiatrist, but he disagreed with the accepted psychoanalytic fashion of the time that claimed that babies related to their mothers only because they provided food.[14] Under this scheme, mothers loved and felt attached to their infants, but these feelings weren't reciprocated by infants, whose behavior was driven not by love but by an instinctual desire to satiate their hunger. In contrast, Bowlby claimed that beyond food, babies also had an innate need for physical, emotional, and psychological connection to their caregivers.

Bowlby's theory was soon born out in the laboratory experiments of Harry Harlow at the University of Wisconsin. Harlow realized that the only way to experiment ethically with the mother-infant relationship was to work with nonhuman primates. He developed a protocol in which newborn rhesus monkeys were removed from their natural mothers and given access to either of two inanimate surrogate mothers—a wire sculpture that had the rudiments of the mother's features with a bottle attached to it, or the identical sculpture covered with soft terry cloth minus the bottle. It became immediately apparent that the infant monkeys far preferred the "terry cloth mother" over the "wire mother," even though its only redeeming feature was that it was soft to the touch, whereas the wire mother was a source of nourishment. Indeed, the infants spent much of their time clinging to their "terry cloth mothers."[15] Over the course of several years, Harlow and his associates also demonstrated that monkeys who grew up without maternal care and ensuing attachment relationships were incompetent social individuals who were unable to parent effectively in adulthood. Harlow concluded that for primate infants, physical contact and emotional connection to their caregivers were at least as important, if not more, than nourishment.

In the wake of Harlow's and Bowlby's pathbreaking findings about the essential role of attachment relationships in healthy child development, decades of follow-up research was conducted that supported and elaborated upon their work. For example, research with premature babies has demonstrated that when these vulnerable infants are held and stroked frequently, they show more rapid neural[16] and physical[17] development than premature babies who are given standard hospital care. Close observations of mothers with their infants reveal that both infants and caregivers play a critical role in the dance that leads to a secure attachment. Immediately after birth, mothers orient themselves to make eye contact with their babies.[18] They recognize the cries of their newborns and can pick out their baby's shirt from a pile of shirts by smell alone.[19] The infant's role in fostering attachment includes the following: babies prefer the sound of the human voice over other sounds, and they demonstrate their attunement to the cadences of speech with corresponding body movements;[20] newborns recognize their mothers' voices and prefer them over the voices of other adults;[21] and babies are more interested in the shape and form of the human face than any other object.[22] As renowned pediatrician Berry Brazelton has demonstrated, the social coordination and mutual regulation of behavior between babies and their caregivers is essential for normal human development.[23] The natural behavioral inclinations of infants and their caregivers foster attachment relationships that develop slowly over a period of several months.[24] In summary, millions of years of evolution have produced an entwined infant-caretaker relationship that is necessary for infants' survival. Survival hinges not only upon receiving nourishment, but also upon physical, psychological, and emotional connection with one's caregivers.

Although Bowlby's attachment theory, Harlow's vivid monkey experiments, and decades of ensuing attachment research underscore the critical importance of an entwined relationship between infant and mother, remarkably, these findings have not had a significant impact on American culture. True, many hospitals have moved to allowing newborns to room with their mothers; but once they are out of the hospital, this culture still views close attachment as at odds with moving children toward independence, which remains the ideal goal. These days, those who adhere to a closer physical and emotional style of parenting are said to be practicing "attachment parenting," which is considered to be new and revolutionary. Lost in the "new" is the fact that attachment parenting has been molded by evolution and was until very recently the only kind of parenting practiced by humans. Indeed, the vast majority of cultures worldwide practice attachment parenting through constant physical proximity with their infants and toddlers. The western style of infant care in which the baby sleeps in a crib, is bottle-fed, pushed about in a stroller, and left to play alone in a crib is in fact the aberration rather than the rule, despite the fact that it has become normative in America.

EVOLVED HUMAN CHILDHOOD

The deeply entwined period of parent-offspring attachment does not end in infancy. In fact, the evolved relationship between caregivers and offspring reaches even further into the human lifespan, making for a whole new lifecycle stage not really seen in other animals.[25] While other mammal offspring quickly reach sexual maturity and move on to make lineages of their own, human children continue to rely on their parents for well over a decade. Fossil evidence shows that childhood as we know it is a recent addition to the human career. The human fossil record reveals that when a major brain expansion appeared about 1.5 million years ago, there was a corresponding lengthening of childhood.

The human childhood years are clearly full of growth and brain maturation. The brain reaches 75 percent of its adult weight by two years of age, and by ten years of age it is 95 percent complete.[26] However, the brain is also a dynamic system that changes in composition and neural networks over time; circuits are turned off and others enhanced, and this re-wiring happens with great vigor all through childhood. Remarkably, the overall growth rate of children, when given adequate nutrition, is similar all over the world. There is typically a rapid rate of growth in height the first year, a slower and steadier increase from one to seven, then a growth spurt followed by regular increases. There is also a major growth spurt right before puberty.[27] Of course, environment and experience then affect all the growth systems (including the brain), which produce wide variation in adult size and shape.[28]

While anthropologists have not reached a consensus about the evolutionary rationale for the lengthening of childhood, we do know that young children continue to depend on adults for their food, clothing, housing, and psychological and moral development, and they expect to be intimately connected to adults for a very long time.[29] Children who must fend for themselves at a young age have high mortality and morbidity rates.[30]

THE INFLUENCE OF CULTURE ON INFANT AND CHILD DEVELOPMENT

Humans are a long-lived, thoughtful, culturally dependent species, and they are also behaviorally flexible. Because of this flexibility, people invent all sorts of ways to live their lives. It is no surprise, then, that different cultural groups have different goals and that those goals are played out in parenting styles that in turn reinforce the prevailing cultural norms within a given group.[31]

Nonetheless, for 95 percent of human history we were all hunters and gatherers. As such, anthropologists have always been interested in how hunters and gatherers manage their lives, and they assume that this subsistence pattern has had a dramatic effect on who we are today. In other words, human behavior and cognition evolved within a context of hunting and gathering, and the modern human brain still contains the evolutionarily selected elements of that kind of lifestyle.

In general, the societal goals of small-scale hunters and gatherers are social integration, mobility, and sharing. There is a particular infant care pattern that reflects these goals. Among the !Kung San of Botswana, for example, babies are held at all times in a sling at the mother's side and fed relatively continuously.[32] Mothers respond to crying within ten seconds, and usually offer the breast. Babies cry as frequently as western babies, but not nearly as long in duration.[33] !Kung babies are also part of a socially dense environment and spend no time alone. The infant caretaking behavior of the !Kung is echoed by all hunters and gatherers in that babies are typically held at all times, fed on cue, sleep with an adult, and spend no time alone.

Childhood for hunters and gatherers is more varied. For example, once they are mobile, !Kung children play in multi-age groups and do not accompany their mothers on gathering expeditions; !Kung children are especially free of all responsibilities. In other indigenous tribes, children accompany their parents while they hunt and gather.

Most people on earth practice a subsistence form of farming called small plot horticulture. Typically, women work small garden plots, children tend to livestock, and men often work away from home. These homes are often polygynous, and several women cooperate to maintain a compound that includes several female-based households.[34] As the Gusii of western Kenya demonstrate, the parental goals in this type of subsistence pattern focus on family integration. Babies are held at all times by the mother or another caregiver, sleep with the mother, and are fed continuously. During childhood, children learn by participating in the household work. The parental role is to observe the children's progress and give corrective feedback; no one provides praise, approval, or rewards, and no one says "good job." To the Gusii, praise would undermine the household hierarchy and make for a conceited and unmanageable child. They feel any child would be motivated by a desire to be like older, obedient, and accomplished children.[35]

One of the best examples of how culture molds the very way we view the nature of children comes from the work of anthropologist Alma Gottlieb on the Beng people of Ivory Coast, in west Africa.[36] Gottlieb discovered that the world of Beng babies was quite unlike that of western infants. According to the Beng, infants come into this world from a place called *wrugbe*, what we might consider an afterlife, or a "before" life. In *wrugbe*, infants have a set of parents who love them. Babies remain in this place, happy, until someone in this life dies and the child is born as a replacement. But birth is really not the beginning of life for the Beng. The journey into this world, as Gottlieb explains it, only begins once the umbilical cord drops off. Beng mothers traditionally apply a special ointment that encourages umbilical healing within three days to speed up the initiation into this world. Once the cord stump is gone, the baby then begins the long and arduous trip away from *wrugbe* and into this world.

The Beng believe that newborns were really alive in their invisible *wrugbe* existence, and that it will take years to be full members of the spiritual community in this life. The job of a parent, the Beng believe, is to make the present as nice as possible so that a baby is not tempted to return to *wrugbe* (i.e., die). The Beng believe that if the baby cries, it is a signal that something is amiss and the child might prefer going back to *wrugbe*. Parents seek advice from their relatives, but if the baby continues to cry, they then consult special baby diviners. These diviners typically tell the parents that the baby is in need of some of the things they had in *wrugbe*, such as cowry shells, coins, or other jewelry. The diviners also remind the parents that their baby was leading a full and happy life elsewhere, and so they had best be more attentive. Otherwise, the baby will not only continue crying, but its *wrugbe* parents will reach into this world and take the baby back.

Gottlieb's work is important because it underscores the fact that the way babies and children are understood in the West is not a universal view. At the same time, despite the rich diversity in cultural beliefs among hunter-gatherer and horticultural societies, we nonetheless see a pattern emerging. Hunter-gatherer and horticultural societies all practice a style of infant care that includes almost constant physical connection and immediate responsiveness to infant cries; in childhood, social integration rather than independence is common.

Parenting practices that emphasize proximity and social integration are normative not only in third world countries. For the Japanese, social integration is also key.[37] The Japanese believe that a baby is a wandering soul that needs to be brought into the family, and so the parents place the baby to sleep between them, symbolically seeing the baby as a river and the parents as protective riverbanks. Japanese babies are also carried at all times and nursed frequently on demand, and parents believe there is no such thing as an unpleasant baby. In early childhood, youngsters are considered important members of the family and the group.[38] Children are encouraged to respect authority rather than express independence and self-reliance, but no matter how a child behaves, he or she is never left out of the group.

The parenting approaches of hunter-gatherers, small plot horti-culturalists, and parents in many industrialized nations contrast sharply with how children are traditionally cared for in most western cultures. The primary goal of western parents—that is, North American and European, but especially American—is independence and self-reliance for children. This push for independence is most striking in infancy, when babies are expected to sleep alone and are fed on a schedule. Western parents also expect infants to "self comfort" when they cry, so many parents delay responses to crying or do not respond at all but believe in a policy of letting the infant "cry it out." This caretaking package results in many hours during which infants are not held and are not part of a social group. Western babies are held 50 percent less than in all non-western cultures and spend 60 percent of the daytime alone, and the West is the only part of the world in which babies are expected to sleep alone.[39] Western babies also spend lot of time on their backs compared with infants from other cultures, and with the advent of pop-out car seats they will be spending considerably more time in the prone position.

CONTRASTING CULTURAL TRADITIONS

In researching parenting practices across cultures, my goal was to consider whether diverse childrearing styles were in keeping with infants' and children's needs acquired through evolution. In doing so, I discovered that western culture (North America and Europe) differed sharply in its parenting practices from the rest of the world—non-industrialized nations in particular.

Overall, in the West we expect babies to be independent, while in all other cultures, adults expect babies to be well integrated into family and society, and no one would consider "independence" and babies in the same breath. Their integration into the life of the family continues during childhood because they are expected to contribute meaningfully to the household. They work at caring for other children, weeding, collecting water and firewood, and tending livestock.[40] Within this system, children are considered assets rather than burdens. By contrast, in western culture, children typically contribute minimally to the family's welfare, and as a consequence, they are viewed as a burden rather than an asset; they tend to be kept apart from the larger culture and treated as a separate class of beings.

The western pattern differs from that of other cultures, in part, because we have a much lower birthrate and because the western work environment typically does not make room for children. We have also demarcated our day into work time, family time, and sleep time, and this pattern does not allow for much overlap in those categories. The western system, like all cultural belief systems and traditions, has opted for certain tradeoffs between parenting and other aspects of adult life. These choices are made sometimes for good reasons and sometimes simply because of cultural history. For example, in most cultures, babies are carried all the time. Obviously, carrying an infant or an older child requires energy expenditure. The tradeoff is that the child rarely cries. In the West, babies are not held all the time, which contributes to their excessive crying, but parents are free to carry other goods.

Parenting styles are constructed from tradition, from culture, and from the goals of parents and the larger society. Unfortunately, though, what might be best for the child physically, biologically, or psychologically is often not considered, or is considered with no real scientific basis. For example, in the West we see a cultural push for adult features and independence and self-reliance that is clearly at odds with the evolved biology of babies. That push for early independence is followed in childhood by directing a child to achieve some future adult goal, whether independence is best for infants and children, who are in essence little dependent primates reaching for a healthy entwined relationship with caretakers. It is ironic that while research on the critical role of attachment relationships for healthy infant development emanated from the West, westerners alone do not put this research into practice.

WHY KIDS MATTER

When I first began to study childhood, I approached the subject from a purely academic standpoint. I was initially interested in how culture interacts with biology during these early human lifecycle stages. But as I spent more time reading ethnographies of other cultures, as I evaluated various studies of childhood physical and social development, and as I went across the country giving talks about the anthropology of childhood, I realized that my subjects were in need of support. Children are the smallest and most vulnerable of our species, and they are the group most in need of our help. In other words, by studying children I found out that the entwined relationship between infants and caretakers could, and should, be extended to all children.

I suggest that we need to think long and hard about how we parent, as individuals and as a society. Today one third of the 6 billion people on earth are under the age of fifteen. Most of these children live in poverty, and they are highly vulnerable to infectious disease, abuse, and war. Currently, the mortality of children under the age of five hovers around 50 percent in most developing countries, and even children in the richest nations are at risk. In the United States, for example, one in five children lives in poverty and 15 percent of American children have no health coverage.[41] Children are also affected deeply by changes in the social fabric.[42] At a time when the composition of the human family is fluid and dynamic, including everything from single-mother households to blended families, children ride the waves of change along with their parents. In an age of global diseases such as HIV/AIDS, spreading civil strife, and rampant poverty—which all so deeply affect children—our very notion of what makes a "good" childhood becomes critical.

We might feel that most of these problems, such as poverty and civil unrest, belong to other countries and cultures, but I suggest that childcare in the West is at risk for other, perhaps even more damaging reasons. We keep our infants physically separate from their caregivers and leave them to cry for hours each day, even though this undermines attachment. We rely on nuclear rather than extended families, and that means children have much smaller social networks to care for them during times of stress.[43] We push children to achieve individually, rather than as a team, thus encouraging competition. In western culture, children are not usually required to contribute to the household well-being, which in contrast to our ideology marks our kids as less independent in day-to-day matters. As a culture, we need to rethink the western parental goals of independence and self-reliance for our children and question whether these goals truly serve children, their parents, or society.

It is important to remember that culture is not some amorphous mantle that hangs on us and overrides all else. We *are* the culture. We can decide whether we want to accept what has gone before, or we can choose to re-think our beliefs about babies and children and change the very way we parent. Mothers and fathers do not have to do what the culture says; it is possible to borrow from other cultures, or borrow back in time, and reject some of the traditions of our own culture in order to better serve our children's irreducible needs.

NOTES

1. Martin, R. D. *Primate Origins and Evolution: A Phylogenetic Reconstruction*. Princeton, NJ: Princeton University Press, 1990.

2. Bogin, B. *Patterns of Human Growth*. Cambridge: Cambridge University Press, 1999.

3. Whiting, B. *Six Cultures: Studies of Child Rearing*. New York: John Wiley, 1963.

4. Talbot, M. "Benjamin Spock, M.D.; A Spock-Marked Generation." *The New York Times Magazine*. January 3, 1999.

5. Fleagle, J. G. *Primate Adaptation and Evolution*. New York: Academic Press, 1988.

6. Small, M. F. *Our Babies, Ourselves: How Biology and Culture Shape the Way We Parent*. New York: Anchor Books, 1998.

7. Smuts, B. B. et al. *Primate Societies*. Chicago: University of Chicago Press, 1987.

8. deWaal, F. *Peacemaking among Primates*. Cambridge: Harvard University Press, 1990.

9. Lovejoy, C. O. "The Evolution of Human Walking." *Scientific American*. November (1988): 118–25.

10. Rosenberg, K. R. "The Evolution of Modern Human Birth." *Yearbook Physical Anthropology* 35 (1992): 89–124.

11. Trevethan, W. R. *Human Birth: An Evolutionary Perspective*. New York: Aldine De Gruyter, 1987.

12. Small, M. F. *Our Babies, Ourselves: How Biology and Culture Shape the Way We Parent*. New York: Anchor Books, 1998.

13. Bowlby, J. *Attachment and Loss*. Vol. 1. London: Hogarth Press, 1969.

14. Blum, D. *Love at Goon Park*. New York: Perseus Books, 2003.

15. Ibid.; Harlow, H. F., and M. K. Harlow. "The Affectional Systems." *Behavior of Nonhuman Primates*. Eds. A. M. Schrier, H. F. Harlow, and F. Stollnitz. New York: Academic Press, 1965, 287–334.

16. Rice, R. D. "Neurophysiological Development in Premature Infants Following Stimulation." *Developmental Psychology* 13 (1997): 69–76.

17. White, J. L., and R. C. Labarba. "The Effects of Tactile and Kinesthetic Stimulation on Neonatal Development in the Premature Infant." *Developmental Psychobiology* 9 (1976): 569–77.

18. Trevethan, W. R. *Human Birth: An Evolutionary Perspective*. New York: Aldine De Gruyter, 1987.

19. Formby, D. "Maternal Recognition of Infant's Cry." *Developmental Medicine and Child Neurology* 9 (1967): 293–98.

20. Condon, W. S., and L. W. Sander. "Neonate Movement Is Synchronized with Adult Speech: Interaction Participation and Language Acquisition." *Science 183* (1974): 99–101. See also Fernald, A. "Human Maternal Vocalizations to Infants as Biologically Relevant Signals: An Evolutionary Perspective." *The Adapted Mind: Evolutionary Psychology and the Generation*

of Culture. Eds. J. Barkow, L. Cosmides, and J. Tooby, Oxford: Oxford University Press, 1992. 391–428; Pinker, S. *The Language Instinct.* New York: William, Morrow and Co., 1994.

21. DeCasper, A. J., and W. P. Fifer. "Of Human Bonding: Newborns Prefer Their Mothers' Voices." *Science 208* (1980): 1174–76; Mehler, J. et al. "A Precursor of Language Acquisition in Young Infants." *Cognition 29* (1990): 143–78.

22. Brazelton, T. B., B. Koslowski, and M. Main. "The Origins of Reciprocity: The Early Mother-Infant Interaction." *The Effect of the Infant on Its Caregiver.* Eds. M. Lewis and L. A. Rosenblum. New York: John Wiley, 1974. 49–76; Brazelton, T. B., J. S. Robey, and G. A. Collier. "Infant Development in the Zincanteco Indians of Southern Mexico." *Pediatrics 44* (1969): 277–90.

23. Brazelton, T. B. et al. "Early Mother-Infant Reciprocity." *Ciba Fd. Symposium 33* (1975): 137–54.

24. Small, M. F. *Kids: How Biology and Culture Shape the Way We Raise Our Children.* New York: Doubleday, 2001.

25. Bogin, B. "Evolutionary Hypotheses for Human Childhood." *Yearbook Physical Anthropology 40* (1997): 63–89.

26. Barnet, A. B., and R. J. Barnet. *The Youngest Minds.* New York: Simon and Schuster, 1998.

27. Bogin, B. *Patterns of Human Growth.* Cambridge: Cambridge University Press, 1999; Tanner, J. M. *Fetus into Man: Physical Growth from Conception to Maturity.* Cambridge: Harvard University Press, 1990.

28. Tanner, J. M. *Fetus into Man: Physical Growth from Conception to Maturity.* Cambridge: Harvard University Press, 1990.

29. Small, M. F. *Kids: How Biology and Culture Shape the Way We Raise Our Children.* New York: Doubleday, 2001.

30. Panter-Brick, C. *Biosocial Perspectives on Children.* Cambridge: Cambridge University Press, 1998; Panter-Brick, C., and M. Smith. *Abandoned Children.* Cambridge: Cambridge University Press, 2000.

31. Whiting, B. *Six Cultures: Studies of Child Rearing.* New York: John Wiley, 1963.

32. Lee, R. B. *The !Kung San: Men, Women, and Work in a Foraging Society.* Cambridge: Cambridge University Press, 1979; Lee, R. B. *The Dobe !Kung.* Eds. G. Spindler and L. Spindler. New York: Holt, Rinehart and Winston, 1984.

33. Barr, R. G. et al. "Crying in !Kung San Infants: A Test of the Cultural Specificity Hypothesis." *Dev. Med. Child Neurol. 33* (1991): 601–10.

34. LeVine, R. A. "Parental Goals: A Cross-Cultural View." *Teachers Coll. Rec. 76* (1974): 226–39; LeVine, R. A. et al. *Child Care and Culture: Lessons from Africa.* Cambridge: Cambridge University Press, 1994.

35. LeVine, R. A., and B. B. LeVine. "Nyansongo: A Gusii Community in Kenya." In *Six Cultures: Studies of Child Rearing.* Ed. B. B. Whiting. New York: John Wiley and Sons, 1963.

36. Gottlieb, A. *The Spiritual Life of Beng Babies*. Chicago: University of Chicago Press, 2004.

37. Smith, R. J. *Japanese Society: Tradition, Self, and the Social Order*. Cambridge: Cambridge University Press, 1983.

38. Ben-Ari, E. *Japanese Childcare: An Interpretive Study of Culture and Organization*. London: Kegan Paul International, 1997.

39. Small, M. F. *Our Babies, Ourselves: How Biology and Culture Shape the Way We Parent*. New York: Anchor Books, 1998.

40. Small, M. F. *Kids: How Biology and Culture Shape the Way We Raise Our Children*. New York: Doubleday, 2001.

41. Ibid.

42. Flinn, M. V., and B. G. England. "Childhood Stress and Family Environment." *Current Anthropology 36* (1995): 854–66.

43. Ibid.

2

Why Parenting Matters

Laura E. Berk

Numerous signs indicate that the quality of parenting in the United States has eroded. America's population of poverty-stricken children and youths—at 16 percent, among the largest in the industrialized world[1]—suffers in manifold ways from a pile-up of stresses that undermine parenting, including family turmoil and instability, chaotic households, and run-down, violent neighborhoods devoid of social supports.[2] But many American children in families with adequate to plentiful incomes are experiencing an increasing array of problems that disrupt their chances for a happy, healthy, successful adult life.

INDICATORS OF ERODED PARENTING QUALITY IN AMERICA

Mediocre Academic Achievement

In worldwide comparisons of academic achievement, American students typically score no better than the international average, and often below it[3]—a disappointing picture confirmed by The Nation's Report Card, a biannual national assessment of educational progress. In the most recent assessment, 37 percent of fourth graders scored below the "basic level" in reading, and 31 percent did so in math. In each domain, less than one third had reached or exceeded a "proficient level" of performance—figures that worsened in junior high and high school.[4] Although quality of school learning experiences contribute greatly to these findings, factors within the home are also involved. For example, American youths devote far less daily time to homework than their counterparts do in high-scoring nations—in high school, only one sixth the time that East Asian students spend and one third of the time that European students spend.[5]

In addition, leisure activities that support academic learning, such as reading and playing educational games, are less common in American than in East Asian homes.

Current estimates indicate that U.S. five- to thirteen-year-olds average only one hour per week reading during their leisure time.[6]

Overloaded, Overscheduled Children

American children aged twelve and younger spend nearly twice as much time in supervised, structured settings than children did two decades ago. Diaries of children's daily activities reveal that today, 75 percent of children's weekday time is programmed, compared with only 40 percent in 1981.[7] Investigators attribute this change to a growing "time crunch" in families—parents' efforts to schedule children while they themselves are scheduled. As children make multiple transitions among school, aftercare, and diverse lessons each day, they lead increasingly hectic, adult-planned lives.

What pursuits lose out? Findings show a 16 percent decline in family mealtimes; a 40 percent decline in religious involvement; a 50 percent decline in outdoor activities, such as walking, hiking, and camping; and a 100 percent decline in family conversations. (Outdoor time and family conversations, however, were infrequent to begin with.[8]) Family togetherness, community participation, and wholesome leisure activities are being sacrificed in favor of a new cultural emphasis on "being busy"—a tradeoff that, very likely, compromises children's development. Regular family meals, for example, are linked to improved childhood nutrition,[9] to language and literacy progress in early childhood,[10] to favorable intellectual development,[11] and to a reduction in behavior problems.[12] Involvement in religious and other community youth groups is associated with a wealth of favorable outcomes, including improved academic performance, reduced antisocial behavior, increased initiative, greater concern for others, and civic responsibility in adulthood.[13]

Furthermore, excessive adult regulation of children's activities may rob children of crucial opportunities to develop self-regulation. On the basis of parental reports, some psychologists have expressed concern that today's children, when not programmed, are easily bored.[14]

Entrenched TV Viewers and Video Game Players

On weekdays, the number-one activity for American children and youths, after sleeping and going to school, is watching television. This pursuit consumes an average of two and a half to three and a half hours per day—substantially more than children devote to interacting with family members or with peers.[15] Another half hour per day is given over to recreational computer use, with school-age children (especially boys) emphasizing video games and adolescents emphasizing various Internet activities.[16]

Although media use can be beneficial, only rarely is TV a positive activity. Frequent viewing is associated with developmental liabilities, including declines in time spent reading, school grades, and concern for others, and increases in gender stereotyping, obesity, and subsequent aggression.[17] Violence and gender stereotypes also abound in video games, which, like TV violence, promote aggression and undermine prosocial behavior.[18]

If parents tend to watch a lot of TV, their children usually do also.[19] Frequent Internet use among adolescents and adults alike is associated with reduced communication with family members and reduced size of their social networks, and with increased loneliness and depression.[20]

Widespread Corporal Punishment of Children

American children are exposed to aggressive models not just in media content, but also in their parents' disciplinary practices. Although many parents are aware that yelling at, slapping, and spanking incite impulsiveness, anger, and hostility in children, physical punishment in the United States is widespread. In a survey of a nationally representative sample of American households, more than half of the parents of infants through twelve-year-olds reported using corporal punishment. Between ages three and seven, when physical punishment of children was highest, more than 80 percent of parents admitted one or more instances of it in the previous year. Moreover, American parents do not limit themselves to a slap or a spank; more than one fourth of physically punishing parents say they used a hard object to hit their child.[21] A wealth of evidence indicates that corporal punishment and physical abuse of children are closely linked.[22]

Research confirms that the more physical punishment children experience, the more likely they are to develop serious, lasting mental health problems, in the form of poor academic performance, depression, and antisocial behavior during childhood and adolescence; and criminality, depressive and alcoholic symptoms, and partner and child abuse in adulthood.[23]

High Rates of Peer Violence and Deviant Behavior

In view of the evidence just reviewed, it is not surprising that large numbers of American youths complain about the behavior of their peers. In a survey of a nationally representative sample of elementary and secondary school students, 74 percent of eight- to eleven-year-olds said teasing and bullying were frequent at their school, and 43 percent said expressions of discrimination and disrespect were. Among ten- to eleven-year-olds, one third mentioned pressure to have sex—and nearly half mentioned alcohol and drug use—as "big problems" for children their age.[24]

Significantly, many young people, even those as young as eight, indicated that they wanted to know more about topics that parents might be reluctant to talk about, such as discrimination, puberty, alcohol, drugs, and HIV/AIDS. Besides asking for information on these issues, 46 percent of twelve- to fifteen-year-olds wanted help with sexual decision-making.[25] Surrounded by disruptive and other problematic peer behaviors, and often manifesting those behaviors themselves, children and adolescents seem to crave sensible adult guidance. Indeed, warm communication, in which parents provide information and convey their values, is associated with teenagers' adoption of their parents' views and with reduced sexual risk-taking and involvement in other deviant activities. Yet with respect to conversations about sex, birth control, and the negative consequences of pregnancy, only about 50 percent of adolescents report having any discussions with their parents.[26]

Worsening Adjustment of Children of Divorce

About 45 percent of American marriages end in divorce, half of which involve children, leaving one fourth of children in single-parent homes at any given time—the highest rate in the industrialized world.[27] Although children's adjustment difficulties in the aftermath of divorce diminish with improved family functioning, problems tend to persist over the years. Compared with children of continuously married parents, children of divorce display poorer academic achievement, self-esteem, and social competence and a higher incidence of school dropout and emotional and behavior problems, including depression, antisocial behavior, early sexual activity, adolescent parenthood, and divorce in their adult lives.[28]

Moreover, three recent, independently conducted meta-analyses found that the adjustment problems of children of divorce have intensified in recent years.[29] Although the precise reasons for this trend are unclear, one speculation is that more parents today are divorcing because they are moderately (rather than extremely) dissatisfied with their married relationships. Perhaps children's difficulty understanding their parents' marital breakups under these conditions, and their grief over the loss of seemingly happy home lives, cause them to be especially puzzled and upset.[30]

Many Chronically Anxious Children

The declining well-being of children of divorce may be partly the result of another trend: American children and adolescents of all walks of life are experiencing more stress than their counterparts of the previous generation. An examination of hundreds of studies of nine- to seventeen-year-olds carried out between the 1950s and the 1990s revealed a steady, large increase in anxiety over this period.[31] A combination of reduced social connectedness and increased environmental dangers (crime, violent media, fear of war, etc.) appeared responsible; measures of both factors were positively correlated with anxiety scores.

Interestingly, whereas societal indicators of diminished social connectedness (divorce, declining family size, etc.) showed strong associations with children's rising anxiety, economic conditions (such as poverty and unemployment) had comparatively little influence.[32] A child's well-being, it appears, is less responsive to whether the family has enough money than to whether it promotes close, supportive bonds with others.

Other changes in the American family also point to a withering of social connectedness. For example, Americans are less likely to visit friends, join community organizations (recall the decline in family religious involvement reported earlier), and volunteer in their communities than they once were.[33] We have seen that parents and children converse and share leisure time less often than they did in the past. Simultaneously, young people's sense of trust in others has weakened. In 1992 only 18.3 percent of high school seniors agreed that one can usually trust people, compared with 34.5 percent in 1975.[34]

Young people's increased anxiety is a natural response to lower-quality relationships. As social connectedness in the United States declined, youth suicide rates rose. Between the 1950s and 1970s, they rose by 300 percent for fifteen- to twenty-five-year-olds; and between 1980 and 1997, by 109 percent for ten- to fourteen-year-olds.[35]

Increasingly Egoistic, Self-Satisfied Children

Paradoxically, while American youths' achievement remains mediocre and their anxiety, antisocial behavior, and adjustment problems have worsened, their self-esteem has become more favorable. Several meta-analyses show that from 1980 into the mid-1990s, the self-esteem scores of elementary school, secondary school, and college students rose sharply.[36] Researchers attributed the gain to American cultural values, which have increasingly emphasized a focus on the self, causing parents to engage in indulgent, self-esteem boosting of children by showering them with compliments, such as "you're great" and "you're terrific," that have no basis in real achievement. Eventually, children see through these statements, mistrust the adults who repeat them, and are riddled with self-doubts and insecurities. According to some critics, too few American parents help their children construct solidly favorable self-images by insisting on worthwhile achievement and socially useful commitments and responsibilities.[37]

An Epidemic of Childhood Obesity

Finally, American children are facing an additional health crisis, one of epic proportions. Although overweight and obesity have increased in many western nations over the past several decades, nowhere is the problem as great as it is in the United States. Fifty percent of American school-age children and adolescents are overweight; half of these overweight youngsters are obese,[38] a condition that places them at risk for serious emotional and social difficulties and life-threatening illnesses. Among the causes of childhood obesity are unhealthy family eating habits. Overly busy, preoccupied parents have replaced healthful family meals with fast foods loaded with sugar and fat. They also permit excessive TV viewing, during which children are sedentary. Also, TV ads encourage children to consume high-calorie snacks.[39] These destructive eating habits get started early. Interviews with more than 3,000 American parents of four- to twenty-four-month-olds revealed that many served their children French fries, pizza, candy, and soda on a daily basis. For example, 60 percent of twelve-month-olds ate candy at least once per day. At the same time, one third ate no fruits or vegetables.[40]

Furthermore, we have seen that contemporary parents spend little time with children in active leisure pursuits. Physical inactivity is pervasive among American youths. Among five- to seventeen-year-olds, only about 40 percent of girls and 50 percent of boys are active enough for good health—that is, they engage in at least thirty minutes of vigorous activity and one hour of walking per day.[41]

PARENTING ATTITUDES AND BEHAVIORS

Assessments of the overall status of American children, as seen through the eyes of parents, are consistent with the disheartening picture just conveyed. Consider the results of the National Survey of America's Families, which tracked changes in the well-being of children from 1997 to 2002 by contacting more than 28,000 families each year, questioning the parent (usually the mother) in the household who was most knowledgeable about the sampled child. Even in this brief period of time, parents—especially economically advantaged parents—reported worrisome changes. For example, although only a minority of parents regarded their children as highly engaged in school to begin with, the percentage dropped further, from 43 percent to 35 percent for six- to eleven-year-olds, and from 38 percent to 31 percent for twelve- to seventeen-year-olds. Higher-income parents also reported increases in emotional and behavior problems, from 4 to 6 percent. Aggravation on the part of parents—those saying that their children "are much harder to care for than most" or "do things that bother them a lot"—rose as well, from 6 to 9 percent.[42]

Of course, not all the negative changes just described are totally the fault of parents. The past few years, to be sure, have been years of reduced funding for education and continued, limited public services that benefit American children and families. But parents, even in their own eyes, are not absolved of responsibility. In yet another nationally representative survey of more than 1,600 parents, 61 percent were critical of their own efforts—that is, they judged the job that they were doing in rearing their children as either "fair" or "poor." More than half believed that parents of previous generations did better.[43]

Although the respondents could easily identify the values they regarded as essential for their children to develop favorably, few felt that they were succeeding in teaching those values. Indeed, parents' beliefs and behaviors were often at odds. For instance, the vast majority stated that they were worried about the impact of negative media images, indicated that it was vital for children to have good nutrition and eating habits, and agreed that "children do better when parents set limits and enforce them." Nevertheless, 51 percent had placed a TV in their child's bedroom—a practice known to increase TV viewing and decrease time devoted to homework and sleeping. A full 91 percent said that their child ate junk food either sometimes or constantly.[44] In terms of parenting practices, only 18 percent described themselves as "parents in chief"—monitoring their children carefully and consistently and being clear about who was in charge. Many more admitted to having parenting difficulties: 17 percent fell into an "overwhelmed" category (felt they could do little to control how their child turned out), 17 percent were "softies"(admitted giving in too quickly to children's desires), and 8 percent were "best buddies" (trying to be their child's best friend). Although the remaining 40 percent could not be easily classified, precious few felt firmly secure about their parenting strategies.[45]

AMERICAN PARENTS: BAFFLED, INSECURE, AND RETREATING FROM CHILDREN

Numerous signs—from parents' diminishing investment in child-rearing, to children's compromised well-being on multiple fronts, to the gut feelings of many parents that they are performing poorly—suggest that American parents have lost their compass when it comes to identifying and implementing effective approaches for bringing up their children. Of course, the meaning of parenting surveys is debatable: some say that they merely reveal how parents perceive themselves, not how parents actually are. But others take the combination of parents' expressed insecurity and children's adverse functioning as deeply worrisome. Their concern is magnified by the ineffective parental behavior they say they observe all around them.[46] American parents' priorities—these experts conclude—have changed: many more are giving short shrift to their child-rearing responsibilities and leading separate lives from their children.[47]

Beneath this trend is an even more fundamental change in parental belief systems: contemporary parents seem to doubt their own power and influence over their children's development. Why is this so? First, societal factors—the current status of public policies that support children and families, and cultural values that sustain parental commitment—have complicated parents' task, making child-rearing far more challenging than in previous generations. Second, theory- and research-based child-rearing advice disseminated to parents is increasingly voluminous but at the same time contradictory. It has failed to offer a clear, consistent vision of good child-rearing to guide daily decision-making and practice. Let's look closely at these sources of parental frustration and confusion.

A CULTURE THAT UNDERMINES PARENTING

The large majority of parents readily agree that American society is an inhospitable environment for rearing children.[48] Yet they are much quicker to point to the negative influences of popular culture (violent media, junk foods, explicit sexuality, and consumerism) than to an even more dire situation: in the United States, family-friendly policies—ones recognized by most western industrialized nations as essential for ensuring psychologically healthy children in today's world—are sorely lacking. American parents, it seems, have accepted their meager lot when it comes to government programs that assist them with their child-rearing responsibilities. Indeed, as American women carved out a significant presence in the workplace during the past three decades, no cultural movement evolved to help them arrive at a comfortable compromise between meaningful work and involvement in their children's lives.

For example, paid, job-protected employment leave for childbirth and child illness, ranging from several months to two years, is available in Canada, western Europe, and even some less-developed nations, such as the People's Republic of China. Yet the U.S. federal government mandates only twelve weeks of unpaid leave, and it limits this paltry benefit to employees in companies with at least fifty workers.[49] Most women, however, work in smaller businesses.[50]

Although an obvious way of reconciling parents' employment needs with young children's rearing needs is to make high-quality, nonparental care widely available and affordable, the United States—unlike Australia and western Europe—has failed to establish a nationally regulated and liberally funded childcare system. In the National Institute of Child Health and Development (NICHD) Study of Early Child Care, the largest investigation of American childcare quality to date (involving ten sites around the country and more than 1,300 families), only 20–25 percent of childcare centers and family childcare homes provided infants and toddlers with sufficiently stimulating experiences to promote healthy cognitive, emotional, and social development; most settings offered mediocre to abysmal care.[51] Childcare conditions for preschoolers were similarly inferior.[52] In fact, so widespread is poor-quality childcare in the United States that American parents have acclimated to it. In another study, over 90 percent of parents whose preschoolers were enrolled in several hundred randomly chosen childcare centers in four states believed that their children's childcare experiences were far better than they actually were.[53] Parents seemed unable to distinguish good from substandard care.

America's weak family-friendly policies are a natural outgrowth of its rugged individualism—its strong bias toward elevating personal over collective, or group, goals. Individualistic values underlie Americans' inclination to be less approving of generous government provision of family services than the citizens of nations that lean toward, or embrace, a collectivistic perspective. As a result, a widespread opinion in the United States is that ensuring quality care for children, and paying for that care, is not a social responsibility. Rather, it is a private, family matter.[54]

Paradoxically, the very individualistic values that have kept the U.S. government at bay where child and family needs are concerned have contributed to diminished parental involvement with and sensible guidance of children. American parents are living ever fuller, busier lives, in which they often accentuate personal fulfillment, professional achievement, and economic success over time spent with children. Over the past decade, the "parental time bind" has been a consistent theme in commentary on American parenting. Reports repeatedly depict U.S. parents as caught up in a ceaseless sprint to reconcile job, marriage, personal, and child-rearing pursuits, resulting in parents feeling so drained at the end of their day that they have little time and energy to give their children much focused attention. In a study of employees at a large midwestern corporation, a majority of parents, whether workers or executives, confirmed the parental state of mind just described: they complained of overly long work days and frenetic lives. At the same time, few had taken steps to make work and family life more compatible. For example, even high earners were not taking the annual twelve weeks of guaranteed, unpaid family leave time available to them, although they could afford to do so.[55]

Examining government household survey data, another investigator of the parental time crunch reported that American employed parents today spend, on average, about 350 more hours a year working compared with 1979. Although the rise affects both mothers and fathers, it is considerably greater for mothers.[56] Parental time diaries show a less extreme increase, but they nevertheless document a substantial rise in work demands and time pressure. The average decline in parents' reported time with children is far less than the average increase in work hours, suggesting that many employed parents find ways to engage with their children. Nevertheless, masked beneath these averages are a sizable number of parents, including both professionals and low-wage earners in long-hour jobs, whose children experience high levels of parental absence.[57] Many such children spend those hours in America's inferior childcare arrangements.

Additionally, children of busy professionals often find themselves caught up in a flurry of scheduled activities, which keep the children nearly as busy as their overextended parents.

As work and other commitments clashed with child-rearing, American parents of recent decades have often rationalized their time scarcity with the comment, "It's quality time with children, not quantity, that counts." The expression "quality time" dates back to the 1970s, a decade that witnessed the largest rise in women's participation in the labor force during this century. In its commonly accepted meaning, quality time is an intense but brief contact, assumed to be as satisfying and as beneficial to the recipient as sustained involvement. But research confirms that quality time is nothing more than a ready salve for the consciences of conflicted parents, who squeeze in a few moments with their children, catch as catch can. In studies following children from infancy into childhood and adolescence, brief episodes of parental stimulation and sensitivity did not result in greater child competence. Instead, positive, supportive parenting that *endured* was linked to favorable child development, including persistence in problem-solving, high self-esteem, socially skilled behavior, closer friendships, and better peer relationships.[58]

Research on workplace and childcare policies confirms the negative impact of minimal parental time investment on children's development. In a series of studies, researchers examined length of maternity leave in relation to employed mothers' psychological well-being and parenting behaviors. Short leaves of six weeks or fewer (the norm in the United States) were associated with maternal anxiety, depression, and negative interactions with infants. In contrast, longer leaves of twelve weeks or more (the norm in the rest of the industrialized world) predicted favorable maternal mental health and sensitive, responsive caregiving.[59]

In a similar vein, long hours in American childcare result in limited daily time with parents and are related to less favorable parent-child interaction during infancy and the preschool years. In the NICHD Study of Early Child Care, researchers repeatedly observed mothers of diverse socioeconomic and ethnic backgrounds playing with their children aged six months to three years. The more time children spent in childcare (which ranged from zero to fifty hours per week), the less positive and responsive their mothers' behavior tended to be. Children experiencing less positive interaction were more negative in mood and less affectionate.[60] At a follow-up at ages four and a half to five, children averaging more than thirty childcare hours per week were rated by their mothers, caregivers, and kindergarten teachers as having more behavior problems, especially defiance, disobedience, and aggression.[61]

These findings are not an indictment of maternal employment or nonparental childcare. Rather, they underscore the importance of considering children's needs in parental work and childcare decisions, and the inescapable need for public policies that enable parents to make work/family arrangements that foster, rather than impede, sustained engagement with children. Childcare quality plays a vital role in this equation: in the NICHD study, mother-child interaction was more favorable when children attended higher-quality childcare.[62] Moreover, in all studies reporting a positive impact of maternal employment on child outcomes (including higher self-esteem, better grades in school, more positive family and peer relations, and fewer gender-stereotyped beliefs), effective parenting mediated these favorable developments. Employed mothers of cognitively competent, well-adjusted children value their parenting role, schedule regular, extended times to devote to their children, and combine warmth with consistent expectations for mature behavior.

The eroded parent-child relationships that result from too little time with children are consistent with the negative trends in American parenting and child well-being summarized earlier in this chapter. Parents who shortchange their children are likely to feel guilty and, therefore, to resort to indulgence. Furthermore, parents who are too exhausted or preoccupied to be physically or psychologically available tend to have youngsters who become discipline problems.[63] Their children's disagreeable behavior heightens parents' fatigue and impatience, increasing the likelihood of parental harshness. Parental permissiveness and punitiveness, in turn, exacerbate children's difficulties. Permissive parenting is linked to impulsive, demanding, dependent child behavior and poor school achievement.[64] Coercive parenting is associated with anger and defiance (especially in boys) and anxiety and withdrawal (especially in girls).[65] Finally, children experiencing either of these maladaptive parenting strategies may eventually rebel, resulting in high rates of antisocial behavior in adolescence.[66]

One analyst of parents' work-family "role overload" concluded, "Many working families are both prisoners and architects of the time bind in which they find themselves."[67] Large numbers of American parents seem to have accepted the status quo of minimal societal supports for child-rearing as inevitable, and even appropriate. As a result, they are too easily co-opted into minimal time with their children, and into detrimental parenting practices.

CHILD-REARING ADVICE: ONE-SIDED, CONFLICTING VIEWS

Although almost all parents feel a need at one time or another for expert advice on how to rear their children, the demand is particularly great today, perhaps because parents, teachers, and the general public sense that children's problematic behavior has increased. The call for parenting advice has led to a proliferation of volumes, in which the methods advocated vary widely. Many of these parenting manuals address discipline and communication, thereby catering to rising numbers of parents with undercontrolled, apathetic, non-goal-directed children. Precious few guidebooks, however, are grounded in the explosion of contemporary child development research that is of significant applied value. Rather, a plethora of opinion is available, some of it playing on parents' self-doubts with such titles as *Parenting for Dummies* and *The Seven Worst Things Parents Do*.[68]

Parenting advice emanating from classic theories—Skinner's, Gesell's, and Piaget's, for example—also offers little comfort, since dramatic shifts in favored theories have occurred during the past half-century. Indeed, this waxing and waning of theories has contributed greatly to discrepancies in expert advice, which (like the theories) has fluctuated between extremes—from an adult-imposed, directive approach to a child-centered, laissez-faire approach and back again. As one critic commented, theories and the popular litera- ture for parents "have done their share to undermine the wavering self-confidence of American parents," as well as to provide scientific justification for nearly any child-rearing tactic a parent might use.[69]

Bipolar tensions in parenting advice continue to the present day, with some titles advocating a philosophy of "feel-good" child- centeredness, and others offering to rescue parents who have allowed their children to ride roughshod over them.[70] Despite a growing con- sensus in the field about parenting techniques that help children develop into competent, caring, responsible adults, the popular par- enting literature continues to lag substantially behind this current knowledge base. It fails to provide parents with a sound, consistent roadmap for rearing children.

DISCOUNTING PARENTS' IMPACT

An especially alarming development in this literature of contra- diction is the recent appearance of expert advice that validates America's refusal to take seriously the importance of parents in its public policies. This new view sidesteps the debate over how best to rear children by claiming that parents' socialization practices have a negligible impact on how children turn out in the long run. The most vocal of these "parenting matters little" advocates is Judith Rich Harris. In her 1998 book *The Nurture Assumption,*[71] Harris declared that child development authorities had grossly overestimated the significance of parental nurturing. Instead, she argued, children's genes and (secondarily) peer groups were the supreme forces in how children turned out.

Harris's message arrived on the scene during a groundswell of scholarly and public interest in biological contributions to human behavior. As a result, her ideas were widely, and mostly favorably, reported in the popular press. In addition, they were immediately endorsed by several prestigious names in the field of psychology. Some supporters were captivated by the revolutionary nature of Harris's thesis, and others by the power of her message to debunk the formerly widespread practice of holding parents solely respon- sible for any problem that might arise in children's lives.

The alluring unorthodoxy of Harris's claims overshadowed the critical voices of numerous child development researchers, whose evidence-based indictments appeared in scholarly journals and other academic outlets largely inaccessible to the everyday citizen.[72] Indeed, in reporting Harris's assertions, the media failed to temper them with the appraisals of reputable detractors—a course that would have undercut the arresting quality of Harris's message and therefore its newsworthiness. The absence of any visible critique has left Harris's claims intact in the minds of many. These include noted figures in the field of psychology who are unfamiliar with the contemporary child development research literature and who continue to disseminate the "parents matter little" doctrine. For example, five years after the release of Harris's book, social psychologist Carol Tavris, writing in *The Chronicle of Higher Education*, included the following on a list of false assumptions that—she confidently asserted—have been "resoundingly disproved by empirical research":

> The way that parents treat a child in the first five years (three years) (one year) (five minutes) of life is crucial to the child's later intellectual and emotional success.[73]

In reality, Harris's position is both misleading and harmful. She exaggerates evidence consistent with her views and overlooks evidence that challenges them. Although her heredity/peer supremacy claims are partly aimed at discrediting parent-blaming, psychological theories pointing to parents as the sole cause of children's ills are old and outdated, harking back to the 1980s and before. That was a time when researchers often ignored the role of children's genetic endowment and overstated findings on parenting effects. Investigators have long since remedied the shortcomings of those early studies. These efforts have yielded a research-based consensus that parents' influence on children, while not exclusive, is nevertheless substantial.

Moreover, Harris's public pronouncement of parental impotence comes at a time when many busy parents are poised to retreat from family responsibilities, and it gives them license to do so. America's unwillingness to invest in humane family supports receives endorsement from the notion that parenting counts for little. If only genes and the peer group matter, then there is no need for generous government commitment to the family. Furthermore, redirecting blame toward children—by asserting that anything good or bad in children's behavior is largely inborn and inevitable—is an even more dangerous excess. It gives tacit permission for parental

indifference, coldness, inconsistency, harshness, and even brutality—
behaviors widely documented to damage children's development.
After all, how parents treat children is irrelevant if parenting is
inconsequential.

PARENTS MATTER GREATLY: CONTEMPORARY
THEORY AND RESEARCH

The contemporary field of child development has moved away
from one-sided perspectives advocating that either nature or nurture largely determines outcomes for children. Rather, a balanced,
inclusive view has coalesced in the field. It asserts that many
elements, both internal and external to the child, are powerful,
interrelated influences on children's development.[74] These include
the child's heredity and biological constitution; the people and
objects in the child's everyday settings of home, childcare center,
school, and neighborhood; the community resources that support
and assist with child-rearing; and cultural values and customs
related to parenting and education. In addition, investigators realize
that the contributions of the child and his or her social environment
to development are interconnected—that they cannot be separated
and weighted in a one-sided, simplistic manner.

To illustrate, Harris's heavy emphasis on heredity is mostly based
on twin studies, which show that identical twins are more similar
than fraternal twins in intelligence and in a wide range of tempera-
mental and personality measures, including shyness/sociability,
irritability, persistence, anxiety, agreeableness, and impulsivity. A
complementary line of evidence indicates that children varying in
brightness and in temperament often *evoke* parental reactions that
act to sustain their biologically based traits—findings that prompted
Harris to conclude that parenting does little to mold children's characteristics. Instead, she argued, parenting is largely a response to, or
an outgrowth of, child behavior. To be sure, a highly verbal child is
likely to receive more parental verbal stimulation than a less verbal
youngster. A friendly, attentive child is likely to be responded to
positively and patiently, whereas an active, impulsive child is more
likely to be the recipient of impatience and coercion.

But study after study reveals that the relationship between
children's traits and the parenting they receive is not just a reactive
one. Child-rearing can modify children's biologically based characteristics. Although parents are unlikely to turn a shy child into
a social butterfly or a fearless risk-taker into an overly cautious

youngster, they can induce substantial change in children's adaptation—either by helping children overcome unfavorable dispositions or by worsening maladaptive ones. After carefully reviewing the literature on parenting effects, one eminent scholar concluded, "The idea that in a long-standing relation such as one between parent and child, the child would be influencing the parent but the parent would not be influencing the child is absurd."[75] Let's look at a sampling of evidence that substantiates the vital significance of parents in children's lives.

ADOPTION RESEARCH

Research on adopted children permits investigators to determine the impact of placing infants who otherwise would have grown up under various conditions of disadvantage with parents who provide consistent affection, stimulation, and guidance. Findings on the malleability of IQ are well known: the test scores of children born to poverty-stricken biological mothers and adopted shortly thereafter into economically advantaged homes remain moderately correlated with the scores of their biological mothers—evidence for the continuing role of heredity. At the same time, follow-ups in middle childhood reveal dramatic gains in IQ—scores well above average and fourteen to thirty points higher than would have been expected had the children remained in their birth homes.[76]

Comparable findings exist for personality and social development. In one such investigation, adopted infants whose biological mothers were imprisoned criminal offenders (and who therefore were assumed to be genetically predisposed to criminality) were followed into adolescence.[77] These teenagers displayed high rates of antisocial behavior only when they had been reared in adverse homes, as indicated by adoptive parents or siblings with serious adjustment problems. In families free of pathology (and the impaired relationships that invariably accompany it), adoptees with a genetic predisposition for criminality did not differ from adoptees without this genetic background. Similarly, children of schizophrenic biological mothers (assumed to be genetically predisposed to mental illness) who were reared by mentally healthy adoptive parents showed little mental illness in adulthood—no more than a control group with healthy biological and adoptive parents. In contrast, psychological impairments piled up in adult adoptees who had been reared by mentally ill adoptive parents.[78]

These findings, and others like them, underscore the bidirectional and interactive effects of nature and nurture. They contribute to a growing literature on children's resilience, which indicates time and again that children at risk for developmental problems who have a warm, supportive relationship with a parent or other adult display more favorable adjustment in adolescence and adulthood.[79]

LONGITUDINAL RESEARCH

In the absence of opportunities to randomly assign children to home environments, the most common approach to examining the long-term impact of parenting on development is a longitudinal design. Statistical procedures are used to estimate the relationship between parenting and future child outcomes, while controlling for child characteristics at the time that parenting was assessed. A growing number of these studies suggest a lasting impact of parenting—one not solely due to the evocative impact of child characteristics on parenting practices.

To cite just one example, in an investigation of more than 500 children, researchers obtained measures of quality of parenting (through interviews with mothers) and of child adjustment in kindergarten (through teacher ratings of children's behavior). Teacher ratings of child adjustment were repeated at grade six, when school grades were also gathered. After many factors (including family background and kindergarten adjustment) had been controlled, supportive parenting at kindergarten age—as indicated by maternal warmth, awareness of and concern about the child's social experiences, and use of calm discussion, guidance, and reasoning in disciplining—predicted academic performance in grade six. Furthermore, supportive parenting appeared particularly important in grade six adjustment for children who had been reared in single-parent and/or low-income families. For example, in mother-headed families where supportive parenting was low, the intensity of children's grade six behavior problems was nearly twice as great as in mother-headed families where supportive parenting was high.

In this investigation, supportive parenting showed little relationship with later adjustment among children reared in two-parent, economically advantaged homes. In most such families, mothers were high in supportiveness, which made the consequences of their good parenting difficult to detect. As the authors noted, parenting is affected by a complex context of situational variables. Its impact appears weaker than it actually is under advantaged family and social conditions, where parenting overall is less variable and more supportive.

INTERVENTION RESEARCH

Indisputable evidence that parenting matters comes from intervention experiments. In an impressive example addressing the impact of parent training on negative parenting behaviors and outcomes associated with divorce, nearly 150 recently separated mothers of first- to third-grade sons were randomly assigned, two thirds to an experimental group and one third to a no-intervention control group.[80] The experimental group experienced a fourteen- to sixteen-session program, one session per week, supplemented by midweek phone calls from the interveners to encourage use of the procedures and to troubleshoot problems. The intervention consisted of intensive teaching of parenting principles, videotapes depicting families using effective parenting techniques to help their children adjust to the divorce transition, and role-play practice. Mothers also received training in managing their own emotions and in ways to deal with family conflict, including ex-spouses, under the assumption that a parent who could better handle the stresses of her own life was more likely to implement good parenting practices. Laboratory observations of mother-son interactions, gathered just before the intervention and at six- and twelve-month follow-ups, were used to assess program effects.

Findings revealed that experimental-group mothers reduced their use of coercive parenting over time, whereas control-group mothers became increasingly coercive. In addition, experimental-group mothers showed less decay in positive parenting during the transition to a single-parent household. Finally, increases in an overall index of effective parenting predicted improved child adjustment, as rated by parents, teachers, and children themselves.

Another similar study, which included 240 families of divorce, each with a nine- to twelve-year-old, demonstrated long-term benefits of a brief but intensive parenting training program.[81] Children whose mothers attended an eleven-week parenting skills class not only showed better immediate adjustment but were functioning more favorably at a six-year follow-up than youths whose parents had not attended the parenting class.

INGREDIENTS OF EFFECTIVE PARENTING

In the studies just reported, and in countless others documenting the relationship of parenting to concurrent and future child outcomes, the features of good parenting are similar. Together, they form the authoritative child-rearing style, a combination of three categories of parenting behaviors that, when implemented over a wide range of situations, generate an enduring, positive child-rearing climate.[82] These ingredients are the following:

1. *Acceptance and involvement.* Authoritative parents are warm, attentive, and sensitive to their children's needs. They take time to establish an enjoyable, emotionally fulfilling bond that draws their child into close connection. This affectionate, caring relationship motivates children—even those who are temperamentally inattentive, impulsive, and difficult to rear[83]—to listen to and follow parents' suggestions and directives, as a means of preserving a gratifying parent-child tie.
2. *Control.* Authoritative parents exercise firm, reasonable control. They consistently insist on mature behavior, enforce their demands, and give age-appropriate reasons for their expectations. By offering explanations, authoritative parents exert control in ways that appear fair and reasonable, not arbitrary, to the child, thereby inducing far more compliance, as well as personal adoption of parental standards, than other child management strategies.
3. *Autonomy granting.* Authoritative parents engage in gradual, appropriate autonomy granting, allowing the child to make decisions in areas where he or she is ready to make choices. Their goal is to nurture a responsible, mature young person. Because authoritative parents are firm and rational early on, they earn the privilege of easing up later, because their children have developed self-control.

Many studies show that these fundamentals of good parenting promote all the elements that make up a well-adjusted child: an upbeat mood, empathy, kindness, honesty, cooperativeness, positive social skills, motivation to learn, and good school performance. Furthermore, authoritative parenting deters emotional and behavior problems. It is effective for children of both genders and of diverse ages, temperaments, and socioeconomic backgrounds.[84] The authoritative style also has broad cultural validity, predicting cognitive and social competence across many ethnic groups and in cultures as different from the United States as China and Korea.[85] Indeed, most cultures sense the value of authoritative parenting. A survey of parenting in over 180 societies found that a combination of warmth and reasonable control is the most common pattern of child-rearing around the world.[86]

Because many forces in addition to parents play roles in children's upbringing, implementing the authoritative style does not ensure a problem-free child. But children whose parents are authoritative are far more likely to develop in healthy ways and are far less likely to have serious difficulties than children of parents who use other approaches. Indeed, supportive aspects of the authoritative style are a powerful source of resilience, helping children surmount biologically based limitations and protecting them from the negative impact of family stress and other environmental threats to development.[87] In sum, a clear, scientifically based set of recommendations for good parenting exists.

POSITIVE PARENTING / POSITIVE PEERS

The "parents matter little" supposition includes a corollary—that next to heredity, the most consequential source of children's development is the peer group. However, no conclusive evidence exists for this conjecture. It is based on an array of selective and equivocal findings, mustered to build a case that parents' influence is confined to how children behave in their presence and does not extend beyond the home.

A large empirical literature documents the interdependence of parental and peer effects on children's social competence and long-term adjustment. Early on, during the preschool years, responsible parents manage their youngsters' peer associations, arranging get-togethers and offering guidance on how to enter a peer group, interact with others, solve peer problems, and keep a positive relationship going. All these parental behaviors are associated with children's social skills.[88] Other aspects of parenting also promote children's peer sociability, even when that is not parents' primary aim. For example, time spent in sensitive, emotionally positive conversations and in play with young children—during which children observe and pick up good social skills—is linked to children's social competence.[89]

In adolescence, parents continue to influence young peoples' choice of peer associates and the quality of their peer relationships. Teenagers with authoritative parents are more likely to spend time with self-controlled, high-achieving peers, whose attitudes, values, and behaviors further strengthen their maturity. In contrast, adolescents whose parents use less-effective child-rearing styles—coercive, permissive, or uninvolved—tend to gravitate toward antisocial, drug-using agemates and to become increasingly like them over time.[90] Recent evidence also demonstrates that secure attachment to and warm interaction with parents predict adolescents' sense of security and positive communication within friendships. Friendship security, in turn, is related to teenagers' sense of security and good communication in dating relationships.[91]

Finally, parents often worry about their children's capacity to resist unfavorable peer pressures during adolescence. But once again, the authoritative style is related to such resistance.[92] Teenagers whose parents are supportive and exert appropriate oversight respect their parents, an attitude that acts as an antidote to negative peer influences.[93] In contrast, adolescents who experience harsh, overbearing parental control or too little control tend to be highly peer-oriented, often relying on friends rather than parents for advice about their personal lives and futures and willing to break their parents' rules, ignore their schoolwork, use drugs, engage in early sexual activity, commit delinquent acts, and hide their talents to be popular with agemates.[94]

Parenting, then, has a potent impact—both directly and indirectly— on peer ties in childhood and adolescence. In fact, the overriding emphasis on peers as a source of development is itself a product of our culture. Compared with other nations, the United States is more peer-oriented; it places greater emphasis on gregariousness and peer acceptance, and its young people spend more of their out-of-school hours with peers.[95] As more American parents with hectic lives retreat from their children, peers take over. Without a constructive link between the values taught at home and the values of the peer group, the consequences of high peer orientation are decidedly harmful, yielding a rise in virtually every youth problem of current concern in the United States.

PARENTING AND CHILD OUTCOMES

"Parenting matters little" advocates downplay or dismiss the parenting/child outcome relationships just reviewed, judging them to be too weak to be meaningful. But recent, well-designed research reveals that links between parenting and children's development are sometimes substantial. For example, in one large-scale study, the correlation between authoritative parenting and adolescents' social responsibility was .76 for mothers and .49 for fathers.[96] Similarly, in a sample of youths with antisocial behavior problems,

parents who engaged in joint problem-solving with their youngsters (they worked out disagreements through rational discussion;
established firm, consistent control; and monitored the adolescents'
whereabouts) reduced lawbreaking by 27 to 42 percent.[97]

When weak associations between parenting practices and children's development are found, they are not necessarily due to the
feeble impact of parenting. Throughout this chapter, we have seen
that the power of good parenting shows up especially strongly under
conditions of biological and/or environmental risk. Examining parenting in undifferentiated samples of children—some of whom require less demonstrative parental support and control because they
are temperamentally easy to rear and because their home, school,
and neighborhood contexts are favorable—underestimates parenting
effects.

But even in such samples, parenting correlates with child outcomes on the order of .20 to .30—associations that, although modest, are consequential. In fact, the strength of this association
equals or exceeds others in the realm of human health that most
Americans accept as meaningful, and that many take as a sufficient basis for changing their behavior. Specifically, the parent-
ing/child adjustment relationship approaches the correlation of
media violence with aggression, equals the correlation of condom
use with sexually transmitted HIV, and exceeds correlations of
passive smoke exposure with lung cancer, asbestos exposure with
laryngeal cancer, and calcium intake with bone mass.[98] America's
uncritical receptiveness to the recent assertion of parents' insig-
nificance—its willingness to take seriously other behavior/health
relationships, but not that between parenting and children's well-
being—is emblematic of diminished parental commitment and
responsibility.

RESTORING AMERICA'S COMMITMENT TO PARENTING

Compared with their agemates of the previous two decades,
American children and youths are less motivated academically;
more programmed and overscheduled; more focused on violence-
filled, gender-stereotyped media; more deviant, antisocial, and
anxious; and more egoistic and self-satisfied. At the same time,
American youngsters are spending less leisure and conversational
time with their parents and are more often targets of parental impatience and punitiveness. They are also growing up in families with

weaker community ties than in the past, as indexed by parents' associations with friends and involvement in community organizations and religious institutions—links that provide social pressures and social supports for good parenting. Furthermore, most American parents view themselves as performing poorly at child-rearing, particularly in transmitting important values and exerting effective control over their children. In line with other assessments of the status of American children, many parents regard their youngsters as vexing problems.

Although the social environment in which American families find themselves—with its endless array of media and products beamed at children, much of which is antithetical to healthy development—tests parents' limit-setting, parents have been given other cultural grounds for withdrawing from sustained involvement with and guidance of their children. Confronted with a widening array of choices for their own lives, many do not select options that protect and promote their children's development, even when they could do so.

Also notable is that American parents are not a strong political force for their own and their children's welfare. Unlike the aged, who have improved their condition through organizing into an energetic lobbying group (the American Association of Retired Persons) to which nearly half of citizens over age fifty belong, American parents as a group have done little to effect change. Whereas the majority of Americans age sixty-five and older vote, only 41 percent of U.S. citizens within the prime child-rearing years (ages twenty-one to thirty-four) go to the polls during presidential election years, and substantially fewer—only 25 percent—do so during the interim, congressional election years. Caught up in a culture of individualism and family autonomy, parents have acquiesced to their low government priority.

Adding fuel to parental bewilderment and retreat from children, the popular advice literature for parents offers little that is consistent to guide them. Among the scientifically couched, contradictory child-rearing messages beamed at parents, the pronouncement that parents do not count—that most of what is wrong with children and youths today can be pinned on children's genetic makeup and, to a lesser extent, on their peers—has captured the most public press. This belittling of parents' roles demolishes the need for parents, as well as other influential adults (such as caregivers and teachers) to invest in children, at a time when children are especially in need of that investment. It also provides society as a whole with the ultimate rationalization for continuing its current course of indifference to child and family needs.

Recently, national columnist Ellen Goodman railed about the murkiness of child-rearing studies, blithely unaware of the consensus of hundreds of investigations of parenting that converge on the same conclusion. "As far as kids are concerned," she cynically remarked, "everything is just a placebo."[99] Perhaps because the research literature confirms what folk wisdom has long assumed—that parental affection, stimulation, supervision, and reasoned direction foster children's competence—researchers have neglected to disseminate, and the media has failed to call attention to, these parenting certainties. Indeed, when all else minimally supports children, committed parents are their last stronghold of protection. Research indicates that parents' personal psychological resources are the most effective factor in buffering children's development from damaging biological and social influences.[100] Thus, the very exposure of children to so many negative forces beyond the family makes parenting more important today than it has ever been.

Although most parents desire information on how to rear children, they do not have access to the best, scientifically grounded advice. If we are to empower parents, we must increase their access to accurate information. Indeed, America's intractability in upgrading its family policies may depend on this unified parenting message, because policymakers look to behavioral scientists for a sense of direction. A strong beginning would be a cadre of respected scientists reaching out to parents with a concise set of parenting principles on which there is common agreement, while dispelling widely publicized, erroneous statements.

Effectively informing parents also requires a new focus of investigation: how best to bridge the gap between parenting research and parenting practice through the collaborative efforts of scientists, government agencies, community organizations, religious institutions, schools, and media. Connecting with the everyday citizen has yet to become an esteemed endeavor among scholars of child development; but some investigators are nevertheless doing so,[101] and fortunately so, as a groundswell of scholarly commitment to renewing parents' vision of themselves as leaders and protectors of their children's development is indispensable for the welfare of America's children.

Finally, as such efforts stimulate "cultures of good parenting," they deliver an extra boost to children's well-being. When many parents in a neighborhood are highly involved in their children's school lives, the impact of parent involvement on children's academic achievement is magnified.[102] When most or all members of a peer group have authoritative parents, adolescents are more likely to encourage one another to resist unfavorable peer pressures.[103] In these and other ways, a communal commitment to effective parenting activates other positive forces, helping to ensure that for our nation's children, good things go together.

NOTES

1. U.S. Census Bureau. (2003). *Statistical abstract of the United States* (123rd ed.). Washington, DC: U.S. Government Printing Office.

2. Evans, G. W. (2004). The environment of child poverty. *American Psychologist, 59,* 77–92.

3. U.S. Department of Education. (2001). *Pursuing excellence: A study of U.S. twelfth-grade mathematics and science achievement in international context.* Washington, DC: U.S. Government Printing Office.

4. National Center for Education Statistics, U.S. Office of Education. (2003). *The Nation's Report Card: Reading and Mathematics.* Retrieved from nces.ed.gov/nationsreportcard/mathematics/results2003/natachieve-g4.asp.

5. Larson, R. W. (2001). How U.S. children and adolescents spend time: What it does (and doesn't) tell us about their development. *Current Directions in Psychological Science, 10,* 160–164.

6. Hofferth, S. L., & Sandberg, J. F. (2001). How American children spend their time. *Journal of Marriage and the Family, 63,* 295–308.

7. Hofferth, S., & Sandberg, J. (1999). *Family life changes in American children's time, 1981–1997.* Retrieved from www.fourhcouncil.edu/Revolution/Resources/Family_Life_Changes.asp.

8. Ibid.

9. Gillman, M. W., Rifas-Shiman, S. L., Frazier, A. L., Rockett, H. R. H., Camargo, C. A. Jr., Field, A. E., et al. (2000). Family dinner and diet quality among older children and adolescents. *Archives of Family Medicine, 9,* 235–240.

10. Beals, D. E. (2001). Eating and reading: Links between family conversations with preschoolers and later language literacy. In D. K. Dickinson & P. O. Tabors (Eds.), *Beginning literacy with language: Young children's learning at home and school* (pp. 75–92). Baltimore, MD: Paul H. Brookes.

11. Bradley, R. H., Caldwell, B. M., Rock, S. K., Ramey, C. T., Barnard, D. E., Gray, C., et al. (1989). Home environment and cognitive development in the first 3 years of life: A collaborative study involving six sites and three ethnic groups in North America. *Developmental Psychology, 25,* 217–235.

12. Hofferth & Sandberg. (See note 6.)

13. Berk, L. E. (1992). The extracurriculum. In P. W. Jackson (Ed.), *Handbook of research on curriculum* (pp. 1002–1043). New York: Macmillan; Bridges, L. J., & Moore, K. A. (2002). Religious involvement and children's well-being: What research tells us (and what it doesn't). *Child Trends Research Brief.* Retrieved from www.childtrends.org; Mahoney, J. L. (2000). Participation in school extracurricular activities as a moderator in the development of antisocial patterns. *Child Development, 71,* 502–516.

14. Hofferth & Sandberg. (See note 6.)

15. Comstock, G. A., & Scharrer, E. (2001). The use of television and other film-related media. In D. G. Singer & J. L. Singer (Eds.), *Handbook of children and the media* (pp. 47–72). Thousand Oaks, CA: Sage.

16. Roberts, D. F., Foehr, U. G., Rideout, V. J., & Brodie, M. (1999). *Kids and media at the new millennium: A comprehensive national analysis of children's media use.* Menlo Park, CA: Kaiser Family Foundation.

17. Anderson, C. A., & Bushman, B. J. (2002). The effects of media violence on society. *Science, 295,* 2377–2379; Donnerstein, E., Slaby, R. G., & Eron, L. D. (1994). The mass media and youth aggression. In L. D. Eron, J. H. Gentry, & P. Schlegel (Eds.), *Reason to hope: A psychosocial perspective on violence and youth* (pp. 219–250). Washington, DC: American Psychological Association; Gortmaker, S. L., Must, A., Sobol, A. M., Peterson, K., Colditz, G. A., & Dietz, W. H. (1996). Television viewing as a cause of increasing obesity among children in the United States, 1986–1990. *Archives of Pediatric and Adolescent Medicine, 150,* 356–362; Signorielli, N. (1993). Television, the portrayal of women, and children's attitudes. In G. L. Berry & J. K. Asamen (Eds.), *Children and television: Images in a changing sociocultural world* (pp. 229–242). Newbury Park, CA: Sage.

18. Anderson, C. A., & Bushman, B. J. (2001). Effects of violent video games on aggressive behavior, aggressive cognition, aggressive affect, physiological arousal, and prosocial behavior: A meta-analytic review of the scientific literature. *Psychological Science, 12,* 353–359; Dietz, T. L. (1998). An examination of violence and gender role portrayals in video games: Implications for gender socialization and aggressive behavior. *Sex Roles, 38,* 425–442.

19. Comstock, G. A., & Scharrer, E. (1999). *Television: What's on, who's watching, and what it means.* San Diego: Academic Press.

20. Kraut, R., Patterson, M., Lundmark, V., Kiesler, S., Mukopadhyay, T., & Scherlis, W. (1998). Internet paradox: A social technology that reduces social involvement and well-being? *American Psychologist, 53,* 1017–1031.

21. Straus, M. A., & Stewart, J. H. (1999). Corporal punishment by American parents: National data on prevalence, chronicity, severity, and duration, in relation to child and family characteristics. *Clinical Child and Family Psychology Review, 2,* 55–70.

22. Gershoff, E. T. (2002). Corporal punishment by parents and associated child behaviors and experiences: A meta-analytic and theoretical review. *Psychological Bulletin, 128,* 539–579.

23. Brezina, T. (1999). Teenage violence toward parents as an adaptation to family strain: Evidence from a national survey of male adolescents. *Youth & Society, 30,* 416–444; Gershoff, E. T. (2002). Corporal punishment by parents and associated child behaviors and experiences: A meta-analytic and theoretical review. *Psychological Bulletin, 128,* 539–579.

24. Kaiser Foundation. (2001). *Talking with kids about tough issues.* Retrieved from www.talkingwithkids.com.

25. Ibid.

26. Jaccard, J., Dodge, T., & Dittus, P. (2002). Parent-adolescent communication about sex and birth control: A conceptual framework. In S. S. Feldman & D. A. Rosenthal (Eds.), *Talking sexuality: Parent-adolescent communication* (pp. 9–41). San Francisco: Jossey-Bass.

27. Hetherington, E. M., & Stanley-Hagan, M. (2002). Parenting in divorced and remarried families. In M. H. Bornstein (Ed.), *Handbook of parenting: Vol. 3. Being and becoming a parent* (2nd ed., pp. 287–315). Mahwah, NJ: Erlbaum.

28. Amato, P. R. (2001). Children of divorce in the 1990s: An update of the Amato and Keith (1991) meta-analysis. *Journal of Family Psychology, 15,* 355–370; Wolfinger, N. H. (2000). Beyond the intergenerational transmission of divorce: Do people replicate the patterns of marital instability they grew up with? *Journal of Family Issues, 21,* 1061–1086.

29. Amato. (See note 28.) Kunz, J. (2001). Parental divorce and children's interpersonal relationships: A meta-analysis. *Journal of Divorce and Remarriage, 34,* 19–47; Reifman, A., Villa, L. C., Amans, J. A., Rethinam, V., & Telesca, T. Y. (2001). Children of divorce in the 1990s: A meta-analysis. *Journal of Divorce & Remarriage, 36,* 27–36.

30. Amato. (See note 28.)

31. Twenge, J. M. (2000). The age of anxiety? Birth cohort change in anxiety and neuroticism, 1952–1993. *Journal of Personality and Social Psychology, 79,* 1007–1021.

32. Ibid.

33. Putnam, R. D. (2000). *Bowling alone: The collapse and revival of American community.* New York: Simon & Schuster.

34. Smith, T. W. (1997). Factors related to misanthropy in contemporary American society. *Social Science Research, 26,* 170–196.

35. National Center for Injury Prevention and Control. (2004). Suicide in the United States. Retrieved from www.cdc.gov/ncipc/factsheets/suifacts.htm.

36. Twenge, J. M., & Campbell, W. K. (2001). Age and birth cohort differences in self-esteem: A cross-temporal meta-analysis. *Personality and Social Psychology Review, 5,* 321–344.

37. See, for example, Damon, W. (1995). *Greater expectations: Overcoming the culture of indulgence in America's homes and schools.* New York: Free Press.

38. U.S. Department of Health and Human Services. (2002b). Obesity still on the rise, new data show. Retrieved from www.cdc.gov/nchs/releases/02news/obesityonrise.htm.

39. Davison, K. K., & Birch, L. L. (2002). Obesigenic families: Parents' physical activity and dietary intake patterns predict girls' risk of over-weight. *International Journal of Obesity and Related Metabolic Disorders, 26,* 1186–1193; Spruijt-Metz, D., Lindquist, C. H., Birch, L. L., Fisher, J. O., & Goran, M. I. (2002). Relation between mothers' child-feeding practices and children's adiposity. *American Journal of Clinical Nutrition, 75,* 581–586; Birch, L. L., & Fisher, J. A. (1995). Appetitive and eating behavior in children. *Pediatric Clinics of North America, 42,* 931–953.

40. Briefel, R. R., Reidy, K., Karwe, V., & Devaney, B. (2004). Feeding infants and toddlers study: Improvements needed in meeting infant feeding recommendations. *Journal of the American Dietetic Association, 104 (Suppl. 1),* S31–S37.

41. U.S. Department of Health and Human Services. (2000). *Promoting better health for young people through physical activity and sports.* Washington, DC: U.S. Government Printing Office; U.S. Department of Health and Human Services. (2001). *CDC School Health Policies and Programs Study, 2001.* Retrieved from www.cdc.gov/nccdphp/dash/shpps/factsheets/fs00_pe.htm.

42. Vandivere, S., Gallagher, M., & Moore, K. A. (2004). Changes in children's well-being and family environments. *Snapshots of America's Families* III, No. 10. New York: Urban Institute. Retrieved from www.urban.org/url.cfm?ID=310912.

43. Public Agenda. (2002). *A lot easier said than done: Parents talk about raising children in today's America.* Retrieved from www.publicagenda.org/specials/parents/parents.htm.

44. Ibid.

45. Ibid.

46. Berk, L. E. (2001). *Awakening children's minds: How parents and teachers can make a difference.* New York: Oxford University Press; Damon, W. (See note 37.); Steinberg, L. (2004). *The 10 basic principles of good parenting.* New York: Simon & Schuster.

47. Guydish, M. (2002, October 31). National survey: Today's parents critical of efforts. *TimesLeader.* Retrieved from www.timesleader.com/mld/thetimesleader/2002/10/31/news/4407738.htm?template=content-Modules/printstory.jsp.

48. Public Agenda. (2002). (See note 43.)

49. Kamerman, S. B. (2000). From maternity to parental leave policies: Women's health, employment, and child and family well-being. *Journal of the American Medical Women's Association, 55,* 96–99.

50. Hewlett, S. (2003). *Creating a life.* New York: Miramax.

51. NICHD Early Child Care Research Network. (2000).

52. Cost, Quality, and Outcomes Study Team. (1995). Cost, quality and outcomes in child care centers: Key findings and recommendations. *Young Children, 50*(4), 40–44.

53. Cryer, D., & Burchinal, M. (1995). Parents as child care consumers. In S. W. Helburn (Ed.), *Cost, quality, and child outcomes in child care centers* (pp. 203–209). Denver, University of Colorado.

54. Halfon, N., & McLearn, K. T. (2002). Families with children under 3: What we know and implications for results and policy. In N. Halfon & K. T. McLearn (Eds.), *Child rearing in America: Challenges facing parents with young children* (pp. 367–412). New York: Cambridge University Press; Rickel, A. U., & Becker, E. (1997). *Keeping children from harm's way.* Washington, DC: American Psychological Association.

55. Hochschild, A. R. (1997). *The time bind: When work becomes home and home becomes work.* New York: Metropolitan Books.

56. Mischel, L., Bernstein, J., & Schmitt, J. (2001). *The state of working America 2000–2001.* New York: Cornell University Press.

57. Schor, J. B. (2002). Time crunch among American parents. In S. A. Hewlett, N. Rankin, & C. West (Eds.), *Taking parenting public: The case for a new social movement* (pp. 83–102). Lanham, MD: Roman & Littlefield.

58. See the evidence on the long-term, developmental consequences of infant-mother attachment, which underscore the importance of both quality and consistency of care: Belsky, J., & Cassidy, J. (1994). Attachment: Theory and evidence. In M. Rutter & D. Hay (Eds.), *Development through life* (pp. 373–402). Oxford, UK: Blackwell; Thompson, R. A. (1998). Early sociopersonality development. In W. Damon (Series Ed.) & N. Eisenberg (Vol. Ed.), *Handbook of child psychology: Vol. 3. Social, emotional, and personality development* (5th ed., pp. 58–65). New York: Wiley.

59. Clark, R., Hyde, J. S., Essex, M. J., & Klein, M. H. (1997). Length of maternity leave and quality of mother-infant interaction. *Child Development, 68,* 364–383; Hyde, J. S., Klein, M. H., Essex, M. J., & Clark, R. (1995). Maternity leave and women's mental health. *Psychology of Women Quarterly, 19,* 257–285.

60. NICHD (National Institute of Child Health and Human Development) Early Child Care Research Network. (1999). Child care and mother-child interaction in the first 3 years of life. *Developmental Psychology, 35,* 1399–1413.

61. NICHD (National Institute of Child Health and Human Development) Early Child Care Research Network. (2003). Does amount of time spent in child care predict socioemotional adjustment during the transition to kindergarten? *Child Development, 74,* 976–1005.

62. NICHD (National Institute of Child Health and Human Development) Early Child Care Research Network. (1997). The effects of infant child care on infant-mother attachment security: Results of the NICHD Study of Early Child Care. *Child Development, 68,* 860–879; NICHD

(National Institute of Child Health and Human Development) Early Child Care Research Network. (1999). (See note 60.)

63. Perry-Jenkins, M., Pepetti, R. L., & Crouter, A. C. (2000). Work and family in the 1990s. *Journal of Marriage and the Family, 62*, 981–998.

64. Barber, B. K., & Olsen, J. A. (1997). Socialization in context: Connection, regulation, and autonomy in the family, school, and neighborhood, and with peers. *Journal of Adolescent Research, 12*, 287–315; Baumrind, D. (1971). Current patterns of parental authority. *Developmental Psychology Monograph, 4*(No. 1, Pt. 2).

65. Hart, C. H., Newell, L. D., & Olsen, S. F. (2003). Parenting skills and social/communicative competence in childhood. In J. O. Greene & B. R. Burleson (Eds.), *Handbook of communication and social interaction skills* (pp. 753–797). Hillsdale, NJ: Erlbaum; Nix, R. L., Pinderhughes, E. E., Dodge, K. A., Bates, J. E., Pettit, G. S., & McFadyen-Ketchum, S. A. (1999). The relation between mothers' hostile attribution tendencies and children's externalizing behavior problems: The mediating role of mothers' harsh discipline practices. *Child Development, 70*, 896–909; Thompson, A., Hollis, C., & Richards, D. (2003). Authoritarian parenting attitudes as a risk for conduct problems: Results of a British national cohort study. *European Child and Adolescent Psychiatry, 12*, 84–91.

66. Barber & Olsen. (1997). (See note 64.); Nix et al. (1999). Thompson et al. (2003). (See note 65.)

67. Hochschild, A. R. (1997). *The time bind: When work becomes home and home becomes work.* New York: Metropolitan Books.

68. Goodkin, S. H., & Goodkin, D. (1995). *Parenting for dummies.* Foster City, CA: IDG Books Worldwide; Friel, J. C., & Friel, L. D. (1999). *The seven worst things parents do.* Deerfield Beech, FL: Health Communications.

69. Johnson, D. (1998, July 18). My blue heaven. *New York Review of Books,* p. 15.

70. Refer to the review of the parenting advice literature in Berk (2001). (See note 46.) Examples of widely conflicting, contemporary advice to parents are David Elkind's (1994) *The hurried child.* Boston: Allyn and Bacon; Thomas Gordon's (1990) *Parent effectiveness training.* New York: American Library; and William Damon's (1995) *Greater expectations.* (See note 37.)

71. Harris, J. R. (1998). *The nurture assumption: Why children turn out the way they do.* New York: Free Press.

72. Collins, W. A., Maccoby, E. E., Steinberg, L., Hetherington, E. M., & Bornstein, M. H. (2000). Contemporary research on parenting: The case for nature and nurture. *American Psychologist, 55*, 218–232; Gardner, H. (1998, November 5). Do parents count? New York Review of Books. Retrieved from www.nybooks.com/articles/684: Maccoby, E. E. (2000). Parenting and its effects on children: On reading and misreading behavioral genetics. *Annual Review of Psychology, 51*, 1–27.

73. Tavris, C. (2003, February 28). Mind games: Psychological warfare between therapists and scientists. *The Chronicle of Higher Education,* p. B7.

74. Horowitz, F. D. (2000). Child development and the PITS: Simple questions, complex answers, and developmental theory. *Child Development, 71*, 1–10; Lerner, R. M. Theories of human development: Contemporary perspectives. In W. Damon (Series Ed.) & R. M. Lerner (Vol. Ed.), *Handbook of child psychology: Vol. 1. Theoretical models of human development* (5th ed., pp. 1–24). New York: Wiley.

75. Maccoby, 2000, p. 18. (See note 72.)

76. Moore, E. G. J. (1986). Family socialization and the IQ test performance of traditionally and transracially adopted black children. *Developmental Psychology, 22*, 317–326; Scarr, S., & Weinberg, R. A. (1983). The Minnesota Adoption Studies: Genetic differences and malleability. *Child Development, 54*, 424–435; Shiff, M., Duyme, M., Dumaret, A., & Tomkiewitz, S. (1982). How much could we boost scholastic achievement and IQ scores? A direct answer from a French adoption study. *Cognition, 12*, 165–196.

77. Cadoret, R. J., Cain, C. A., & Crowe, R. R. (1983). Evidence for gene-environment interaction in the development of adolescent antisocial behavior. *Behavior Genetics, 13*, 301–310.

78. Tienari, P., Wynne, L. C., Moring, J., & Lahti, I. (1994). The Finnish adoptive family study of schizophrenia: Implications for family research. *British Journal of Psychiatry, 164*, 20–26.

79. Masten, A. S. (2001). Ordinary magic: Resilience processes in development. *American Psychologist, 56*, 227–238.

80. Forgatch, M. S., & DeGarmo, D. S. (1999). Parenting through change: An effective prevention program for single mothers. *Journal of Consulting and Clinical Psychology, 67*, 711–724.

81. Wolchik, S. A., Sandler, I. N., Millsap, R. E., Plummer, B. A., Greene, S. M., Anderson, E. R., et al. (2003). Six-year follow-up of preventive interventions for children of divorce: A randomized controlled trial. *Journal of the American Medical Association, 288*, 1874–1881.

82. Gray, M. R., & Steinberg, L. (1999). Unpacking authoritative parenting: Reassessing a multidimensional construct. *Journal of Marriage and the Family, 61*, 574–587; Hart, Newell, & Olsen. (2003). (See note 65.); Russell, A., Mize, J., & Bissaker, K. (2002). Parent-child relationships. In P. K. Smith & C. H. Hart (Eds.), *Handbook of childhood social development* (pp. 205–222). Oxford, UK: Blackwell.

83. Kochanska, G., Gross, J. N., Lin, M.-H., & Nichols, K. E. (2002). Guilt in young children: Development, determinants, and relations with broader system standards. *Child Development, 73*, 461–482; Fowles, D. C., & Kochanska, G. (2000). Temperament as a moderator of pathways to conscience in children: The contribution of electrodermal activity. *Psychophysiology, 37*, 863–872; Kochanska, G. (1997). Multiple pathways to conscience for children with different temperaments: From toddlerhood to age 5. *Developmental Psychology, 33*, 228–240.

84. Baumrind, D., & Black, A. E. (1967). Child care practices anteceding three patterns of preschool behavior. *Genetic Psychology Monographs, 75*,

43–88; Gray & Steinberg. (1999). (See note 82.); Herman, M. R., Dornbusch, S. M., Herron, M. C., & Herting, J. R. (1997). The influence of family regulation, connection, and psychological autonomy on six measures of adolescent functioning. *Journal of Adolescent Research, 12,* 34–67; Luster, T., & McAdoo, H. (1996). Family and child influences on educational attainment: A secondary analysis of the High/Scope Perry Preschool data. *Developmental Psychology, 32,* 26–39; Mackey, K., Arnold, M. K., & Pratt, M. W. (2001). Adolescents' stories of decision making in more and less authoritative families: Representing the voices of parents in narrative. *Journal of Adolescent Research, 16,* 243–268; Steinberg, L. D., Darling, N. E., & Fletcher, A. C. (1995). Authoritative parenting and adolescent development: An ecological journey. In P. Moen, G. H. Elder Jr., & K. Luscher (Eds.), *Examining lives in context* (pp. 423–466). Washington, DC: American Psychological Association.

85. Steinberg, L. (2001). We know some things: Parent-adolescent relationships in retrospect and prospect. *Journal of Research on Adolescence, 11,* 1–19; Chen, X., Dong, Q., & Zhou, H. (1997). Authoritative and authoritarian parenting practices and social and school performance in Chinese children. *International Journal of Behavioral Development, 21,* 855–873; Chen, X., Liu, M., & Li, D. (2000). Parental warmth, control, and indulgence and their relations to adjustment in Chinese children: A longitudinal study. *Journal of Family Psychology, 14,* 401–419; Mantzicopouilos, P. Y., & Oh-Hwang, Y. (1998). The relationship of psychosocial maturity to parenting quality and intellectual ability for American and Korean adolescents. *Contemporary Educational Psychology, 23,* 195–206.

86. Rohner, R. P., & Rohner, E. C. (1981). *Parental acceptance-rejection and parental control: Cross-cultural codes. Ethnology, 20,* 245–260.

87. Pettit, G. S., Bates, J. E., & Dodge, K. A. (1997). Supportive parenting, ecological context, and children's adjustment: A seven-year longitudinal study. *Child Development, 68,* 908–923.

88. Ladd, G. W., LeSieur, K., & Profilet, S. M. (1993). Direct parental influences on young children's peer relations. In S. Duck (Ed.), *Learning about relationships* (Vol. 2, pp. 152–183). London: Sage; Laird, R. D., Pettit, G. S., Mize, J., & Lindsey, E. (1994). Mother-child conversations about peers: Contributions to competence. *Family Relations, 43,* 425–432; Mize, J., & Pettit, G. S. (1997). Mothers' social coaching, mother-child relationship style, and children's peer competence: Is the medium the message? *Child Development, 68,* 312–332.

89. Russell, A., Pettit, G. S., & Mize, J. (1998). Horizontal qualities in parent-child relationships: Parallels with and possible consequences for children's peer relationships. *Developmental Review, 18,* 313–352; Lindsey, E. W., & Mize, J. (2000). Parent-child physical and pretense play: Links to children's social competence. *Merrill-Palmer Quarterly, 46,* 1479–1498; Pettit, G. S., Brown, E. G., Mize, J., & Lindsey, E. (1998). Mothers' and fathers' socializing

behaviors in three contexts: Links with children's peer competence. *Merrill-Palmer Quarterly, 44,* 385–394.

90. Mounts, N. S., & Steinberg, L. (1995). An ecological analysis of peer influence on adolescent grade point average and drug use. *Developmental Psychology, 31,* 915–922.

91. Furman, W., Simon, V. A., Shaffer, L., & Bouchey, H. A. (2002). Adolescents' working models and styles for relationships with parents, friends, and romantic partners. *Child Development, 73,* 241–255.

92. Fletcher, A. C., Darling, N. E., Steinberg, L., & Dornbusch, S. M. (1995). The company they keep: Relation of adolescents' adjustment and behavior to their friends' perceptions of authoritative parenting in the social network. *Developmental Psychology, 31,* 300–310; Mason, C. A., Cauce, A. M., Gonzales, N., & Hiraga, Y. (1996). Neither too sweet nor too sour: Problem peers, maternal control, and problem behavior in African American adolescents. *Child Development, 67,* 2115–2130.

93. Sim, T. N. (2000). Adolescent psychosocial competence: The importance and role of regard for parents. *Journal of Research on Adolescence, 10,* 49–64.

94. Fuligni, A. J., & Eccles, J. S. (1993). Perceived parent-child relationships and early adolescents' orientation toward peers. *Developmental Psychology, 29,* 622–632.

95. Fuligni, A. J., & Stevenson, H. W. (1995). Time use and mathematics achievement among American, Chinese, and Japanese high school students. *Child Development, 66,* 830–842; Larson, 2001. (See Note 5.)

96. Hetherington, E. M., Henderson, S. H., & Reiss, D. (1999). Adolescent siblings in stepfamilies: Family functioning and adolescent adjustment. *Monographs of the Society for Research in Child Development, 64*(4, Serial No. 259).

97. Patterson, G. R., & Forgatch, M. (1995). Predicting future clinical adjustment from treatment outcome and process variables. *Psychological Assessment, 7,* 275–285.

98. See correlations presented in Bushman, B. J., & Anderson, C. A. (2001). Media violence and the American public: Scientific facts versus media misinformation. *American Psychologist, 56,* 477–489. Original sources: Paik, H., & Comstock, G. (1994). The effects of television violence on antisocial behavior: A meta-analysis. *Communication Research, 21,* 516–546; Smith, A. H., Handley, M. A., & Wood, R. (1990). Epidemiological evidence indicates asbestos causes laryngeal cancer. *Journal of Occupational Medicine, 32,* 499–507; Weller, S. C. (1993). A meta-analysis of condom effectiveness in reducing sexually transmitted HIV. *Social Science and Medicine, 36,* 1635–1644; Wells, A. J. (1998). Lung cancer from passive smoking at work. *American Journal of Public Health, 88,* 1025–1029; Welten, D. C., Kemper, H. C. G., Post, G. B., & van Staveren, W. A. (1995). A meta-analysis of the effect of calcium intake on bone mass in young and middle aged females and males. *Journal of Nutrition, 125,* 2802–2813.

99. Goodman, E. (2003). Studies on child-raising continue to confound. *Boston Globe Archives*. Retrieved from www.boston.com/news/globe/editorial.opinion/oped/goodman.

100. See, for example, Belsky, J. (1984). The determinants of parenting: A process model. *Child Development, 55*, 83–96; van IJzendoorn, M. H., Goldberg, S., Kroonenberg, P. M., & Frenkel, O. J. (1992). The relative effects of maternal and child problems on the quality of attachment: A meta-analysis of attachment in clinical samples. *Child Development, 63*, 840–858.

101. For example, Hirsh-Pasek, K., & Golinkoff, R. M. (2003). *Einstein never used flash cards*. New York: Rodale, which explains to parents how to support early brain development with developmentally appropriate learning activities; Steinberg, L. (2004). *The 10 basic principles of good parenting*. New York: Simon & Schuster, which provides parents with ten research-based techniques for helping children nurture strengths and overcome weaknesses.

102. Darling, N., & Steinberg, L. (2000). Community influences on adolescent achievement and deviance. In J. Brooks-Gun, G. Duncan, & L. Aber (Eds.), *Neighborhood poverty: Context and consequences for children* (Vol. 2, pp. 120–131). New York: Russell Sage Foundation.

103. Fletcher, A., Darling, N., Steinberg, L., & Dornbusch, S. (1995). The company they keep: Relation of adolescents' adjustment and behavior to their friends' perceptions of authoritative parenting in the social network. *Developmental Psychology, 31*, 300–310.

Part II

How American Culture Is Failing Our Kids

3

The War against Parents

SYLVIA ANN HEWLETT AND CORNEL WEST

We parents are so used to being trampled on, sneered at, or just plain ignored that we often fail to understand how embattled we are. But occasionally some especially flagrant example of parent-bashing grabs our attention and we catch our breath. For a fleeting moment we glimpse ourselves from the outside in, and see and hear the contempt and carelessness American society routinely throws our way.

A few months after my (Sylvia Ann Hewlett) book *When the Bough Breaks* came out in paperback, I was invited to discuss issues of parental overload and child neglect on the Larry King radio show. In the early 1990s this was one of those hugely popular call-in radio shows that reached vast numbers of people across the country. It aired between 10 p.m. and 2 a.m., and all kinds of people called in to talk to Larry: lonely truck drivers spinning along interstate highways, trying to stay awake; security guards and insomniacs killing the dead hours in the middle of the night; etc. Most of the call-ins on this particular show were eminently forgettable, but one seared my consciousness in ways I will never forget.

Gary called in to talk to Larry King and me. He was twenty-seven years old and lived in Phoenix, Arizona. Gary wanted to talk about what was going on in his family. He and his wife had just put their three-week-old baby daughter into a kennel.

"A kennel!" we cried in unison, shocked and disbelieving. "You put your baby in a kennel?"

"Hold on," Gary said, becoming defensive. "Let me explain."

Gary and his wife, Brenda, both worked full time. He was a maintenance person at a local office complex; she worked as a checkout clerk at a convenience store. Together they earned $23,000 a year, a sum of money that "didn't go a whole distance in Phoenix." After taxes, their joint take-home pay was just over $400 a week, half of which went to pay the rent. When their daughter Jenny was born, they found themselves dealing with some heavy-duty problems. To begin with, neither of their jobs carried medical insurance, and consequently Jenny's birth triggered some huge bills: $3,930, to be precise. As Gary put it, "Jenny will be three years old before we have paid off the obstetrician." Another problem was that neither of them was entitled to parenting leave. They worked for small employers and did not qualify for job-protected leave under the terms of the Family and Medical Leave Act, which excludes businesses with fewer than fifty employees. Brenda couldn't simply quit her job, as Gary's paycheck did not even cover rent and utilities.

They coped with the actual birth by fudging and lying through their teeth. Brenda called in sick for ten days and then used up a week of accumulated vacation. When Jenny was two and a half weeks old, they hit the daycare market in Phoenix and found that the only thing they could afford was informal family daycare, which in their neighborhood boiled down to a private home where two elderly women, unlicensed and untrained, looked after eighteen babies and toddlers. When Gary dropped Jenny off, he discovered to his horror that the other children were strapped into car seats, watching television, dirty and disconsolate. Despite a frantic search, Gary and Brenda had up until then failed to find something better. Their budget was $40 a week, tops, and this was what $40 bought you on the private daycare market in Phoenix. In Gary's caustic words, "Dogs and cats have a better deal—at least kennels are tightly regulated in this city and are required to live up to some kind of standard of cleanliness and care."

Gary's parting shot was bitter: "We're not welfare cheats, we're just regular Americans working as hard as we know how to do the right thing for our kid. Why is it so difficult? Why is everything stacked against us? We feel such shame that we can't do better by our baby." His voice rose in raw sharp pain as he faded off the air.

There was a short silence as Larry King and I struggled to absorb the meaning of Gary's poignant words. Larry then cleared his throat and offered some tentative sympathy. What a stressful situation. How could any family deal well with such an impossible set of circumstances? My inadequate contribution was that as tragic as Gary's story was, it was far from being exceptional. In a nation of plummeting wages and threadbare social supports, hundreds of thousands of Americans are in precisely the same situation when they embark on the serious business of raising a child. Unlike new parents in other rich nations, American moms and dads are expected to do a stellar job without the benefits of a living wage, medical coverage, decent childcare, or parenting leave.

Caring, nurturing, cherishing—the essential components of good parenting—have less and less support in our society. These non-market values and activities have been pushed to the margins by the dominant forces of American life. The stakes could not be higher as the painful struggle of individual adults such as Gary and Brenda is much more than a private tragedy. When parents are so seriously disabled that they cannot perform their central functions, the results are disastrous for our nation—and the fallout on children is quite lethal.

The current generation of American children is spinning out of control. Hundreds of thousands are hurting and killing; millions more are failing to thrive. Child poverty rates are up and SAT scores are down, teen suicide rates have doubled since the 1970s, and child homicide rates have quadrupled since the mid-1980s.[1] In the words of one blue-ribbon commission, "Never before has one generation of American children been less healthy, less cared for, or less prepared for life than their parents were at the same age."[2] There is an urgent and desperate need to pay attention to this state of affairs, for children are not some fringe group, some bit players. Children are 100 percent of our collective future, and if we continue on our present course, this great nation will most surely tear itself to shreds.

Highlighting our problems—and our national shame—is the fact that most of these terrible trends are unique to the United States. In Germany, France, and Japan, for example, child poverty rates and school dropout rates are extremely low and heading down, and child homicide is virtually unknown. A child is twenty times more likely to be killed in New York than in Paris or Bonn, and seventy times more likely to be killed in Dallas than in Tokyo.[3]

So why has America visited such treachery on its children?

At the center of our children's agony is an enormous erosion of the parenting role. Moms and dads are increasingly unable to look after their children, with the result that our entire web of care is breaking down, blighting the lives of young people. A 1997 study sponsored by the Ad Council shows that fully two thirds of Americans now see teenagers as rude, irresponsible, and wild. They place the blame squarely on the shoulders of parents. Children are out of control because parents are failing to do their job.[4]

The fact is, too many parents have tuned out. Too many children have been left home alone, to raise themselves on a thin and cruel diet of junk food, gangster rap, and trash talk shows. More and more babies are being born without a skin—with none of that protective armor that in the past was provided by loving parents and supportive communities. Increasingly, these exposed, "skinless" children are being buffeted by a ruthless market and a poisonous culture. Many of the more vulnerable have become infected or burned, their bodies and their souls stunted and seared by the onslaught of neglect and greed.

However devastating this burgeoning tide of parental neglect, simply heaping blame on overburdened moms and dads will not solve our problems. Modern-day mothers and fathers, like those before them, struggle to put children at the center of their lives. But major impediments and obstacles stand in their way, undermining their most valiant efforts. From early in the morning till late at night, America's parents are battered by all kinds of pressures, most of which are not of their making. The truth is, the whole world is stacked against them. If parents cannot give a childhood to their children, it is not their fault.

Over the course of the last thirty years, public policy and private decision-making have tilted heavily against the altruistic nonmarket activities that make up the essence of parenting. In recent years, big business, government, and the wider culture have waged an undeclared and silent war against parents. Adults raising children have been hurt by managerial greed, pounded by tax and housing policy, diminished by psychotherapy, and invaded and degraded by the entertainment industry. A myopic government increasingly fails to protect or support parents, while an unfettered market is allowed to take up more and more private space. Our leaders talk as though they value families but act as though families were a last priority. Sooner or later, worn-out moms and dads get the message that devoting their best time to raising children is a mug's game—a lonely, thankless undertaking that cuts against the grain of all that is valued in our society. Despite the fact that the parental role and function are enormously important, we have constructed a public morality where all the kudos go to work and achievement outside the home. We live in a nation where market work, centered on competition, profits, and greed, increasingly crowds out nonmarket work, which is centered on sacrifice, commitment, and care. In today's world, what really counts in America is how much you get paid and what you can buy.

Small wonder, then, that parenting is a dying art. Small wonder, then, that parents have less and less time for their children;[5] and time is, of course, at the heart of the enterprise. Being a "good enough" parent requires providing a child with the gifts of love, attention, energy, and resources, generously and unstintingly over a long period of time. It involves nourishing a small body, but it also involves growing a child's soul—sharing the stories and rituals that awaken a child's spirit and nurturing the spiritual bonds that create meaning and morality in that child's life. The Greeks had a name for it: they called this cultivation of character and virtue in a young person *paideia*. But none of these practical or sacred tasks are easily accomplished by demeaned and devalued parents. In contemporary America, mothers and fathers are set up to fail.

Today's parents understand what the score is. In their guts, they know they have been left high and dry by a society intent on other agendas, and they are trying quite desperately to respond. From parental rights propositions to ordinances that would hold parents legally accountable for the actions of their children, they are struggling to regain their footing, reestablish their bearings, and take back control. However, despite this new awareness, few recognize how fierce the external pressures have become. Regular moms and dads have a hard time comprehending the degree to which business, government, and our culture are bitterly antagonistic toward them.

A HOSTILE MEDIA

Just think of the sound bites of our culture. In the opening episode of the popular 1990s television show *My So-Called Life*, the lead character, a depressed fifteen-year-old, says to herself, "Lately I can't seem to even look at my mother without wanting to stab her repeatedly." In an article titled "Father Knows Squat," the *Washington Post* points out that in the media, parents are one of the few remaining groups that are "regularly ridiculed, caricatured, and marginalized."[6] On television, parents tend to be blustering bores, miserly boobs, overprotective fools, or just plain dopey and twerpy. Strong, effective parents are hard to find on television today. Primetime seems to be heavily featuring dysfunctional families and irresponsible dads: In *Gilmore Girls*, for example, dad is out of the picture and mom was sixteen when she had her daughter, who is now in her first year at Yale. In *One Tree Hill*, the main character lives with his mother and goes to school with his half-brother; his dad doesn't acknowledge or support his son, who was born when the parents were still in high school. Strong, effective parents are hard to find on television today.

Contemporary black culture tends to be more muted and cautious in its criticism of parents. Precisely because the black family is in such desperate straits and serious parent-bashing is dangerously close to the bone, the media are forced to reflect at least some positive images, particularly of Mom. "Dear Mama," a 1996 hit song by the late rap artist Tupac Shakur, is a case in point. In this ode, Tupac describes his mother as a "crack fiend" and a "black queen." At the same time, the song is imbued with love and longing when he acknowledges her extraordinary devotion to him in the face of appalling circumstances.

GOVERNMENT TILTS AGAINST PARENTS

The political establishment can be as hostile as the media. In recent years, government has pulled the rug from under adults raising children, because neither the right nor the left of our political culture values or supports the work that parents do.

Many conservatives refuse to recognize the ways in which market values destroy family values. In elemental ways, they do not get it. They fail to understand that we need to rein in free enterprise if we are going to create the conditions that support parents and nurture children. A free and unfettered labor market, for example, can seriously undermine family life by exerting enormous downward pressure on wage levels for young, child-raising adults. This is exactly what has happened over the last twenty years. Successive administrations, abandoning any notion of a social contract, have gotten out of the business of maintaining the value of the minimum wage, providing legal protection for labor unions, or placing limits on out-of-control corporate greed.[7] Every day we read in the newspapers of thousands of workers being downsized or laid off while senior managers are cushioned by golden parachutes or special deals. Recent events at Levi Strauss are a good example:

"Facing up to corporate miscalculations and sluggish sales of its blue jeans," Levi Strauss & Co. announced plans late in 1997 to lay off one third of its U.S. labor force and close eleven plants. At the same time, the company confirmed that in 1996 it paid retiring president Thomas Tusher more that $125 million as part of a closely held stock buyback program.

Commenting on the size of Tusher's options award, the compensation expert Graef "Bud" Crystal said, "That's a lot of jeans, but it doesn't make these jaded eyes pop out of their sockets." He noted that other executives had received higher awards; for example, Disney's chief executive, Michael Eisner, had just received 8 million stock options in a package that could be worth $771 million in a decade. "What's interesting here," Crystal added, "is the disconnect between finding out that someone got that much money at the same time that you're seeing so many employees about to be laid off."

By apparel industry standards, the 6,395 workers whom Levi Strauss let go were decently treated—they collected eight months' pay plus three weeks' pay for each year of service—but these severance packages pale in comparison with Thomas Tusher's golden deal. Tusher was paid $105.8 million in accumulated stock options and $21.5 million as a "gross tax offset bonus" to help cover the taxes on that income.[8]

The Levi Strauss story is not that unusual; today, millions of workers are experiencing severe economic pressure, despite record-breaking profits and a huge increase in executive compensation. These trends have profoundly weakened family life. Fathers and mothers like Gary and Brenda have been forced to work longer and harder just to maintain living standards, and children have been pushed to the edge.

Sagging wages, mounting insecurity, and lengthening workweeks make up the vanguard of the war against parents. Rich folks have done breathtakingly well in recent years, while everyone else has gone on the skids. For example, Michael Eisner was paid $204.2 million in 1996. At the median wage—now $33,538, down from $35,959 in 1989—a regular person would have to work 6,182 years to make that much money.[9] It's hard to see how we can sustain a democracy with these kinds of numbers—and it is clearly hard to sustain high-quality parenting.

Conservatives who espouse family values face a Herculean challenge on the economic front. Are they prepared to redistribute income and wealth in order to relieve the pressures on young families? It seems unlikely. Redistribution requires government action and interference with market mechanisms, and today's conservatives are virulently opposed to both. Those on the right simply do not understand that government must play a pivotal role if we are to develop the social supports we need to counter the family-destroying and parent-displacing properties of the market. Bolstering the earning power of child-raising adults is just one of the ways in which government must intervene if moms and dads are to be effective and wholehearted parents. Such intervention is taken for granted elsewhere. France and Germany, for example, have developed tax codes that give huge privileges to families with children. Other rich democracies seem to understand that parenting cannot be left to the tender mercies of the marketplace.

Not so very long ago, conservatives were willing to provide parents with serious help on the child-raising front by spearheading various kinds of family-friendly policies. Remember the 1950s, that golden age of the American family? Well, we often forget that the fifties family was a creature of supportive government programs, at least some of which were put in place by President Eisenhower, an unabashed conservative. That was an era when children were this nation's most important tax shelter; parents were able to claim a deduction of $6,500 (in current dollars) for each dependent child.[10] It was a time when the GI Bill and the Highway Act significantly subsidized the education and housing needs of millions of American families. George W. Bush and Dick Cheney, however, are singularly out of touch with the degree to which Ozzie and Harriet were bolstered by public policy and depended on the public purse.

But myopia is not limited to today's conservatives. Liberals are also destroying the parental role. Many on the left fail to understand that we need to rein in untrammeled individualism if we are to recreate the values that nurture family life. The extraordinary emphasis in left-wing circles on the rights and freedoms of the individual has seriously compromised those altruistic, other-directed energies that are the stuff of parenting. Liberal divorce laws, for example, have produced a situation in which adults can choose marriage partners two, three, or four times with no particular penalty, regardless of how many children are betrayed or abandoned. Liberal welfare policies permit fifteen- and seventeen-year-olds to bear and raise children out of wedlock—indeed, through Aid to Families with Dependent Children (AFDC), now called Temporary Assistance for Needy Families (TANF), government supports these teenagers, albeit grudgingly. The new freedom of individuals to choose single parenthood is, of course, not limited to poor teens. High-profile showbiz moms such as Jodie Foster, Cynthia Nixon, Camryn Manheim, Rosie O'Donnell, and Diane Keaton have made single motherhood a chic thing to do—the ultimate liberated act of a strong woman.

African-American celebrities tend to be more supportive of conventional family structures than their white peers. Whitney Houston and Snoop Doggy Dogg, for example, are both deeply committed to marriage and the two-parent family and have hung in there with their respective spouses in the face of considerable scandal. Indeed it's hard to identify a black movie star who has chosen to flaunt single parenthood. Perhaps because of the way in which out-of-wedlock births have devastated their community, black celebrities have felt the need to protect and defend the family.

Despite this qualification, the overwhelming message from progressive, liberal folks in Hollywood is, *Who needs a husband to have a child?* The problem here is that there are real conflicts between adult rights to freedom of choice and a child's well-being. While some Hollywood celebrities may not want to deal with a male partner, most children do much better in life when they can count on the loving attention of both a mother and a father.

At the end of the day, both conservatives and liberals clobber children. Take your pick, right or left, it doesn't matter; in contemporary America both ideologies are dangerously blind when it comes to creating the conditions that allow men and women to give real priority to the difficult and glorious business of cherishing children.

PARENTING: THE ULTIMATE NONMARKET ACTIVITY

Whatever their political orientation, our leaders seem to have little understanding of how much the decks are stacked against parents in our materialistic, individualistic age. At the heart of the matter is the fact that from a purely economic standpoint, raising a child has become the ultimate nonmarket activity, as various types of market logic have moved against mothers and fathers. Adults have never viewed children solely or even primarily as financial assets, but through history and across cultures, parents have often reaped at least some material reward from raising children—help with planting or harvesting, support in old age, and so on. None of these economic reasons for raising children hold true today. On the contrary, in the modern world, children are hugely expensive and yield little in the way of economic return to the parent. Estimates of the cost of raising a child to eighteen are now in the $145,000 range—and this figure does not include college or graduate school![11] Despite this significant investment, the grown-up child rarely contributes earnings—or any other kind of material support—to the parental household. Today, children "provide love, smiles, and emotional satisfaction, but no money or labor."[12]

Of course, large numbers of well-meaning moms and dads may still elect to invest large quantities of money and time in child-raising, but for the first time in history their loving energies are not reinforced by enlightened self-interest. Instead, they must rely entirely on large reserves of altruistic love—large enough to last for more than two decades per child. This is a tall order in a society that venerates the market. We are asking parents to ignore the logic of their pocketbooks and buck the dominant values of our age. If they routinely fall down on the job, who can blame them? Contemporary moms and dads are trapped between the escalating requirements of their children, who need more resources (in terms of both time and money) for longer periods of time than ever before, and the signals of a culture that is increasingly scornful of effort expended on others. Parents often feel as though they are expected to read from two or three scripts that diverge completely in terms of how they lead their lives. Should they take on a second job to pay for college or should they stay home in the evening to do a little bonding and turn off the TV? Or should they do neither of the above, but rather work two jobs and spend the extra income on health-club memberships? Life is short, and paying at least some attention to oneself is a good idea. Besides, a trimmer figure might make all the difference in the next round of promotions. It is easy for a bewildered parent to become paralyzed as he or she is besieged by a host of contradictory demands.

FREE FEMALE LABOR

For more than a century, a variety of scholars and social commentators have paid tribute to the nonmarket work done by women in American society. In the 1880s and 1890s, the social feminist Jane Addams stressed the moral heft of women's traditional roles. Indeed, much of her political activism was directed toward securing for women the right to stay at home and care for their children rather than being forced into the labor market. She saw "the home as the original center of civilization."[13]

Much more recently, the psychologist Carol Gilligan has made a distinction between the voices of men and women. In her highly acclaimed 1982 book, *In a Different Voice*, she describes how men gravitate toward the instrumental and the impersonal and emphasize abstract principles, while women lean toward intimacy and caring and give priority to human relationships. Gilligan points out that the female "care" voice is not inferior to the male "instrumental" voice, as it is often treated in psychological theory; it is simply different—different and enormously important. Over the decades this voice of care has played a critical role in producing a healthy equilibrium between individual and community in American society. Because it balances self with other and tempers market values with nonmarket values, it has gone some distance toward redeeming the urgent greed that is the spirit of capitalism.

Prior to the 1960s, when more families were organized along traditional lines than is true today, women provided this voice of care, which knitted together family and community. At least in the middle classes, a clear division of labor between the sexes allowed women to devote huge amounts of time to nourishing and nurturing: they read bedtime stories, helped with homework, wrapped presents, attended parent-teacher conferences, and taught Sunday school. But in the 1970s, the myriad selfless tasks that were the stuff of raising kids and building communities went by the board as American society underwent a sea change. Traditional patterns were broken by a liberation movement that often encouraged women to clone the male competitive model in the marketplace, and by a new set of economic pressures that increasingly required both parents to be in the paid labor force to sustain any semblance of middle-class life.

Before getting too nostalgic about traditional roles, however, we should remember that the sacrificial load carried by at-home women was often hard to bear. Many spent their entire lives laboring to serve the needs of others. Gilligan tells us that the main change wrought by feminism was that it "enabled women to consider it moral to care not only for others but also for themselves." She quotes Elizabeth Cady Stanton telling a reporter in 1848 "to put it down in capital letters: SELF-DEVELOPMENT IS A HIGHER DUTY THAN SELF-SACRIFICE."[14] Despite her appreciation of the importance of women's traditional roles, Jane Addams was also convinced that women must undergo a struggle for identity and recognition. She thought that the great challenge facing women was to hold in fruitful tension the "I" of the self, the "us" and "ours" of the family, and the "we" of citizens of the wider civic world.[15] The character Nora struggled with this challenge in Henrik Ibsen's *A Doll's House* (1879), and women have been struggling with it ever since.

The insights of Addams and Gilligan reflect the lives of middle-class white women and have little to do with the lives of poor women, particularly poor black women. Since the beginning of this nation, women of color have toiled both in the workplace—often in a white woman's kitchen—and in their own homes. In a very real sense, their contribution to family and community has been even more heroic than that of middle-class women. In sustained and steadfast ways, they have looked after the children of affluent white women in addition to their own, and they have received very little in the way of recompense or recognition. Black women thus have done double duty and been doubly invisible.

This brief historical excursion helps explain why the shortcomings of our nation on the parent-support front were until recently cloaked by the existence of a deep and largely invisible reservoir of free female labor. For generations, women spent huge chunks of their lives making the nonmarket investments in family and community that underpin our nation. By nurturing children and by nourishing a web of care that included neighborhood and township, women created the competence and character upon which our democracy and our economy depended. Thus, the invisible labor of women comprised nothing less than the bedrock of America's prosperity and power. In addition, as women grew and tended our stock of human and social capital, they masked the contradictions inherent in our political culture. Conservatives had the luxury of cultivating a blind faith in markets because women (unacknowledged and unappreciated though they were) provided the all-important nonmarket work; and liberals had the luxury of cultivating a taste for self-fulfillment—at least white men did—because women reached out to others.

Today, it is clear that relying on free and invisible female labor as the wellspring of our social and human capital no longer works. Modern women are intent on a fair measure of self-realization, and besides, the economic facts of family life preclude a return to traditional structures. Falling male wages and sky-high rates of single parenthood make it hard to spin out a scenario in which large numbers of women (or men) have the option of staying home on a full-time basis.

It is ironic to note that the nurturing, caring roles that are so underappreciated by contemporary culture are very much factored in by the market. Career interruptions triggered by childbirth and the special demands of the early childhood years cost women dearly in terms of earning power. A study by the Rand Corporation shows that a two- to four-year break lowers earning power by 19 percent.[16] Of course, if we were to expand our programs of family support—paid parenting leave, job sharing, and the like—more women would be able to stay on their career ladders during the child-bearing years.

FATHERS UNDER SIEGE

The inability of our nation to give value to or even recognize the work of parents has penalized men and women in different ways. If the work done by mothers has been rendered invisible—or used to exact a price in the labor market—fathers have come under special attack by programs and policies oblivious to the importance of the father-child bond. Over the last thirty years, divorce reform and the onerous conditions attached to welfare benefits have conspired to make it extremely difficult for a large proportion of American men—somewhere between a third and half—either to live with or to stay in effective touch with their children. Aid to Families with Dependent Children is a case in point. In retrospect, it seems clear that AFDC, the nationwide program that for three decades provided the lion's share of income support for poor families, was set up so as to deliberately exclude fathers. The rules held that if an "able-bodied man" resided in a household, a woman with dependent children was unable to claim benefits for herself and her children.[17] This caused men to be literally pushed out of the nest. Not only did the AFDC regulations create a huge disincentive to marry, they made it extremely difficult for poor men to become fathers to their children. These government-sponsored rules help explain why out-of-wedlock births in the black community leapt from 21 percent in 1960 to 69.8 percent in 1996.[18]

In recent years men have experienced a tremendous loss of power in the workplace and in the family, which is a large part of the reason why millions of men are turning to Promise Keepers and the Nation of Islam. Demoralized, displaced men are seeking solace in brotherhood and turning inward to their gods. Jesus or Allah might just come through for them in a way that is increasingly problematic for employers or government.

The antifather bias in our public policies has found its clearest expression in the demonization of deadbeat dads. Public outrage on this subject was triggered by a 1989 Census Bureau report enti-tled "Child Support and Alimony," which described how more than a quarter of all noncustodial fathers were absent from their children's lives and paid nothing in the way of child support.[19] Shocking and shameful as these findings were, some factors were overlooked. To begin with, almost 40 percent of the "absent fathers" described in this report had neither custody nor visitation rights and therefore no ability to connect with their children. It seems odd to call them by the pejorative term "absent" when they have no right to be present. In addition, a little-known study by the Depart-ment of Health and Human Services shows that noncustodial moth-ers have a far worse record of child-support compliance than noncustodial fathers: almost half of all noncustodial mothers pay nothing toward the support of their children.[20] It seems that once a parent—male or female—has lost touch with a child, that parent is unlikely to contribute financial support. It is probably unrealistic to think we can keep in place all the obligations of traditional parent-hood without its main reward: loving contact with a child.[21] Yet, rather than create policies that help noncustodial parents connect with their children, all we seem capable of doing is cracking down some more on deadbeat dads—thin stuff in a country that leads the world in fatherlessness.

One thing we do know: the huge increase in fatherlessness goes some distance toward explaining why so many youngsters are out of control. There is now a weight of evidence connecting fatherlessness to child poverty, juvenile crime, and teen suicide.

THE PARENT-CHILD BOND

This brings us to the heart of the matter: if the center of this nation is to hold, we have to learn to give new and self-conscious value to the art and practice of parenting. It can no longer be left to invisible female labor or the tender mercies of the market. Make no mistake about it: the work of moms and dads is of the utmost importance to our nation. At a fundamental level of analysis, the parent-child bond is the strongest and most primeval of all human attachments. When it weakens and frays, devastating consequences ripple through our nation, because this elemental bond is the ulti-mate source of connectedness in society.

H. F. Harlow, the animal psychologist, demonstrated in a famous series of studies of infant monkeys the extraordinary importance of parental love. Taking a group of newborn monkeys from their parents, he placed them with artificial surrogates—a wire mesh "mommy" and a terry-cloth "mommy." Despite the fact that the infant monkeys were supplied with all the ingredients for physiological development—nourishment, water, proper temperature, and protection against disease—they failed to flourish. In Harlow's study, the deprived infants became zombies, developing odd, autistic behavior of the kind one sees in severely retarded persons. To Harlow, they did not seem fully alive. While the baby monkeys enormously preferred the terry-cloth mommy to the wire mesh mommy, avoiding the cold wire mesh and clinging fiercely to the warm, cuddly terry cloth, even the terry-cloth mommy was a long way from being enough.

These artificial surrogates failed to provide loving, tender, responsive care, and thus the baby monkeys grew up not knowing the give-and-take of talk and touch, of feeding and fondling, of learning and playing. The infants survived and eventually grew into adults, but strange, abnormal adults who could not relate to their own kind or reproduce.[22] The implication of Harlow's research for humans is clear: the mere fact of physical survival does not guarantee a person. The full development of a human being requires something much deeper and more complicated than food and water; it requires sustained and sustaining love. According to the psychiatrist Willard Gaylin, "It is necessary to care for a child with love, in order to initiate a similar capacity in the child."[23]

Who will provide this transforming love? The obvious candidates are parents, because it is mothers and fathers, above other adults, who tend to fall crazily in love with their children. As the child psychologist Urie Bronfenbrenner has shown, children thrive on huge amounts of "irrational, emotional attachment," most often the gift of a mother or a father but in exceptional cases provided by a devoted grandparent or some other caregiver.[24] This is the magical force that provides the basis for self-love and self-esteem. Once a child has learned to love himself or herself, that child is able to care deeply about others. Thus parental love not only contributes powerfully to the development of a fully human being, it also nourishes and sustains the larger society. The connections are straightforward enough: caring about the well-being of others is the foundation of compassion, conscience, and citizenship. When a child is deprived of parental love, that youngster is liable to grow up in an infantilized state—very much like Harlow's zombies—never developing a love of self, never developing the ability to reach out to others. This is a recipe for violence, against oneself and against others, for anger and aggression remain raw and exposed, untempered by a commitment to anyone or anything. It is also a recipe for civic collapse. How do you persuade a young person who is profoundly careless of his own or of others' well-being to join a Boys and Girls Club or to vote in our democracy?

I (Cornel West) remember meeting one of these disconnected, tortured youngsters at a talk I gave at a community center in Newark, New Jersey. After the event, a young man sixteen or seventeen years old came up to me and said, "Professor West, I hear you're a pretty smart brother, you write this deep stuff, it must take a lotta talent and a lotta work to do something like that. Well, I've got talent too. I'm the smartest guy in my class. But the rub is, I can't find any motivation. I don't see why I should try to do what you do. More and more I feel I belong on the streets, hustling, dealing, and hurting like everyone else. That's the way to survive where I live."

He then asked a question. "Brother, what made you want to keep doing all that hard work, what made you believe in some kind of different future?" So I talked about my dad encouraging and disciplining me, my mom reading poetry to me, my older brother helping me with my homework, and my younger sisters cheering me on. The young man listened closely and then, in obvious pain, said, "Here's the score—I'm in this world by myself. My mother's strung out and tuned out. I have brothers, but I don't know them, and as for my father, where he is nobody knows. I sure have never seen him."

I remember feeling totally helpless. I had no recipe to heal these open wounds. The only thing I could think of doing was to bow before the enormity of his misery, kiss the young brother's hand, and mumble some words of empathy. "My God, I can't imagine— it's beyond my experience. You've got things you can teach me— you've been somewhere I've never been. I've read a ton of books on alienation, but I cannot grasp what you are living.... I cannot understand what it must be like to have never been loved." I then simply told him to stay strong and don't forget to pray.

This bleak and bitter encounter in Newark reflects the agony of a child who was born without a skin, without the tender love of an attentive parent. For this young man, the parent-child bond— the relationship that transmits self-love and the capacity to love others—had never developed, and the consequences were quite deadly.

A WORLD UPSIDE DOWN

This young man is not alone. In modern America, across race, gender, and class, millions of children are in terrible trouble. Consider the following facts:

- The homicide rate for children aged fourteen to seventeen has risen 172 percent since 1985.
- One fifth (20.5 percent) of all children are growing up in poverty—a 36 percent increase since 1970.
- The number of homeless children among high school seniors is up 44 percent since 1992.
- SAT scores have slipped 27 points since the early 1970s.
- The rate of suicide among black teenagers has more than tripled since 1980.
- Obesity among children aged twelve to seventeen has doubled since 1970.[25]

Some of these statistics (poverty, homelessness) describe the pain of disadvantaged kids; others (obesity, SAT scores) describe the anguish of middle-class kids. Problems triggered by divorce, teen pregnancy, school failure, and substance abuse are no longer confined to the ghetto. They reach deep into the middle class; they belong to "us" as well as to "them." Out-of-control children aren't always other people's kids. They come in all sizes, shapes, and colors, and from affluent neighborhoods as well as down-at-heel city 'hoods. Kids who do bad things have highly educated parents as well as barely literate ones. A recent Carnegie Corporation report describes the depth and reach of our child-related problems: "Nearly half of American adolescents are at high or moderate risk of seriously damaging their life chances. The damage may be near term and vivid, or it may be delayed, like a time bomb set in youth."[26]

Youth Violence

The enormous surge in youth violence is perhaps the most cruel—and most costly—manifestation of our inability to nurture our young. Children are now responsible for a staggering 20 million crimes a year. Between 1985 and 1994, among those aged fourteen to seventeen, arrests for murder increased by 172 percent, and for other violent crimes (rape, robbery, and aggravated assault) by 46 percent. While violent crime among teenagers has been escalating, comparable crime rates for adults have been falling quite rapidly: between 1990 and 1994, homicide rates among adults aged twenty-five and older declined 18 percent.[27] There are now two crime trends in America, one for adults and one for children, and they are moving in opposite directions. One poorly understood fact is the hefty price tag attached to juvenile crime, as society ends up paying for a lifetime spent in and out of jail. A recent study estimates the cost to taxpayers of one violent young person at $1.5 million.[28]

In a day and age when we associate crime with young black men, it is important to stress that increases in juvenile crime apply across the board, in "all races, social classes, and lifestyles." Although young black males are four to five times more likely to be arrested for violent crime than white youths of the same age, the increase in the rate of arrests is far higher for white youths than for black: a 44 percent increase compared to a 19 percent increase between 1988 and 1993.[29]

> Daphne Abdela, age 15, moved in a private school underworld in New York City where belonging means playing thug, getting wasted, and committing crimes. In her case, these crimes might well have included murder. In June 1997, she and her buddy Chris Vasquez, also 15, were arraigned in connection with the stabbing death of a 44-year-old real estate agent named Michael McMorrow. The killing occurred in the vicinity of the stately apartment building on Central Park West where Daphne lived. Daphne reportedly told the police that after the murder she and Chris mutilated the body, cutting off the dead man's nose and almost severing a hand in an attempt to hide his identity. Then they tried to sink McMorrow's 220-pound frame in the park's lake, gutting it first, Daphne told police, "because he was a fatty."

Daphne cannot claim to be black, brown, or disadvantaged. She is a highly privileged youngster, even by the standards of Manhattan. Before her arrest she lived in a $3 million home and was driven to school by the family chauffeur.[30]

When we look into the future, the picture becomes bleaker still. Demographic trends indicate that when it comes to juvenile crime, the worst may be yet to come. A "baby boomlet" in the late 1980s and early 1990s means that there are now 40 million children under age ten in the United States. We can therefore expect the adolescent population to swell by a quarter over the next decade. Since so many of these children are growing up below the poverty line in fragmented families, there is every reason to expect a new surge in juvenile crime.

Suicide

If thousands of American youngsters are being killed or injured at the hands of their peers, thousands more are lost in their own nightmares. These are the children who self-destruct, seeing suicide as their only way out. Their numbers too are soaring. Between 1960 and 1994, the suicide rate among teens nearly tripled, making suicide the third leading cause of death for young people. Black children and very young children seem to be at risk in new and dreadful ways: the suicide rate among black males aged ten to fourteen went up a staggering 240 percent between 1980 and 1995.[31]

Poverty

A particularly shameful fact is that the United States has the highest percentage of children living in poverty of any rich nation: 20.5 percent, a figure that represents a 36 percent increase since 1970 and compares with 9 percent in Canada, 4 percent in Germany, and 2 percent in Japan.[32] Children quite simply have not shared in America's prosperity in recent years. Very young children are particularly badly off: for those under six years of age, the poverty rate is 23 percent, which means that over 5 million preschoolers now live below the poverty line.[33] Bad as these figures are, they are expected to get considerably worse as the effects of welfare reform kick in. The Urban Institute predicts that an additional 1.1 million children will have slithered into poverty in 1997 alone. Black and Hispanic children are disproportionately represented in the poor population—47 percent of black children and 34 percent of Latino children are poor, but in recent years the poverty rate has grown twice as fast among whites as among blacks. Significantly, in 1996, 69 percent of poor children lived in families where at least one adult was at work—up from 61 percent in 1993.[34] In the late 1990s, getting a job did not necessarily pull a family out of poverty.

Substance Abuse

Substance abuse is also on the increase among teens. The use of illegal drugs by adolescents increased significantly between 1992 and 1995. This represents a reversal of earlier downward trends.

In 1996 the government reported troubling increases in drug use in all age groups. For example, between 1992 and 1995, the use of marijuana by high school seniors increased by 63 percent, while the use of inhalants such as glues, aerosols, and solvents by eighth-graders increased 28 percent.[35]

Plummeting Educational Achievement

On the educational front the news is equally grim, since under-achievement and failure continue to dog the steps of American youngsters. Across the nation, combined average Scholastic Aptitude Test (SAT) scores have fallen significantly since 1972, despite a recent re-centering exercise, which had the effect of rais-ing nominal scores. Data collected by the National Assessment of Educational Progress, which has been testing national samples of students aged nine, thirteen, and seventeen each year since 1969, show "few indications of positive trends" in reading and writing.[36] American children are also at or near the bottom in most interna-tional surveys measuring educational achievement, coming in seventh out of ten countries in physics and tenth—dead last—in average mathematics proficiency.

Another disturbing fact is that only 69.7 percent of American stu-dents who enter ninth grade earn a high school diploma four years later, a figure that has slipped seven percentage points since 1970.[37] Most policymakers see this as a national disgrace in an age when other advanced nations have near universal secondary school edu-cation. In Japan, for example, 90 percent of seventeen-year-olds graduate from high school.

Emotional Problems

Not only is a large proportion of American youth growing up badly educated and ill prepared for the world of work, but a significant number are further handicapped by increasingly serious emotional problems. According to the Carnegie Corporation, today's youngsters are having trouble coping with stresses in their lives: "Many are depressed, and about a third of adolescents report they have contemplated suicide."[38] Since 1971, the number of adolescents admitted to private psychiatric hospitals has increased fifteenfold. Experts in the field explain this alarming trend by point-ing to a constellation of pressures ranging from long workdays to divorce to absent fathers, which have left many parents too thinly stretched to provide consistent support for their children. The pressures on single mothers are particularly severe. Indeed, in many instances the stress is so great that parenting breaks down and becomes inconsistent and erratically punitive.

One thing seems clear enough from this brief survey: not only are American children failing to thrive, but in several critical respects, their condition and life circumstances are steadily deteriorating. Overall, they lead more dangerous and more poverty-stricken lives than children did thirty, twenty, or even five years ago. They are also less likely to succeed in school and more likely to experiment with drugs, and many are depressed and seriously self-destructive. It is particularly distressing to realize that children in America are at much greater risk than children elsewhere in the advanced industrial world. Although the United States ranks second worldwide in per capita income, this country does not even make it into the top ten on any significant indicator of child welfare.

LINK TO PARENTS

Parental love and parental attention are enormously powerful in determining what happens to a child. Genetic endowment may determine eye color and a third to half of raw intelligence, but whether a child acquires discipline and self-esteem and becomes a well-adjusted, productive person is largely a function of parental input and how well both parent and child are supported by the wider community.[39]

Unfortunately, there is much less of this precious parenting energy than there used to be. The last three decades have seen a sharp decline in the amount of time parents spend caring for their children. Stanford University economist Victor Fuchs has shown that the amount of parental time available to children fell considerably in the 1970s and 1980s; white children lost ten hours a week of parental time, while black children lost twelve hours.[40] Using a more recent data set, economist Edward Wolff demonstrated that over a thirty-year time span, parental time declined 13 percent.[41] The time parents have available for their children has been squeezed by the rapid shift of mothers into the paid labor force, by escalating divorce rates and the subsequent abandonment of children by their fathers, and by an increase in the number of hours required on the job. The average worker is now at work 163 hours a year more than in 1969, which adds up to an extra month of work annually.[42]

The increasing inability of adults to devote significant time to children has left millions of youngsters fending for themselves, coping more or less badly with the difficult business of growing up. True, some children continue to be raised in supportive communities by thoughtful and attentive parents, but this is not the overall drift of society. Contemporary America is populated by over-worked, stressed-out parents who are increasingly unable to be there for their children. There is now a ton of literature telling parents how to parent. Walk into any bookstore and you will encounter shelf upon shelf of advice manuals detailing the skills and techniques of parenting. However, despite the claims of the experts, there is no one recipe for raising children, no magic bullet that guarantees a well-developed child. In the wise words of the Harvard psychologist Jerome Kagan, precisely how a parent feeds an infant or disciplines a teenager is less important than "the melody those actions comprise."[43] The feelings that parents bring to the role—their pleasure in parenting, their respect for the child—are extremely important. But most important is ensuring adequate time for the role. Melodies cannot work their magic unless they are given time and space. If a divorced father hasn't seen his son in six weeks or if a mother is working a sixteen-hour day, it's almost impossible to conjure up the sustained, steadfast attention that is the stuff of good parenting. Child-raising is not some mysterious process; adults have been engaged in it since the beginning of time, long before we had experts or manuals. At the heart of the matter is time, huge amounts of it, freely given. Whatever the child-raising technique, a child simply does better with loving, committed, long-term attention from both mom and dad.

A weight of evidence now demonstrates ominous links between absentee parents and an entire range of behavioral and emotional problems in children. A study that surveyed 5,000 eighth-grade students in the San Diego and Los Angeles areas found that the more hours children were left by themselves after school, the greater the risk of substance abuse was. In fact, home-alone children as a group were twice as likely to drink alcohol and take drugs as children who were supervised by a parent or another adult family member after school. The study found that this increased risk of substance abuse held true regardless of the child's sex, race, or economic status.[44]

In a similar vein, a recent survey of 90,000 teenagers—the largest and most comprehensive study ever conducted on adolescent behavior—found that youngsters are less likely to become violent or use drugs if they are closely connected to their parents.[45] This study found that the mere physical presence of a parent in the home after school, at dinner, and at bedtime significantly reduced the incidence of risky behavior among teenagers, a finding reinforced by recent research at the Harvard School of Public Health. Jody Heymann and Alison Earle show that parental evening work has extremely negative effects on the home environment and on children's cognitive and emotional development.

A 1997 report prepared for the Department of Justice demonstrates the scope of these negative effects. According to FBI data, the peak hours for violent juvenile crime are now 3 p.m. to 8 p.m.[46] This can be attributed to a huge drop-off in the number of parents available to supervise their children after school. In 1970, 57 percent of school-age children had at least one parent at home on a full-time basis; by 1995, this figure had fallen to 29 percent.[47] Experts estimate that somewhere between 5 and 7 million latchkey children go home to an empty house after school and that fully a third of all twelve-year-olds are regularly left to fend for themselves while their parents are at work.[48] These children are at a significantly greater risk of truancy, school failure, substance abuse, and violent behavior than children who have a parent at home. Children, especially adolescents, crave excitement, and if they are not supervised by parents or involved in some organized activity, they are likely to become involved in something dangerous to themselves or others.

Besides insulating a child from risk and warding off potential harm, parents make a large contribution to a child's success in school. Twenty years ago, Chicago sociologist James S. Coleman demonstrated that parental involvement mattered far more in determining student achievement than any attribute of the formal education system. Across a wide range of subject areas, in literature, science, and reading, Coleman estimated that the parent was almost twice as powerful as the school in determining achievement at age fourteen.[49] The importance of parent involvement in the educational process has been further confirmed by psychologist Lawrence Steinberg, who completed a six-year study of 20,000 teenagers and their families in nine different communities. Steinberg argued convincingly that underachievement and failure in American schools "owes more to conditions in the home than to what takes place within school walls." One out of every three parents is "seriously disengaged" from his or her adolescent's education, and this is the primary reason why so many American students perform below their potential—and below students in other rich countries.[50]

In his research, Coleman revealed that good parenting not only improved academic performance, but was also essential to the development of human capital—that combination of attributes (skills, knowledge, work habits, and motivation) that makes for a competent young person. For at least a generation, economists and business leaders have wrung their hands over the sorry state of America's human capital, and they have good reason to be concerned. More than a quarter of all eighteen-year-olds fail to complete high school, and many of these youngsters lack the basic skills and discipline necessary to hold down the simplest job. According to one survey, fewer than half of all American youngsters can determine the correct change after purchasing a hamburger and a Coke at McDonald's. This distressing fact tells us something about the inadequacy of our educational system, but it tells us even more about the inability of many parents to come through for their children.

In addition, a great deal of recent scholarly attention has been given to the depletion of our social capital—that store of trust, connectedness, and engagement in community life. Robert Putnam, Francis Fukuyama, Jean Bethke Elshtain, and Michael Sandel, among others, have expressed great concern that "the moral fabric of community is unraveling around us. From families and neighborhoods to schools, congregations, and trade unions, the institutions that traditionally provided people with moral anchors and a sense of belonging are under siege."[51] These scholars have advanced a variety of reasons to explain why so many Americans are newly isolated, distrustful, and depoliticized, newly "bowling alone" rather than in leagues.[52] All kinds of culprits have been put forward, including television-watching and political scandal. But despite a noisy, high-profile debate, no one has gone upstream to the source of the problem—the huge erosion of the parental role. When parenting breaks down, the mechanism that transmits self-love is shattered, and this seriously compromises society's ability to pass from one generation to the next the values of compassion and commitment to others, which are the essential raw material of community-building and citizenship.

Therefore, the erosion of the parental function has immense implications in both the public and the private spheres: it jeopardizes our society as well as our souls. When parenting breaks down, it is an unmitigated disaster for the individual child. But it is much more than that, for the altruistic energy of moms and dads contributes enormously to our store of human and social capital and thus conditions the strength of our economy and the vitality of our democracy.

So how do we turn this thing around? How do we somehow give new and self-conscious value to the art and practice of parenting? It is not a simple matter, this task of creating a public morality and a political culture that will support the heroic work of mothers and fathers. The obstacles are enormous.

On the left, we rub up against a fierce attachment to untrammeled lives. Over the last thirty years we grownups have gotten used to being extraordinarily free. We have cut ourselves loose from most moral and religious constraints and acquired a new set of emotional and sexual liberties. Many of us revel in an unprecedented range of choice. In the spirit of Tom Wolfe's *Bonfire of the Vanities*, we have tasted our new freedoms and find them "quite glorious."[53]

On the right, we rub up against a blind faith in markets and a deep distrust of state intervention. In recent years conservatives have badmouthed government so thoroughly that it has become extraordinarily difficult for anyone on the right to acknowledge that government is capable of doing any good—that it can be instrumental in providing indispensable social support and in creating a public morality that supports the sacrificial energy of parents. Conservatives seem light-years away from acknowledging that contemporary parents need enormous amounts of help—not grudging help, not marginal help, but big-time heavy lifting—if they are to conjure up the altruistic energies that allow children to thrive. In the manner of the fifties, this help should be directed to strengthening rather than displacing moms and dads.

We must also remember that the nuances of this project are critical. No progressive person wants family if "family" translates into oppressive husbands and abused wives. And no progressive person wants community if "community" translates into "black jelly beans" sticking "to the bottom of the bag."[54] Texaco, after all, developed an extremely strong and vital corporate culture, but this culture was also irredeemably ugly, contaminated by systematic discrimination against people of color. However, rejecting racism, patriarchy, and homophobia need not mean retreating to a version of the liberal project in which freedom is boiled down to the ability to function as a lone individual within a heavily competitive market society. Most grownups fail to flourish in such a thin universe, and children are seriously damaged. Unless a child is protected and cherished by the selfless energies of at least one loving adult who is uniquely committed to him or her, that young person will grow up without a skin, buffeted, bleeding, and seared.

This daunting and complex set of challenges boils down to one pivotal question: can we find the political will? Can we find the key that will unlock a new and potent source of activist energy? We are, after all, talking about radical change.

We think we have found the answer. Our solution involves putting mothers and fathers front and center on the national stage. By tapping into the latent strength of our democratic processes, we craft a parents' movement that will send America's 62 million parents to the polls. This will have the magical effect of tilting our entire political culture in a direction that supports and values adults raising children. By mobilizing behind a single agenda, which we call "A Parents' Bill of Rights,"[55] and by speaking with a single voice, moms and dads can transform both our public morality and our political culture to give new and massive support to the work they do. It is important to stress that parent power can be a powerful healing force in American society. The deep and desperate concerns of parents cross the usual divides of gender, race, and class and thus feed a common vision and seed a common ground in ways that are rare and precious in our centrifugal society.

As we embark on this extraordinary journey, let us appreciate the enormous weight of the task at hand. The project of giving new status and support to mothers and fathers has extraordinary potential because of the ways in which the parent-child bond is the most fundamental building block in human society. When this is hollowed out, the wellspring of care and commitment dries up, and this has a huge impact beyond the home: community life shrivels up, and so does our democracy. America's stock of social and human capital becomes dangerously depleted. If we can produce this magical parent power, we can go to the very heart of our darkness and make the center hold.

APPENDIX: A PARENTS' BILL OF RIGHTS

Mothers and fathers are entitled to
1. Time for their children
   - Paid parenting leave
   - Family-friendly workplaces
   - A safety net

2. Economic security
   - A living wage
   - Job opportunities
   - Tax relief
   - Help with housing

3. A pro-family electoral system
   - Incentives to vote
   - Votes for children

4. A pro-family legal structure
   - Stronger marriage
   - Support for fathers
   - Adoptions assistance

5. A supportive external environment
   - Violence-free neighborhoods
   - Quality schooling
   - Extended school day and year
   - Childcare
   - Family health coverage
   - Drug-free communities
   - Responsible media
   - An organizational voice

6. Honor and dignity
   - An index of parent well-being
   - National Parents' Day
   - Parent privileges

NOTES

This chapter originally appeared as "Parents and National Survival," from *The War against Parents* by Sylvia Ann Hewlett and Cornel West. Copyright © 1998 by Sylvia Ann Hewlett and Cornel West. Reprinted by with permission of Houghton Mifflin Company, New York. All rights reserved.

1. An index measuring the social health of children is at its lowest point in twenty-five years. See 1996 *Index of Social Health* (New York: Fordham Institute for Innovation in Social Policy, 1996), p. 6.

2. National Commission on the Role of the Schools and the Community in Improving Adolescent Health, *Code Blue: Uniting for Healthier Youth* (Washington, DC: National Association of State Boards of Education/ American Medical Association, 1990), p. 3.

3. Centers for Disease Control and Prevention, "Rates of Homicide, Suicide and Firearm-Related Death among Children—26 Industrialized Countries," *Morbidity and Mortality Weekly Report 46*, no. 5 (Feb. 7, 1997): 101–5. According to this study, the number of child homicides in the United States is five times higher than the *combined* figure for twenty-five other developed countries.

4. Steve Farkas and Jean Johnson, *Kids These Days: What Americans Really Think about the Next Generation*, a report from Public Agenda, sponsored by Ronald McDonald House Charities and the Advertising Council, 1997, p. 13.

5. The language of these sentences owes much to the work of the advisers to the Task Force on Parent Empowerment, particularly Enola Aird and Nancy Rankin.

6. Megan Rosenfeld, "Father Knows Squat," *Washington Post*, Nov. 13, 1994, p. G1.

7. Even with the September 1995 hike in the minimum wage, it still has only 63 percent of the buying power it had in the 1960s. See Edward N. Wolff, "The Economic Status of Parents in Postwar America," paper prepared for the Task Force on Parent Empowerment, Sept. 20, 1997, p. 27.

8. Summarized from Kenneth House, "No. 2 at Levi's Cashed Out at $107 Million; Executive's Package Set Bay Area Record," *San Francisco Chronicle*, Nov. 12, 1997, p. Ai and Ralph King Jr., "Levi's Ex-President Got 1996 Payment of $125 Million," *Wall Street Journal*, Nov. 14, 1997, p. B6.

9. David Cay Johnston, "Tracking Executives' Compensation," *New York Times*, Apr. 14, 1997, p. D6. For median wage data, see U.S. Census Bureau, Historical Income Tables–Persons, Table P29, www.census.gov.

10. Allan Carlson, president, Rockford Institute, telephone interview, Feb. 10, 1998. This $6,500 figure represents the same percentage of the 1996 median family income as $600 did in 1948. See also Ben J. Wattenberg, "The Easy Solution to the Social Security Crisis," *New York Times Magazine*, June 22, 1997, p. 30.

11. This figure describes the average expenditure on a child from birth to eighteen years, in a husband-wife household with an income in the $33,700–$56,700 range. See U.S. Department of Agriculture, Center for Nutrition Policy and Promotion, *Expenditures on Children by Families, 1995 Annual Report*, Publication No. 1528 (Washington, DC: GPO, 1995).

12. Viviana A. Zelizer, *Pricing the Priceless Child: The Changing Social Value of Children* (New York: Basic, 1985), p. 3.

13. Jane Addams, *Democracy and Social Ethics* (Cambridge, Mass.: Belknap/Harvard University Press, 1964).

14. Carol Gilligan, *In a Different Voice: Psychological Theory and Women's Development* (Cambridge, Mass.: Harvard University Press, 1982), pp. 129, 149.

15. Jean Bethke Elshtain, *Democracy on Trial* (New York: Basic, 1995), p. 129.

16. Gus A. Haggstrom, Linda J. Waite, David E. Kanouse, and Thomas J. Blaschke, "Changes in the Life Styles of New Parents" (Santa Monica, Calif.: Rand Corporation, Dec. 1984), p. 61.

17. Diana DiNitto, *Social Welfare: Politics & Public Policy* (New York: Allyn & Bacon, 1995), pp. 169–70. See detailed discussion of AFDC in Chapter 6.

18. Stephanie Ventura, demographer, National Center for Health Statistics, telephone interview, Dec. 10, 1997.

19. U.S. Bureau of the Census, *Child Support and Alimony: 1989*, Current Population Reports, series P60, No. 173 (Washington, DC: GPO, 1991).

20. Daniel R. Geyer and Steven Favasky, "Custodial Fathers: Myths, Realities, and Child Support Policy," *Journal of Marriage and the Family* 55 (Feb. 1992): 73–89.

21. For an in-depth discussion, see Jack Kammer, "What Do We Really Know about Child Support?" *Crisis* (Jan. 1994): 16.

22. Harry F. Harlow, "Love in Infant Monkeys," *Scientific American*, June 1959, pp. 68–74.

23. Willard Gaylin, "In the Beginning: Helpless and Dependent," in Willard Gaylin, Ira Glasser, Steven Marcus, and David J. Rothman, eds., *Doing Good: The Limits of Benevolence* (New York: Pantheon, 1978), p. 10.

24. Urie Bronfenbrenner, "Discovering What Families Do," in *Rebuilding the Nest: A New Commitment to the American Family* (Milwaukee, Wis.: Family Service America, 1990), p. 31.

25. James Alan Fox, *Trends in Juvenile Violence: A Report to the United States Attorney General on Current and Future Rates of Juvenile Offending* (Washington, DC: Bureau of Justice Statistics, March 1996); Centers for Disease Control, "Rates of Homicide . . . among Children," pp. 101–5; Select Committee on Children, Youth, and Families, *U.S. Children and Their Families*, p. 31, and National Law Center on Homelessness and Poverty, *Blocks to Their Future: A Report on the Barriers to Preschool Education for Homeless Children*, Sept. 1997; Lloyd D. Johnson et al., *National Survey Results on Drug Use from the* Monitoring the Future *Study*, 1975–1996 (Washington, DC: National Institute on Drug Abuse, 1997), Table 20–1; Karen W. Arenson, "Students Continue to Improve, College Board Says," *New York Times*, Aug. 23, 1996, p. A16; Centers for Disease Control, *Morbidity and Mortality Weekly Report*, Apr. 21, 1995, and *Suicide Deaths and Rates per 100,000, United States*, 1989–1995, unpublished data; National Center for Health Statistics, *Health United States 1996–1997*, July 1997, Table 73, p. 193.

26. Carnegie Council on Adolescent Development, *Great Transitions: Preparing Adolescents for a New Century* (New York: Carnegie Corporation of New York, Oct. 1995), p. 10.

27. Fox, *Trends in Juvenile Violence*.

28. Fox Butterfield, "Survey Finds That Crimes Cost $450 Billion a Year," *New York Times*, Apr. 22, 1996, p. A8.

29. Barbara M. Jones, "Guns, Drugs, and Juvenile Justice: Three Aspects of the Crisis in Youth Violence," paper prepared for the Task Force on Parent Empowerment, Apr. 17, 1996, p. 1.

30. Nancy Jo Sales, "Lost in the Park," *New York*, June 16, 1997, pp. 24–29; N. R. Kleinfield et al., "Lives Tangle in Park's Hidden World," *New York Times*, June 1, 1997, p. 1.

31. Centers for Disease Control, "Suicide among Children, Adolescents, and Young Adults—United States, 1980–1992," vol. 44, no. 15, Apr. 21, 1995, pp. 289–90; National Center for Health Statistics, Mortality Data Tapes, "Suicide Deaths and Rates per 100,000, United States, 1989–1995."

32. Sylvia Ann Hewlett, *Child Neglect in Rich Nations* (New York: UNICEF, 1993), p. 1.

33. U.S. Bureaus of the Census, *1997 March Current Population Survey*, App. C., Table 20.

34. Joe Dalaker, statistician, Bureau of the Census, telephone interview, Oct. 15, 1997.

35. *National Survey Results on Drug Use*; National Institute on Drug Abuse, "Facts about Teenagers and Drug Abuse," NIDA Capsule Series (C-83-07), 1996; "Monitoring the Future Study: Trends in Prevalence of Various Drugs for 8th Graders, 10th Graders and High School Seniors," NIDA Capsule Series (C-94-01), 1996.

36. National Center for Education Statistics, NAEP *1994 Trends in Academic Progress* (Washington, DC: GPO, Nov. 1996), p. iv.

37. National Center for Education Statistics, *Digest of Education Statistics, 1997*, Table 99, "High School Graduates Compared with Population 17 Years of Age, by Sex and Control of School: 1869–70 to 1996–97," p. 108, Dec. 31, 1997.

38. Carnegie, *Great Transitions*, p. 10.

39. David C. Rowe and Robert Plonim, "The Importance of Nonshared (E1) Environmental Influences in Behavioral Development," *Developmental Psychology 17*, no. 5 (1981): 517–53.

40. Victor R. Fuchs, *Women's Quest for Economic Equality* (Cambridge, Mass.: Harvard University Press, 1988), p. 111.

41. Edward N. Wolff, "The Economic Status of Parents in Postwar America," paper prepared for the Task Force on Parent Empowerment, Sept. 20, 1996, p. 9.

42. Juliet B. Schor, *The Overworked American: The Unexpected Decline of Leisure* (New York: Basic, 1992), p. 29.

43. Jerome Kagan, *The Nature of the Child* (New York: Basic, 1984), p. 108.

44. J. L. Richardson et al., "Substance Abuse among Eighth-Grade Students Who Take Care of Themselves after School," *Pediatrics 84*, no. 3 (Sept. 1989): 556–66.

45. Michael D. Resnick et al., "Protecting Adolescents from Harm," *Journal of the American Medical Association* (Sept. 1997): 823–32; S. Jody

Heymann and Alison Earle, "Family Policy for School Age Children: The Case of Parental Evening Work," Malcolm Wiener Center for Social Policy and the John F. Kennedy School of Government, Harvard University, April 1996, H-96-2.

46. James Alan Fox and Sanford A. Newman, "After-School Crime or After-School Programs: Turning in to the Prime Time for Violent Juvenile Crime and Implications for National Policy," a report to the U.S. Attorney General, Department of Justice, Sept. 10, 1997, p. 3.

47. Howard Hayghe, supervisory economist, Bureau of Labor Statistics, telephone interview, Jan. 13, 1998.

48. Fox and Newman, "After-School Crime," p. 6.

49. James S. Coleman, "Effects of School on Learning: The IEA Findings," paper presented at Conference on Educational Achievement, Harvard University, Nov. 1973, p. 40.

50. Laurence Steinberg, "Failure Outside the Classroom," *Wall Street Journal*, July 11, 1996, p. A14; Laurence Steinberg et al., *Beyond the Classroom: Why School Reform Has Failed and What Parents Need to Do* (New York: Simon & Schuster, 1996), p. 119.

51. Michael Sandel, "Making Nice Is Not the Same as Doing Good," *New York Times*, Dec. 29, 1996, p. E9.

52. Robert D. Putnam, "Bowling Alone: America's Declining Social Capital," *Journal of Democracy 6*, no. 1 (Jan. 1995): 65–78. See also Putnam, "The Strange Disappearance of Civic America," *American Prospect* (Winter 1996): 34–48.

53. Bill Moyers, *Bill Moyers: A World of Ideas* (New York: Doubleday, 1989), p. 60.

54. "Excerpts from Tapes in Discrimination Lawsuit," *New York Times*, Nov. 4, 1996, p. D4.

55. A copy of our Parents' Bill of Rights is printed in an appendix at the end of this chapter. For a full discussion of the Parents' Bill of Rights, please see Sylvia A. Hewlett and Cornel West, *The War against Parents* (New York: Houghton Mifflin Company, 1998).

4

The Impact of Media Violence on Developing Minds and Hearts

Gloria DeGaetano

I'll finish her off by ripping out her heart.

No, cut off her head.

But I want to rip her heart out.

I want to see her head fly off.

Oh, all right, let's see her head roll. There! Look at all that blood. Cool.

Is this a conversation between two psychopaths? No. This exchange took place between two sixth-grade boys when they played the video game Mortal Kombat 2 in 1993. Things have gone downhill since then. Today's video games display even more horrific violence, with sharper images and more realistic graphics. American children spend a daily average of six hours and thirty-two minutes consuming visual electronic media.[1] Images of brutality fill up much of their leisure time.

ENTERTAINMENT VIOLENCE AND ATTITUDE FORMATION

While youngsters watch violent cartoons, take in the latest horror flicks, and play violent video games, their fundamental beliefs or attitudes about the world are taking shape. An attitude can be formed through conscious, intentional deliberation as may occur when serving on a jury,[2] or an attitude can be catalyzed unconsciously, guided predominantly by emotional arousal rather than thoughtful analysis.

Advertisements are intentionally constructed to shape attitudes by appealing to primitive emotions while keeping thinking to a minimum. Similarly, screen violence wields its persuasive power by eliciting primal fears, base instincts, and a natural curiosity about death and destruction. Through relentless depictions of hatred, rage, revenge, and brutality, the media portray a highly skewed image of human nature, emphasizing our basest tendencies, while ignoring our capacity for reflection, empathy, morality, and spirituality.

Images of human suffering and property destruction carefully constructed to elicit strong emotional reactions promote antisocial and often extremely deranged attitudes in children. These attitudes not only affect present behaviors, but they become the foundation and the filter through which children process new information. Video game researcher Jeanne Funk puts it this way: "Individuals tend to process information differently depending on how consistent new information is with pre-existing attitudes."[3] Attitudes gleaned from sensational screen violence permeate every aspect of children's lives and can lead to depression, anxiety, and numerous other mental health problems. As our children's minds and hearts are filled with media violence in most of their leisure moments, they can even develop cognitive scripts that mimic psychopathic language. Taking pleasure in violent entertainment, they talk to themselves and to each other as if they were cold-blooded murderers.

MEDIA RATING SYSTEMS FAIL TO PROTECT CHILDREN

Although the television, movie, and gaming industries have created their own rating systems with which to guide consumer choices, they are largely unsuccessful in protecting children from violence—perhaps this is akin to putting the wolves in charge of the henhouse.

Video Game Ratings Fail

Teens and elementary age children routinely play "M" video games (recommended for age seventeen and over). A recent study found that 73 percent of fourth-grade boys and 59 percent of fourth-grade girls listed violent games as their favorites.[4] In a "mystery shopper" study conducted by the U.S. Federal Trade Commission, underage children (ages 13–16) unaccompanied by an adult attempted to purchase games rated "M." They were successful in 85 percent of the 380 stores sampled. The study also found that over 90 percent of surveyed companies producing M-rated games targeted children under seventeen in their marketing campaigns.[5] Of course, if a game is purchased by an older family member, it is nearly impossible to regulate its use once it enters the home.

Teachers are often shocked to overhear their students talking about the gory details of popular M-rated games. One preschool educator told me, after viewing an educational video about violent video games, that now she understood what a four-year-old boy was telling her about "the dukem game" he played with his older brother. She was beside herself with worry when she realized that the little fellow was regularly playing the video game *Duke Nukem*. This is an extremely violent and disgusting video game in which the player assumes the role of the hero, Duke Nukem. As Duke, the player performs "heroic" deeds such as shooting monks hanging from rafters with ropes around their necks and blowing up people into little piles of blood and gore. The game includes an image of a Japanese woman opening and closing her kimono to expose her naked breasts; when the player shoots her she explodes into a bloody mass. The game shows scantily clad women of various nationalities chained to columns and whispering, "Kill me, kill me."[6]

Grand Theft Auto III, released by Rockstar Games, was one of the most popular teen games in 2001. Playing this game means one can engage in sex with a prostitute and then bludgeon her to death after she comments on "how big you are." *Grand Theft Auto III* attracted special notoriety, as it was one of the first "cop killer" games in which a player shoots police officers up close in the face or sets them on fire and listens to them scream as their flesh burns.[7] In *Soldier of Fortune* (2000)—a game British Columbia rated X and put in pornography sections of bookstores—players realistically rip arms from sockets and see bone and sinew dangling while blood gushes from the wounds. In other video games, urinating on women and setting black men on fire while noting, "It smells like chicken," are just a few of the racist, demeaning, and troubling images and messages conveyed.[8]

One of the latest games to come onto the scene, *Manhunt* (2004), moves screen violence up yet another notch. In this game, the player kills to vicariously satisfy "the Director," who whispers commands into the player's ear via an optional headset, urging the player to move beyond any reticence he or she may have in experiencing the "thrill" of maiming and destroying. The ultra-realistic violence sets *Manhunt* apart on the gaming scene, unnerving even those in the industry. "It ... shows people stuff they haven't seen in games before, but in slasher flicks," said Greg Kasavin, executive editor of GameSpot.com. "There's a lot of blood, people getting strangled and killed with household weapons."[9]

Like television, video games didn't start out being so obscenely violent and antisocial. The first ones developed had unwritten rules to adhere to a semblance of civilized standards. Nolan Bushnell, the founder of Atari, explains that "we had an internal rule that we wouldn't allow violence against people. You could blow up a tank or you could blow up a flying saucer, but you couldn't blow up people."[10] Today, things have clearly changed. There are no rules, written or unwritten. In fact, shooting, blowing up, and torturing people are the main events in today's violent video games.

Some games give extra points for headshots. These are the modern-day equivalent of the Three Stooges, who whacked each other on the heads, or cartoon characters that regularly bang heads. Joseph Strayhorn, MD, author of *The Competence Approach to Parenting*, worries about the effects of even cartoon depictions of head injury:

> [T]he act of one person's hitting another person in the head is one of the most obscene acts that we can conjure up. The brain is the seat of the personality, and it is a delicate organ. It is easily injured by blows to the skull. One hard blow to the head can result in seizures for the rest of the [child's] life, or in permanent damage to the basic processes of thinking and feeling and behaving. Brain injury is a very prevalent horror in our society. Dorothy Lewis, a psychiatrist and an internationally recognized expert on violence, has looked at very violent delinquents and has found a high prevalence of brain abnormalities in them, the type that are often caused by blows to the head. Many of these delinquents have histories compatible ... of child abuse, specifically blows to the head.... Yet in movies like the *Teenage Mutant Ninja Turtles* we see almost continuous blows delivered to heads, and we give the movie[s] a PG rating.[11]

Television Ratings Fail

Sixty-one percent of television content is violent, and children's programming has the most violent content of all. Television exposes

American children to at least 10,000 violent acts each year. By age twelve, children will have seen 20,000 murders and 80,000 injurious assaults on TV alone, not counting the acts of extreme violence they will have witnessed in electronic games and movies. Although television programs are rated, 65 percent of eight- to eighteen-year-olds have televisions in their bedrooms, as do 32 percent of children aged two to seven, and 26 percent of children under two, and so a majority of children have extensive control over their viewing choices.[12]

The wildly popular programs produced by the World Wrestling Entertainment Corporation (WWE) are among the most egregious sources of TV violence. Its programs depict frequent head blows, sadistic bullying, and male sexual domination over women through brute force. Although many of their programs are rated (PG-14), WWE explicitly targets young viewers by marketing everything from underwear to action figures to children as young as preschoolers.

More than half of the violent incidents portrayed on television feature physical aggression that would be lethal or incapacitating if they were to occur in real life, and yet at least 40 percent of the violent scenes include humor.[13] Also, the perpetrator of the violence is usually the most attractive or charismatic character on the screen. Youth tuning into MTV, for instance, will find that attractive or seductive models are the aggressors in more than 80 percent of violent music videos.[14]

Movie Ratings Fail

The movie rating system likewise lacks clout. A study from the Harvard School of Public Health found that movies that the Motion Picture Association of America currently rates PG-13 are similar in content to R movies a decade ago. Whereas *Forrest Gump* with Tom Hanks exemplified PG-13 movies in 1994, *Minority Report* with Tom Cruise, a hard-edged cop film depicting a terrifying futuristic world, was rated PG-13 in 2002.[15]

Teens, and even elementary-age children, frequently see R-rated movies. In one study, more than half of all fifteen- to sixteen-year-olds had seen the majority of the popular R-rated movies at the time.[16] In too many instances, even young children are exposed to violent films. Canadian researchers discovered that a father was tucking his seven-year-old son into bed at night and then leaving him to watch Freddie Krueger (*Nightmare on Elm Street*) videos. In describing a deliberate attempt to reduce his own fear, he told the researchers, "It was easy. I pretended I was Freddie Krueger. Then I wasn't scared. Now that's what I always do and I'm never scared."[17]

RESEARCH ON THE IMPACT OF MEDIA VIOLENCE

More than 2,500 studies conducted over the course of four decades have demonstrated a definitive relationship between watching violent entertainment and real-life aggression.[18] As far back as 1972, the Surgeon General of the United States issued a warning that TV violence was harmful to the mental health of children and adults. Since that time, numerous professional organizations including the American Academy of Pediatrics, the American Medical Association, and the American Psychological Association have issued similar warnings and position statements.[19]

Dr. Craig Anderson, a professor of psychology at Iowa State University and a pioneer in violent video game research, states unequivocally, "The effect of exposure to violent video games on subsequent aggressive behavior in children ... is larger than: (a) the effect of exposure to passive tobacco smoke on lung cancer; (b) the effect of calcium intake on bone mass; and (c) the effect of homework on academic achievement."[20]

Not all depictions of violence are equally detrimental to children. Studies show that if the perpetrator is not glamorized, regrets his or her actions, or is punished, and the violence is shown to have negative consequences, then witnessing such acts is less likely to initiate imitation or antisocial attitudes. But these conditions are rarely met in violent screen entertainment.

Depictions of violence that have been shown to encourage violent attitudes and behavior are ubiquitous in the media and include the following:

- Plots that are driven by quick-cut scenes of gratuitous violence delivered in rapid-fire sequence with graphic technical effects.
- Graphic sadistic revenge, torture techniques, and inhumane treatment of others in a context of humor, trivialization, glibness, and/or raucous "fun."
- Explicitly depicted violent acts shown through special effects, camera angles, background music, or lighting to be glamorous, heroic, "cool," and worthy of appreciation and imitation.
- Depictions of people holding personal and social power primarily because they are using weapons, or using their bodies as weapons,

and dominating other people through threat of violence or through actual violence.

- Extraneous, graphic, gory, detailed violent acts whose intent is to shock without a sense of empathy or revulsion.
- Violent acts shown as an acceptable way to solve problems or presented as the primary problem-solving approach.
- News programs that explicitly detail murder and rape, with information and graphic images not necessary for understanding the central message.[21]

In the sections to follow, I will detail some of the specific ways in which screen violence impacts children's brains and behaviors.

The Impact of Screen Violence on Young Children

Like sunflowers turning toward the afternoon sun, young children are drawn to emotionally charged images. In fact, those are mostly what they remember when they watch screens. A study of preschoolers demonstrated that one visually vivid but incidental scene in an educational program informed their synopsis of the entire program. The program they watched was about the construction and uses of canals. In one scene, canal boat operators covered their heads to avoid having spiders land on them as they went through tunnels. When asked to summarize the program, the children stated that it was about spiders jumping down on people as they went through tunnels. Not one youngster mentioned the intended educational content.[22]

Children aged eight and under are especially vulnerable to violent imagery because they lack the mental mechanisms to either filter or interpret what they are seeing. In addition, young children have difficulty distinguishing reality from fantasy. Dr. Alvin Poussaint, professor of psychiatry at Harvard Medical School, believes that exposing children to violent images is similar in its impact to "physical or sexual abuse ... or living in a war zone. None of us would willingly put a child into those situations, yet we do not act to keep them from watching movies about things we would be horrified to have them see *off* the screen."[23]

Increasing Aggression

A number of recent reports are pointing to an increase in both the amount and the intensity of violent behavior that is being witnessed in preschool and kindergarten settings. "I'm clearly seeing

an increasing number of kindergartners and first-graders coming
to our attention for aggressive behavior," says Michael Parker, program director of psychological services at the Fort Worth Independent School District, which serves 80,000 students. The incidents
have occurred not only in low-income urban schools but in middle-
class areas as well. Says Parker, "We're talking about serious talking back to teachers, profanity, even biting, kicking and hitting
adults, and we're seeing it in five-year-olds."

This alarming trend has been confirmed by a survey that was
conducted by Partnership for Children, a child-advocacy group.
Ninety-three percent of the thirty-nine schools that responded to
their survey said kindergarteners today had "more emotional and
behavioral problems" than were seen five years earlier. More than
half the daycare centers said "incidents of rage and anger" had
increased over the past three years. "We're talking about children,
a three-year-old in one instance, who will take a fork and stab
another child in the forehead. We're talking about a wide range of
explosive behaviors, and it's a growing problem," says John Ross,
who oversaw the survey.[24]

The effects of media violence on children reach well into children's adult years. Research has established that the amount of violent television that children watch at eight years of age is a strong
predictor of the likelihood that they will commit serious crimes, be
physically abusive to their spouses, and use violence to punish their
own children in adulthood.[25] The relationship between watching
TV violence and committing later aggression persists even when
the effects of socio-economic status, intellectual ability, and quality
of parenting are taken into account.[26]

Increasing Fear

In addition to inciting aggressive behavior, violent images can
also terrify young children with lasting effects. Yet, children as
young as three years old were taken to see *Kill Bill Vol. 1*—an ultra-
violent movie, even by director Quentin Tarantino's estimation.
One theater manager stated, "I've seen parents take little kids into
the worst stuff in the world. It's horrible."[27]

Dr. Joanne Cantor, who has studied fright reactions of young
children to screen violence, states,

> efforts at prevention are well worth the hassle when weighed against
> the difficulty of reassuring a young child who has been frightened

by something on TV or in a movie … many of these responses are remarkably intense, and they can be very hard to undo…. There have been several case studies in medical journals telling about young people who had to be hospitalized for several days or weeks after watching horror movies … one reported that two children had suffered from post-traumatic stress disorder … as a result of watching a horror movie on television. One of the children described in the article was hospitalized for eight weeks.[28]

Derailed Brain Development

Human brain development is exquisitely dependent upon and responsive to environmental stimulation. It goes without saying that immersing children in a two-dimensional world of screens for hours each day over the course of several years—as opposed to the three-dimensional world of experience—will dramatically alter their brains.[29] While behavioral evidence to this effect has existed for decades (see section above), a newly minted scientific discipline called video-game neurology is now providing direct evidence that engaging with violent visual electronic media does indeed assault the brain. It is fitting that brain research has so far focused on the impact of video games, because scientists have suspected that playing them may have a more potent impact than television or movie viewing. As John Murray, professor of psychiatry at Kansas State University, explains, "In a video game, the player is the character. That identification makes the effect of game images far more intense and lingering."[30]

Video-game neurology—using magnetic resonance imaging (MRI) to systematically examine how playing video games impacts the brain—is confirming these suspicions. In a recent study of five children aged eight to thirteen, Murray and his colleagues observed the following: increased blood flow to the right brain hemispheres, indicating emotional arousal; activation of brain areas that sense danger and energize the body for "fight or flight"; and activation of the prefrontal cortex, which suggests that the children were physically preparing to imitate the boxing moves they had just observed in the game. In addition, the posterior cingulate region of the brain was aroused, indicating that the images were being stored as vivid, persistent, and traumatic memories. Based on these results, Dr. Murray concluded that the brain "treats entertainment violence as something real … [and] stores this violence as long-term memory."[31]

Other studies have also found that children's "fight or flight" response is engaged while playing violent video games, as evidenced by elevated blood pressure, heart rate, and norepinephrine (adrenaline) levels. With the aid of an MRI technique called independent component analysis, researchers at Johns Hopkins University found that players using high-speed driving simulators experienced deactivation in brain areas that sense risk and counsel caution. "These gamers first learned, then reinforced two lessons: faster is better, and peril can successfully be ignored."[32] Researchers at Iowa State University found that the brain's "orientation reflex," which heightens and rivets the senses to a sudden change in the environment such as a bright flash or a loud noise, was activated in the brains of video gamers as often as in the brains of soldiers in combat.

When emotionally charged, ever-changing screen images grab children's attention and alert their brains to danger repeatedly, over the course of several hours, their bodies are kept in an adrenaline-fueled state of readiness—easy to startle, quick to blow up. At the same time, cortical functioning is reduced: there's no time to think with the constant barrage of fast-paced, violent images. There is no problem for the child to solve; no deliberation is necessary. The violence takes care of whatever is not working. Violent imagery, in effect, keeps young brains on alert, producing hypervigilant children who have trouble listening carefully and responding thoughtfully.

Children who engage often with violent screen entertainment may come to dislike activities that require methodical thinking. Self-direction, intrinsic motivation, and internal control become increasingly alien. Thinking becomes plodding and difficult in contrast to the ease of violence. Avoiding mental challenges means the young cortex lacks the necessary exercise to develop higher-level thinking. Over time, thinking and self-creation become "boring" and violence and virtual death become "cool." Now the child is "hooked" but lacks the cortical development, and often the literacy skills, to resist the physiological lure of sensational screen violence. The lesson that violence is "fun" can't easily be unlearned. Expecting youngsters who equate violent entertainment with pleasure to resist other forms of screen violence as they grow older is like expecting adults to ignore the flashing lights of an ambulance. It can't be done.

When young children spend so much time in an artificially induced alarm state—with the consequent hyperactivity and noradrenaline pulsing through their veins—they may revert to low noradrenaline levels and predatory behaviors by puberty. One explanation for the change may be that brain cells exposed to constant stress burn out, dropping to a lower level of activity to save themselves. Animal studies show that overexposure to stress can kill brain cells. Dr. Bruce Perry, who has extensively researched the effects of trauma on young human brains, observes that "it's really scary to watch the transition from high arousal to low arousal … they (youth) develop this incredible icy quality of being emotionless."[33] Adolescents who copy crimes they see on television do so without remorse and with cold-blooded calculations. They even detect and correct the flaws that may have caused the television crime to fail.[34]

According to Dr. Donald Shifrin, a pediatrician and longstanding media representative for the American Academy of Pediatrics, video-game playing mimics drug-seeking behaviors:

> When youngsters get into video games the object is excitement. The child then builds tolerance for that level of excitement and seeks greater and greater levels. Initially there's experimentation, behavior much like seeking a drug for increasing levels of excitement. Then there is habituation, when more and more of the drug is actually necessary for these feelings of excitement.[35]

Even non-violent video games lead children to seek increased levels of excitement, since the basic construct of these games is stimulus-response. Dr. Shifrin believes so strongly in the ease with which children can be conditioned to video game technology that he states emphatically, "There is no need to have a video game system in the house, especially for young children. There is no middle ground for me on this. I view it as a black-and-white issue like helmets for bike safety."[36]

Constant excitement equals stress. By late adolescence, kids who have played video games daily run the risk of burnout, a complete shutdown of emotional responsiveness. Rollo May has written, "Human freedom involves our capacity to pause between stimulus and response and, in that pause, to choose the one response toward which we wish to throw our weight. The capacity to create ourselves based upon this freedom is inseparable from consciousness or self-awareness."[37]

It takes time for the reasoning cortex to become engaged, to assess, and to choose. A mature, well-functioning pre-frontal lobe can act as the dampening switch to impulsive behaviors, initiating that pause. But with untimely introduction of video games, young brains do not get the practice of pausing and thinking through an intended action. Instead, the brain is prompted, and eventually conditioned, to react without thinking. Caught up in low brain-reactive states, children don't acquire the metacognitive skills to become self-aware. If, however, they have developed an inner life and prefrontal capabilities *before* they begin playing video games, they are less likely to be attracted to violent, fast-paced games and more likely to seek out thoughtful games that challenge them to reason and respond creatively.

Normal kids in normal homes aren't about to become killers after playing video games. Nonetheless, Dr. Anderson—one of the pre-eminent researchers on the effects of exposure to violent video games—cautions that children who use these games heavily are more likely to use excessive aggression in relatively benign situations such as being jostled in a lineup. Dr. Anderson emphasizes that there are a multitude of subtle but serious consequences for children who are heavy users of violent video games: "The people who are willing to interact with them, the types of interactions they have, and the types of situations made available to them all change. Interactions with teachers, parents, and non-aggressive peers are likely to decline in frequency and quality, but interactions with 'deviant' peers are likely to increase."[38]

Screen Viewing

While it may seem intuitive that violent entertainment is unhealthy for children, it is of critical importance to understand that the *process* of engaging with visual electronic media *regardless of the content* is also cause for concern. As stated earlier, children in the United States spend an average of six hours and thirty-two minutes in front of a screen daily.[39] Staring at two-dimensional images cannot stimulate the brain in the way that physical and tactile experiences such as art, dance, and sports do. A field trip "online" does not begin to exercise the child's brain to the extent that a walk through a nature trail does. Simultaneous activation of a full range of the child's senses is absolutely necessary for optimal neocortex development and maturation of the prefrontal lobe.[40]

Television's emotionally intense, rapid-fire imagery rivets children to the screen by repeatedly engaging their brains' "orienting response" while tuning out the rest of the world. If you are in doubt about this, try engaging the attention of a youngster who is watching television. Reading requires children to conjure up the visual and auditory images of the people and places they are reading about, whereas television leaves nothing to the imagination. As a result, TV viewing keeps children in a state of sensory deprivation—riveted to the screen, immobilized, tuned out. For this reason, children who watch television for extended periods of time often become hyperactive and aggressive when "burning off steam" as they re-engage with the real world.

In her book *Smart Moves: Why Learning Is Not All in Your Head*, Dr. Carla Hannaford explains the brain processes catalyzed by sensory experiences:

> As sensory experience floods our systems, it travels through the brain stem and the reticular activating system and on to the thalamus of the limbic system. All pathways from the sensory nerve endings to the neocortex pass through the thalamus, except for smell. The thalamus not only monitors sensory input and adds emotional context to the information, it has direct connections with all areas of the neocortex…. These subtle, invisible transactions among sensory/emotional/motor areas of the brain allow us to create meaning from our experience. In the process of developing the base patterns which organize our experience, different lobes of the cerebrum are involved: the occipital lobe for visual understanding, the temporal lobe for hearing and gravitational understanding, and the parietal lobe for touch, pressure, pain, heat and cold sensations and proprioception all over the body…. Through [these] base patterns we construct models of the way things work, make predictions, organize physical responses, and come to more complexity of understanding as we assimilate new learning.[41]

There is a body of research that demonstrates that the more children watch television, the more they choose television violence, the less they read, and the less successful they are in school. This downward spiral leads to poor study habits, frustrating school experiences, and an overall inability to persevere through mental challenges. Seeking thrills and quick reinforcement though fast-paced, violent video games becomes the next step as these children narrow their entertainment choices to be in sync with their limited literacy and cognitive abilities and their heightened need for excitement.[42]

EFFECTIVE PARENTAL STRATEGIES TO COUNTER SCREEN VIOLENCE

Thousands of studies conducted over the course of four decades tell us in no uncertain terms that violent visual media have a devastating impact on our children's fundamental beliefs, and on their social, emotional, and intellectual development. Recent MRI research demonstrates that children's brains are being rewired as a result of engaging with violent entertainment.

Despite the compelling evidence that screen entertainments are undermining our children's development, this research is not reaching parents, and their parenting choices reflect it. One study found that 90 percent of teens in grades eight through twelve reported that their parents never checked the ratings of video games before allowing their purchase, and only one percent of the teens' parents had ever prevented a purchase based on its rating. Furthermore, 89 percent reported that their parents never limited time spent playing video games.[43] As stated earlier, a majority of children have TVs in their rooms, and therefore dominion over the programs they watch, and the length of time that they watch them.

Parents, however, can only make decisions based on the information that is available to them. According to Dr. Anderson, "As the state of scientific knowledge supporting a significant and causal link between media violence and aggression grew stronger, news media reports about the link actually grew weaker."[44] It comes as no surprise that the media are not keen to disclose that spending hours each day engaged with it is damaging children's brains!

Misinformation and misguided debate lock our collective attention on the wrong focus. Look up a professional journal article on some aspect of media violence research from a decade ago and you will see the same messages given by researchers today. We waste precious time and our children suffer with escalating behavioral and mental health problems while arguments continue about whether or not media violence is harmful. In reality, that debate is over and needs to be buried. We need to help parents focus their attention and efforts on what will work.

Based on the available research, I urge parents to do the following:

- Limit children to one hour or less of screen time per day and eliminate screen time for children under the age of two, in keeping with the recommendations of the American Academy of Pediatrics.[45]
- Protect children aged eight and under from all forms of screen violence until they are capable of distinguishing between fantasy and reality.
- Wait until children are at least eleven years of age—when the cortex is more developed—before introducing video games.

The following guidelines can help parents to implement these three recommendations:

- Observe children after they watch cartoons with violent content and after they watch educational shows. Which programming better supports children's ability to play non-violently, to be creative, instead of destructive, to be calm and curious when learning?
- Monitor all videos and video games that come into the home environment. Essentially, introducing these into the home is like introducing another environment. Is their content compatible with the values and attitudes of the home environment?
- Take the TV out of children's and teens' bedrooms and replace it with an aquarium, a terrarium, a bonsai garden—anything that is alive and will need the children's care and nurturance.
- Discuss TV, movies, and video game content frequently, paying attention to their antisocial or prosocial messages.
- Ask older children and teens this question often: how is this (TV program, movie, video game) making you a more competent and caring person?
- Affirm children and teens when they say "No" to peers and refuse to go along with the crowd, thereby making an unpopular but developmentally appropriate media entertainment choice.
- Make and enforce family rules about media use. Strive to keep to the American Academy of Pediatrics recommendations of one hour or less of all screen time per day and no screen time for children under the age of two.
- Allow time for children and teens to reflect and think through ideas. Make this a parental mantra: "Take your time and think about it. Then let's discuss it."
- Keep the TV off in the room where a child is playing or doing homework. Allow for the child to enter his or her mental landscape without external distractions from screens.
- Consider family media literacy as a high priority and offer many daily opportunities for children and teens to voice their opinions about media content and choices.

These choices and actions would provide the necessary "fuel" to launch a collective paradigm shift in how we as a society and how individual families approach media violence. These choices are extremely difficult for most parents to accomplish because our culture has been co-opted by the very media that market these entertainments to our children. Until the American Academy of Pediatrics, American Medical Association, and American Psychological Association guidelines about media violence are in our newspapers daily, parents and caregivers who implement them will be making "countercultural" choices on behalf of their children.

CONCLUSION

Parents are the key players in stemming the tide of media violence in their children's lives. They can monitor, protect, manage, and teach. They can empower their children like no one else can. Professionals in turn need to empower parents with relevant information, compelling reasons, and a sense of urgency to heed what we know about the impact of cumulative exposure to all forms of screen violence. If we wish our children and teens to grow up using their minds and valuing their hearts in their interactions with others, we need to catalyze parents to become transformational change agents in their homes; and we need to appreciate, support, and affirm their efforts to parent well in a media age.

NOTES

1. M. L. Mares, *Children's Use of VCR's*, American Academy of Pediatrics Policy Statement Social Science, 557, 1998, pp. 120–131.

2. Jeanne B. Funk, "Violent Video Games: Who's at Risk?" in *Kid Stuff: Marketing Sex and Violence to America's Children*, eds. Diane Ravitch and Joseph Viteritti, The Johns Hopkins University Press, 2003, p. 175.

3. Ibid.

4. Craig A. Anderson, "Video Games and Aggressive Behavior," in *Kid Stuff: Marketing Sex and Violence to America's Children*, eds. Diane Ravitch and Joseph Viteritti, The Johns Hopkins University Press, 2003, p. 147.

5. Ibid., p. 146.

6. David Grossman and Gloria DeGaetano, *Stop Teaching Our Kids to Kill: A Call to Action against TV, Movie, and Video Game Violence*, Crown, 1999, p. 78.

7. *Game Smart*, an educational video by Mothers against Violence in America, 2003.

8. Ibid.

9. Matt Slagle, "Manhunt Redefines Video Game Violence," *Add Technology* (January 27, 2004).

10. Anderson, "Video Games and Aggressive Behavior," p. 144.

11. Joseph Strayhorn, "Media Violence," www.psyskills.com/media-violence.htm, p. 10.

12. D. F. Roberts, U. G. Foeh, V. J. Rideout, and M. Brodie, *Kids and the Media at the New Millennium: A Comprehensive National Analysis of*

Children's Media Use, The Henry J. Kaiser Family Foundation Report, 1999.

13. Joel Federman, Ed., *The National Television Study*, Vol. 3: *Executive Summary*, Regents of the University of California, 1998, pp. 29–42.

14. Ibid., p. 32.

15. S. Waxman, "Study Finds Film Ratings Are Growing More Lenient," *New York Times* (July 14, 2004).

16. Federman, *National Television Study*, p. 18.

17. Wendy Josephson, *Television Violence: A Review of the Effects on Children of Different Ages*, National Clearinghouse on Family Violence, Health Canada, 1995.

18. Victor C. Strasburger and Edward Donnerstein, "Children, Adolescents, and the Media: Issues and Solutions," *Pediatrics*, 103 (January 1999): 130.

19. Ibid.

20. Anderson, "Video Games and Aggressive Behavior," p. 155.

21. Grossman and DeGaetano, *Stop Teaching Our Kids to Kill*, pp. 121–122.

22. Josephson, *Television Violence*.

23. Poussaint, Alvin, "Taking Movie Ratings Seriously: The Risks Faced by Children Allowed to Watch Film Meant for Adults Are as Real as Those from Alcohol, Tobacco, or Abuse," *Good Housekeeping* (April, 1997), pp. 74.

24. Quoted in Gloria DeGaetano, *Parenting Well in a Media Age*, Personhood Press, 2004, pp. 22–23; from Emily Yearwood-Less, "Viciousness of Youth Attacks Increase while Numbers Remain Static," *Canadian Press* (Sunday, December 7, 2003).

25. L. D. Eron and L. Rowell Huesmann, "The Control of Aggressive Behavior by Changes in Attitudes, Values, and the Conditions of Learning," in *Advances in the Study of Aggression*, eds. R. J. Blanchard and D. C. Blanchard, Academic Press, Inc., Orlando, FL, 1984.

26. L. Rowell Heussmann, Jessica Moise-Titus, Cheryl-Lynn Podolski, and Leonard D. Eron, "Longitudinal Relations between Children's Exposure to TV Violence and Their Aggressive and Violent Behavior in Young Adulthood: 1977–1992," *Developmental Psychology*, 39(2) (2003): 201–221.

27. David Schmader, "Friday, October 10," *The Stranger* (October 16–22), p. 4.

28. Joann Cantor, *Mommy, I'm Scared: How TV and Movies Frighten Children and What We Can Do to Protect Them*, Harcourt Brace and Company, San Diego, 1998, p. 140.

29. J. M. Healy, *Failure to Connect: How Computers Affect Our Chidren's Minds—and What We Can Do About It*, Touchstone, New York, 1998.

30. W. I. Atkinson, *Globe and Mail*, Toronto (Saturday, March 13, 2004).

31. Ibid.

32. Ibid.

33. Bruce Perry, "Incubated in Terror: Neurodevelopmental Factors in the Cycle of Violence," in *Children, Youth and Violence: Searching for Solutions*, ed. Joy D. Osofsky, The Guilford Press, New York, 1995.

34. Josephson, *Television Violence*, p. 40.

35. Grossman and DeGaetano, *Stop Teaching Our Kids to Kill*, p. 70.

36. Ibid.

37. Rollo May, *The Courage to Create*, Bantam Books, New York, 1975, p. 117.

38. Anderson, "Video Games and Aggressive Behavior," p. 160.

39. Mares, *Children's Use of VCR's*, pp. 120–131.

40. Healy, *Failure to Connect*.

41. Carla Hannaford, *Smart Moves: Why Learning Is Not All in Your Head*, Great Ocean Publishers, Arlington, VA, 1995, pp. 73–74.

42. Gloria DeGaetano, "Cycle Effects from Long-Term Viewing of Television Violence," in *Screen Smarts: A Family Guide to Media Literacy*, Gloria DeGaetano and Kathleen Bander, Houghton Mifflin, New York, 1996, p. 57.

43. Anderson, "Video Games and Aggressive Behavior," p. 149.

44. Ibid., pp. 151–152.

45. American Academy of Pediatric Website, "Television and the Family," http://www.aap.org/family/tv1.htm.

5

The Commercialization of Childhood

SUSAN LINN

The well-worn phrase "It takes a village to raise a child" is an evocative means of arguing for the necessity of community involvement in child-rearing. It also reminds us that children's experiences beyond the family—in the neighborhood or community—can have a powerful impact on their growth and development. Unfortunately, the village raising our children has been co-opted by electronic media, a ubiquitous force in children's lives. On average, children between the ages of two and eighteen spend almost forty hours a week outside of school consuming media,[1] most of which is commercially driven. Nor is marketing limited to the time children spend outside of school. In 2000, a report from the Government Accounting Office called marketing in schools a "growth industry."[2] Exclusive beverage contracts, corporate-sponsored teaching materials, book covers featuring ads, and corporate-sponsored newscasts are just a few of the ways that marketing infiltrates educational settings.[3]

JUST SAYING NO IS NOT ENOUGH

The advertising industry spin is that parents should bear sole responsibility for protecting children from marketing and that parents are to blame for the consequences of commercialism.[4] "I think it's all the parents' fault," an older woman comments during a call-in radio show about marketing to kids. "They are too indulgent these days. They need to learn to say no." I often hear comments like this when I talk about children and the marketplace. I don't agree. After years of exploring advertising and advertising practices as they affect children, I have come to the following conclusion: telling parents to "just say no" to every marketing-related request they feel is unsafe, unaffordable, unreasonable, or contrary to family values is about as simplistic as telling a drug addict to "just say no" to drugs.

As I listen to parents and think about my own experiences, I am reminded of a conversation I had with a colleague of mine who worked with families in a neighborhood saturated with gangs. He talked about the anguish of parents who found that, despite all their best efforts, they couldn't compete with the seductive offerings of a toxic street culture. The culture of marketing that saturates all our communities, from the poorest to the richest, is similar in that it is pervasive and alluring and competes with parental values for children's hearts and minds.

Educators and healthcare professionals have long known to look beyond the child to the influence and values of family, neighborhood, and peer group. But now we have to consider the influence and values of Madison Avenue and the commercial world as well. Children are bombarded from morning to night by messages designed not to make their lives better but for the sole purpose of selling them something.[5]

THE DEREGULATION OF ADVERTISING

The 1970s were a progressive decade for media regulation. During this time, the Federal Trade Commission (FTC) gained the authority to regulate deceptive and unfair advertising, including advertising to children.[6] Under these early regulations, program-length commercials that were the result of developing and marketing products and TV programs together were prohibited. In addition, the Federal Communications Commission (FCC) regulated children's television and placed a limit on the number of advertising minutes per hour.[7] These policies helped to stem the tide of advertising to children.

In 1978, prodded by pressure from advocacy groups such as *Action for Children's Television*, the FTC proposed banning television advertising to children under eight. The ban never came to be. Bowing to corporate interests, in 1980 Congress took away the

FTC's power to regulate advertising.[8] In 1984 the FCC deregulated children's television, ending the ban on program-length commercials. Technological advances in the 1980s that enabled electronic media to proliferate coincided with the advent of deregulation, thus multiplying the flood of advertising that was soon to engulf children. Programs such as *Masters of the Universe* were used to market whole lines of toys. Today, most of the best-selling toys are linked to media.[9]

In 1990, Congress passed the Children's Television Act, which set new limits on the amount of time per hour that could be devoted to commercials. In 1999, spearheaded by the Center for Media Education, the Children's Online Privacy Protection Act (COPPA) made it illegal to collect personal information from children under twelve online. Aside from a few such laws, marketing to children in the United States is virtually unregulated.

We must not underestimate the amount of marketing to which children are exposed. The average child sees more than 40,000 commercials each year on television alone.[10] Even public television allows commercials before and after programming. Many children's television programs, including those on PBS, are funded through brand licensing, a practice that allows companies to market toys, clothing, and accessories based on characters associated with a program. Children are often alone when they watch television, meaning that no adult is present to help them process the marketing messages permeating the medium. Thirty-two percent of children two to seven have televisions in their rooms, as do 65 percent of children eight to eighteen[11] and 26 percent of children under two.[12]

While television is the most prevalent medium in children's lives, children's access to the Internet—where the lines between content and marketing can be significantly blurred—is growing.[13] Companies lure children with "advergaming": products are incorporated into computer and video games as a means of advertising, allowing companies to keep children's attention focused on specific brands much longer than a traditional commercial can.[14] One site, called Candystand (www.candystand. com) consists of games featuring Kraft products such as Lifesavers, Crème Savers, and Jello pudding bites.[15] Popular sites for young children, such as Neopets, include product placement of brands ranging from McDonald's to Disney.[16] The video game Crazy Taxi includes stops at Pizza Hut and Kentucky Fried Chicken.[17]

SCHOOLS FOR SALE

Poor children—a population in which children of color are disproportionately represented—are even more inundated with marketing. They watch more television than their middle class counterparts,[18] and the schools they attend receive less state and local funding than other schools, making them more vulnerable to in-school marketing as a means of filling the funding gap.[19]

Derek White, an executive from the clothing catalogue company Alloy, explained in an interview that school administrators "are becoming more open to commercialism and thinking about how they can reduce budgetary problems." As a result, "[b]rands are learning to create curriculum-based programs when possible or appropriate, bring mobile tours to schools, infiltrate locker rooms and sports fields, and sample, sample, sample."[20]

Schools in poorer neighborhoods are more likely to make use of a corporate news program called Channel One, which "donates" video equipment in exchange for daily feeds of commercially based news broadcasts that students are required to watch.[21] Schools that sign on with Channel One contract to show the broadcasts—consisting of ten minutes of content and two minutes of commercials—on 90 percent of school days and in 80 percent of the classrooms.[22] Unlike watching TV at home or a friend's house where they can elect to turn down the sound, or stretch their legs, thousands of children are required to watch two minutes of daily commercials—as part of their school curriculum—for violent movies, junk food, and credit cards.

CUTTING OUT THE MIDDLE-MAN: DIRECT MARKETING TO CHILDREN

With unfettered access to millions of children, corporations now aggressively market to them directly instead of targeting parents. From 1992 to 1997, the amount of money spent on marketing to children doubled from $6.2 billion to $12.7 billion.[23] In 2002, estimates were at $15 billion.[24] Marketing to children is no longer confined to toys and sugared cereals. Encouraged by studies showing that children aged two to fourteen directly and indirectly influence purchases valued at about $600 billion per year,[25] companies traditionally associated with adult consumers, such as airlines and automobile companies, are marketing to children as well. For instance, the airline Delta Express painted a likeness of the Cartoon Network's *PowerPuff Girls* on one of its airplanes. The promotion, which ran for six months in 2001, included a Delta Express/PowerPuff Girls' banner ad on the Cartoon Network's Website. Stacy Geagan, who was a manager in marketing communications at Delta Express, explained in *Advertising Age* that Delta ran the campaign because it wanted to "appeal to parents via the children."[26] In 2001, American Isuzu launched its SUV, the Axiom, through a promotion with the Disney film *Spy Kids* and McDonalds.[27]

In addition to capturing a share of the current market, a common rationale for corporate advertising to children is the dream of lifelong devoted consumers. James McNeal, a psychologist who has written extensively about the children's market, describes the phenomenon this way:

> We have living proof of the long-lasting quality of early brand loyalties in the cradle-to-grave marketing at McDonald's, and how well it works.... We start taking children in for their first and second birthdays, and on and on, and eventually they have a great deal of preference for that brand. Children can carry that with them through a lifetime.[28]

DIRECT MARKETING HARMS CHILDREN

For those of us who devote our lives to promoting the well-being of children, the corporate view of childhood as nothing more than a market segment is appalling. By instinct and training, we place the well-being of children and families above all else—and certainly above financial gain. But putting aside our philosophical—or visceral—outrage, there is mounting evidence that this avalanche of marketing is causing children harm.

Childhood obesity,[29] family stress,[30] increased materialistic values,[31] and discontent with body image[32] have all been associated with marketing. In addition, children with particular concerns seem to be more vulnerable to manipulation. For instance, obese children may be more susceptible to feel-good messages in food commercials,[33] and girls with eating disorders may be more susceptible to the influence of super-thin models.[34]

PSYCHOLOGY IN BED WITH BIG BUSINESS

It's ironic, especially for mental health professionals, that child psychologists and child psychology are central to the success of marketing campaigns that target children. In 1992, the ethical standards of the American Psychological Association stated that psychologists should "apply and make public their knowledge of psychology in order to contribute to human welfare."[35] Yet, psychologists who help companies market successfully to children routinely employ principles and practices of child psychology—from developmental theory to diagnostic techniques—for the sole purpose of increasing the companies' profits.

Developmental psychology, the study of how children develop and change over time, traditionally provides the underpinnings for practices and policies designed to protect children or to promote their well-being. In recent years, it has also served as the foundation of what the advertising industry calls market segmentation, or target marketing. Jean Piaget's work in children's cognitive development, Erik Erikson's work in psychosocial development, and even Lawrence Kohlberg's work on moral development are cited in treatises on marketing to children, with titles such as: *What Kids Buy and Why: The Psychology of Marketing to Kids*. Dan Acuff, who is president of the market research company Youth Market Systems, expounds on the relevance of child development to marketing and product development:

> We have divided or segmented the youth target ... in accordance with a wide variety of scientific research such as that of Piaget, Erikson, and Kohlberg.... It is an in-depth understanding of the child consumer that provides the only real access to approximating a "winning formula" for the development of products and programs that succeed with kids.[36]

Piaget's studies of how children's understanding of the world evolves are the cornerstone of countless school programs and teaching methods.[37] Erik Erikson's constructs of psychosocial tasks—and the consequences of failure to successfully navigate those tasks—provide the foundation for parent education, especially around early childhood education, and are used to help therapists understand their clients' needs.[38]

Both Erikson and Piaget write about children with such care and respect that it seems the height of cynicism—not unlike commercials featuring images of Gandhi to sell Apple computers—to use their work to hone marketing techniques for what advertisers frequently call the "kid market." In fact, in today's cutthroat competition for "share of mind,"[39] marketing experts are practically evangelical in their devotion to developmental psychology.

To snag a preteen audience, advertisers are hiring child psychologists and other experts to understand the segments and nuances of the youth market. "Only a decade ago, advertisers lumped all kids into one broad category. Now they realize age segmentation is essential," says Tim Coffey, CEO of WonderGroup, a youth consultancy in Cincinnati. At WonderGroup, the red-hot "tween" market (ages eight to twelve) is subsegmented. "After all," says Mr. Coffey, "a 12-year-old is 50 percent older than a kid who is 8."[40]

Obviously, anyone is free to read books about psychology or take courses in child development. But since, in the world of marketing, knowledge of how children change and develop over time is used (or misused) to exploit children's vulnerabilities, shouldn't we question the ethics of trained psychologists who, presumably for a substantial fee, pass on their expertise to executives whose goal is to become more effective at exploiting children for profit?

For instance, Saatchi and Saatchi, a global marketing company, hired psychologists and anthropologists to do a study on Generation Y, as the new crop of preteens and teens is described in the marketing world. Reports to the industry urged companies to market to these children's need to belong and to have a group identity:

> Generation Y also has a strong need for community. In order to win these consumers, children's business retailers should change their goal to selling a community experience, instead of selling a product. The retailer must move to a "community" mentality where the Generation Y consumer becomes empowered, and they get involved.... These findings, the result of an exhaustive study conducted by ad agency giant Saatchi & Saatchi over a six-month period, have particularly significant implications for children's business retailers: change your goal from selling a product to creating a hip, community experience ... and you'll win the loyalty of what Saatchi & Saatchi calls today's "connexity" kids.[41]

Anyone who works with teens and preteens is aware that adolescence is a time of great turbulence, insecurity, and rebellion. The challenge for caretakers is to help them safely navigate the turbulence. But for marketers, adolescent vulnerabilities provide grist for the profit mill: "Playing off teen insecurities is a proven strategy. But even that won't get you very far if you're using a stale campaign and yesterday's slang," says observer Shelly Reese.[42]

In an article on selling prom-related items, the newsletter *Selling to Kids* provides tips for retailers based on "intensive work with psychologists," encouraging them to exploit teenage vulnerabilities. "There's no end to teen narcissism: focus on the fantasy," is one bit of advice offered. Says Rachel Geller, chief strategic officer of New York-based Gepetto Group, "Teens are ... an oppositional subculture, interested in shutting out the adult world. However, there are enormous opportunities for the marketer who is able to understand both the reality and fantasy of teen life."[43]

None of the articles quoted question the ethics, or the psychosocial impact, of inundating teenagers with images and messages designed to foster insecurities as the primary motivation for action. Marketing agencies are as relentless in their quest for knowledge about children as any academic institution, and they are certainly better funded! In fact, it is ironic that most of the research being done on children is in the corporate world. As one marketing expert states, "We've probably done more recent original research on kids, life stages and recognition of brands than anybody."[44] But what's missing in reports of data collected for market research, or how that data are used, are the questions that should be central to all psychological research conducted with children: "Am I using this information to make children's lives better? How will this application of child psychology benefit children?" Whatever their private concerns may be, it seems that no one in the advertising industry questions publicly whether children benefit from marketing messages that play to their vulnerabilities. In fact, marketers, for the most part, say that concerns about the impact of marketing on children are overblown.

In a 1997 article in *BusinessWeek*, Tom Kalinske, former CEO of Sega of America and Mattel, Inc., said, "I have a high regard for the intelligence of kids." The article went on to explain that "Kalinske and others in the industry believe that kids today are more sophisticated consumers than the generations that preceded them, well able to recognize hype and impervious to crude manipulation."[45]

By championing children's "intelligence" and "sophistication" as a rationale for the escalating onslaught of child-targeted marketing, marketing experts reveal that their alleged love affair with psychology is as superficial and deceptive as the ads they create. Paul Kurnit, president of an agency that specializes in marketing to children, expanded on this point of view in *KidScreen*, explaining that "It's a point of fact that today's child is more savvy than ever before about what it's like to live in a commercial society.... And what parents are telling us is that kids are requesting brands and are brand-aware almost as soon as their verbal skills set in."[46]

The problem is that the industry confuses the trappings of sophistication with maturation. That babies and toddlers request or recognize brands in no way reflects that they are "savvy" about marketing, which implies a capacity to decode and resist advertising messages. It does suggest that very young children are highly susceptible to marketing, a fact that is borne out by academic research.[47] Until they reach four or five, children have trouble differentiating between a commercial and programming on television.[48] It's not until the age of about eight that children are able to recognize that the intent of ads is to persuade them to want or buy something.[49]

The marketing industry's embrace of the notion that children are leap-frogging through development at breakneck speed is simplistic, potentially harmful, and self-serving. Girls are entering puberty at an earlier age.[50] There's evidence that they are beginning to abuse drugs, alcohol, and tobacco at younger ages.[51] But there is no evidence that their emotional development is keeping pace with their bodies or their behavior—and we don't know what meaning children make of their experience with the trappings of maturation.

How does a seven-year-old understand the plastic sexuality of Britney Spears? How do ten-year-olds cope with pressure to dress and act in sexually provocative ways? According to the toy industry, proof of children's sophistication lies in statistics showing that children are leaving some traditional toys behind at a younger age and trading them in for video games and pop culture icons. The toy industry's solution to this problem is to market dolls that are representations of pop culture. That may solve their sales problems on several levels. Media-based toys are a gold mine both for toy companies and for media companies. But we don't know the impact that dolls based on sexy pop stars may have on the emotional/social development of young girls. Nor can we discount the likelihood that targeting children with marketing campaigns for more "sophisticated" toys contributes to their apparent disinterest in more traditional playthings.

Children's alleged sophistication about media and marketing is also used as justification for product placement—the growing trend of embedding products into the props, scenery, and sometimes the plot of television shows, movies, and video games. Product placement has even infiltrated books: now there are board books for babies that look just like a Cheerios or Froot Loops box, a package of M&Ms, or other snack food products. Julie Halpin, CEO of WPP Group's Geppetto Group, sees such books as a relatively benign marketing tactic. "For the marketer it's creating affinity for the brand," Halpin says. "For parents, the kid is learning to count. There's no downside."[52]

But when childhood obesity is a major public health problem,[53] it is hard to see that inculcating babies' affinity for brands of candy is really so benign. There are laws prohibiting product placement within television programs directly targeted to children. But there are not similar laws for films aimed at children. For instance, the popular film *Spy Kids* showed a McDonald's meal. Television programs such as *American Idol*—which is a teen favorite and watched by lots of pre-teens as well[54]—include product placement for all sorts of products. Coca Cola paid $20 million to have the judges on the popular program drink the cola out of cups sporting the company's logo and to paint the traditional "green room" where performers wait before they appear, a Coca Cola red.[55] On *Gilmore Girls*, a program popular with tweens, Kellogg's Pop Tarts are served for breakfast.[56] Interestingly enough, *Gilmore Girls* was created through a consortium of corporations called the Family Friendly Programming Forum—including many, such as Kellogg, from the food industry. The stated mission of the Forum is to create programming that is good for families to watch together: programming that is free of excessive violence and explicit sexuality, but not free from marketing food.[57]

The advertising industry's use of psychology as a tool to manipulate children should provide special incentive for psychologists to take a stand against child-targeted marketing. But anyone who cares about children has cause for serious concern. In addition to the threat it poses to their physical and mental health, marketing also undermines children's social and spiritual well-being. For instance, the values inculcated by marketing messages, such as impulse buying, unthinking brand loyalty, and a "me first" mentality, are antithetical to values such as critical thinking and cooperation that are essential to democracy. The message central to almost all marketing campaigns—that a particular product can bring us happiness—is contrary to the teaching of all mainstream religions.

STEMMING THE TIDE OF CORPORATE MARKETING

Stemming the tide of corporate marketing aimed at children is not going to be easy. Consumerism and a belief in the sanctity of free market capitalism are so entrenched in American society that many people dismiss child-targeted marketing as just another legitimate means for corporations to turn a profit. In that sense, children can be viewed as similar to other populations, such as minorities, workers, and women, who have been subject to commercial exploitation in this country. In doing so, it becomes clear that the history of other social struggles in this country contains important lessons. One family, one teacher, one psychologist, or one advocacy group alone cannot combat a $15 billion industry.

Certainly, the need for systemic change does not relieve parents or professionals of individual responsibility to the children in our charge. To start, we can monitor our own investment in consumerism as well as our responses to advertising. We can institute ongoing dialogues with children about consumerism. We can set limits on their access to electronic media, which is a prime venue for commercial marketing. There is no reason, for instance, for children to have television sets in their bedrooms. Nor does television need to be on during meals. Media literacy can be taught in schools and at home, although it is important to note that there is no evidence to date that helping children decode marketing actually has an impact on purchasing behavior.

Marketing to children is a societal problem and needs to be treated as such. There is mounting evidence that concern among parents and professionals has been growing enough to translate into grassroots actions and efforts. In recent years, for instance, the California-based Center for Commercial Free Public Education has been successfully helping communities challenge the soft drink industry's campaign for exclusive pouring rights in schools. Dads and Daughters, in Minnesota, has forced corporations such as Campbell's to take commercials particularly harmful to girls off the air. The Center for the New American Dream in Pennsylvania works directly with families to help them find alternatives to commercialism. In 2000, the American Psychological Association, in response to concerns expressed by psychologists collaborating with the advocacy organization Commercial Alert, set up a task force to investigate the ethics of psychologists working with companies that market to children.

Most recently, these organizations and others have joined together with educators and mental health professionals in a coalition called Campaign for a Commercial Free Childhood, enabling each small organization to reach a broad base of support for actions ranging from a successful campaign to stop CNN from adding commercials to their classroom news broadcasts to pressuring the publishing company Scholastic, Inc. to withdraw from sponsoring the Golden

Marble Awards, the advertising industry's celebration of marketing to children.

Like any complex social problem, the issues arising from corporate marketing will not be easily resolved. Because marketing in this country is so pervasive that people are often unconscious of its effects, parents and professionals alike need to be educated about its impact. At the same time, we need to advocate for research funding that is not conducted and owned by corporations. We need to continue grassroots efforts to influence the marketing policies of particular corporations, and also to influence public policy.

The village raising our children is dominated by a culture of greed that has a powerful negative impact on all aspects of children's lives. It is unrealistic to think that staying cocooned within our classrooms, offices, or health centers is adequate for mitigating the impact of marketing that targets children. Only when professionals concerned with the health and well-being of children join together with parents and social advocates will we begin to effect change.

NOTES

1. Donald F. Roberts, Uhla G. Foehr, Victoria Rideout, et al., *Kids & Media @ the New Millennium* (Menlo Park, CA: The Henry J. Kaiser Family Foundation, 1999).

2. General Accounting Office, *Public Education: Commercial Activities in Schools: Report to Congressional Requesters* (Washington, DC: General Accounting Office, 2002), p. 26.

3. Alex Molnar, *Giving Kids the Business: The Commercialization of America's Schools* (Boulder: Westview Press, 1996).

4. Susan Linn, *Consuming Kids: The Hostile Takeover of Childhood* (New York: The New Press, 2004).

5. Ibid.

6. Dale Kunkel, "Children and Television Advertising," in *The Handbook of Children and Media*, eds. Dorothy G. Singer and Jerome L. Singer (Thousand Oaks, CA: Sage Publications, 2001), pp. 375–393.

7. Tom Engelhardt, "Saturday Morning Fever: The Hard Sell Takeover of Kids' TV," *Mother Jones*, 11(6) (1986): 38–48, 54.

8. Kunkel, "Children and Television."

9. Diane Levin and Susan Linn, "The Commercialization of Childhood: Understanding the Problem and Finding Solutions," in *The Psychology of Consumer Culture*, eds. Tim Kasser and Allen Kanner (Washington, DC: American Psychological Association, 2004), pp. 213–232.

10. Kunkel, "Children and Television."

11. Roberts et al., *Kids & Media*.

12. Victoria Rideout, Elizabeth Vandewater, and Ellen Wartella, *Zero to Six: Electronic Media in the Lives of Infants, Toddlers and Preschoolers* (Menlo Park, CA: The Henry F. Kaiser Family Foundation, 2003), p. 5.

13. Roberts et al., *Kids & Media*.

14. Chris Powell, "Get in the Game," *Marketing Magazine 108*(27) (2003): 11.

15. www.candystand.com. Accessed March 29, 2004.

16. Elizabeth Winding, "Immersed in Child's Play: Marketing: A Website That Offers Virtual Pets Has Found a Successful Way of Advertising to Children," *Financial Times (London) 17* (2002): 17.

17. Gene Emery, "Brand Names Popping Up in Games Are Free Advertising—For a Reason: 'You Don't Pick Up a Facial Tissue, You Pick Up a Kleenex,' marketer says." In *Vancouver Sun* (31 January 2002): F2.

18. Velma D. Lapoint and Priscilla Hambrick-Dixon, "Commercialism's Influence on Black Youth," in *The Psychology of Consumer Culture*, eds. Tim Kasser and Allen Kanner (Washington, DC: American Psychological Association, 2004), pp. 233–350.

19. Alex Molnar, "School Commercialism Hurts All Children, Ethnic Minority Group Children Most of All," *Journal of Negro Education 72*(4) (2003): 371–378.

20. Derek White, executive vice president of Alloy, quoted in Carrie MacMillan, "Readin,' Writin,' and Sellin,'" *Promo 15*(10) (1 September 2002): 24.

21. Michael Morgan, *Channel One in the Public Schools: Widening the Gaps* (Oakland, CA: Unplugged, 1993), p. 4.

22. Consumers Union, "Evaluations," in *Captive Kids: A Report on Commercial Pressures on Kids in School* (Washington, DC: Consumer Union, 1993), p. 3. Available at www.consumersunion.org/other/captivekids/evaluations.

23. Patricia Winters Lauro, "Coaxing the Smile That Sells: Baby Wranglers in Demand in Marketing for Children," *New York Times* (1 November 1999): C1+.

24. David Barboza, "If You Pitch It, They Will Eat," *New York Times* (3 August 2003): sec. 3, p. 1.

25. Packaged Facts, *The Kids Market* (New York: MarketResearch.com, March 2000).

26. Janis Rosenberg, "Brand Loyalty Begins Early," *Advertising Age 72*(2) (12 February 2001): 2+.

27. Laura Clark Geist, "To Isuzu, It's Axiomatic: Sell Family, Sell SUV," *Automotive News Detroit* (12 March 2001).

28. Karen Stabiner, "Get 'Em While They're Young: With Kid Flavors, Bright Colors and Commercials That Make Children Masters of Their Universe, Advertisers Build Brand Loyalty That Will Last a Lifetime," *Los Angeles Times Magazine* (15 August 1993): 12.

29. Gerard Hasting, Martine Stead, Laura McDermott, et al., *Review of Research on the Effects of Food Promotion to Children: Prepared for the Food*

Standards Agency (Glasgow: University of Strathclyde Center for Social Marketing, 2003).

30. Linn, *Consuming Kids*, pp. 31–40.

31. Tim Kasser, *The High Price of Materialism* (Cambridge: Massachusetts Institute of Technology, 2002), pp. 91–92.

32. Jean Kilbourne, *Deadly Persuasion: Why Women and Girls Must Fight the Addictive Power of Advertising* (New York: The Free Press, 1999), pp. 128–155.

33. M. K. Lewis and A. J. Hill, "Food Advertising on British Children's Television: A Content Analysis and Experimental Study with Nine-Year-Olds," *International Journal of Obesity 22* (1998): 206–214.

34. Josep Toro, Manuel Salamero, and E. Martinez, "Assessment of Sociocultural Influences on the Aesthetic Body Shape Model in Anorexia Nervosa," *Acta Psychiatrica Scandinavica 89*(3) (1994): 147–151.

35. American Psychological Association, "Ethical Principles of Psychologists and Code of Conduct," *American Psychologist 47* (1992): 1597–1611. The 1992 version of the American Psychological Association's Ethical Principles of Psychologists and Code of Conduct, General Principles, Principle F, Social Responsibility, reads: "Social Responsibility Psychologists are aware of their professional and scientific responsibilities to the community and the society in which they work and live. They apply and make public their knowledge of psychology in order to contribute to human welfare. Psychologists are concerned about and work to mitigate the causes of human suffering. When undertaking research, they strive to advance human welfare and the science of psychology. Psychologists try to avoid misuse of their work. Psychologists comply with the law and encourage the development of law and social policy that serve the interests of their patients and clients and the public. They are encouraged to contribute a portion of their professional time for little or no personal advantage." The 2003 version does not have a section on social responsibility. A comparison of the 1992 and the 2003 versions can be found at www.apa.org/ethics/codecompare.html.

36. Dan S. Acuff, with Robert H. Reiher, *What Kids Buy and Why: The Psychology of Marketing to Kids* (New York: The Free Press, 1997), p. 16.

37. Hans G. Furth and Harry Wachs, *Thinking Goes to School: Piaget's Theories in Practice* (New York: Oxford University Press, 1974).

38. Karen Mencke Paciorek and Joyce Huth Munro, eds., *Sources: Notable Selections in Early Childhood* (New York: McGraw-Hill/Dushkin, 1998).

39. Judann Pollack, "Foods Targeting Children Aren't Just Child's Play: Shape-Shifting Foods, 'Interactive' Products Chase Young Consumers," *Advertising Age* (1 March 1999): 16.

40. Fay Rice, "Superstars of Spending: Marketers Clamor for Kids," *Advertising Age* (12 February 2001): S1.

41. Amy Frazier, "Landmark Study Identifies Generation Y Preferences," *Selling to Kids* 4(4) (3 March 1999).

42. Shelly Reese, *Marketing Tools* (5 July 1997).

43. Rachel Geller, chief strategic officer of the Geppetto Group, quoted in Amy Frazier, "Prom Night Means Teen Independence, Buying Spree for Parents and Kids: Geppetto Group Finds Teens Ready to Break Away, Buy, Buy, Buy," *Selling to Kids* 3(8) (15 April 1998).

44. Paul Kurnit quoted in Duncan Hood, "Is Advertising to Kids Wrong? Marketers Respond," *Kidscreen* (November 2000): 15–18.

45. David Leonhardt and Karen Kerwin, "Hey Kid, Buy This! Is Madison Avenue Taking 'Get 'Em While They're Young' Too Far?" *BusinessWeek* (30 June 1997): 62.

46. Kurnit quoted in Hood, "Is Advertising to Kids Wrong?"

47. D. Borzekowski and T. Robinson, "The 30-Second Effect: An Experiment Revealing the Impact of Television Commercials on Food Preferences of Preschoolers," *Journal of the American Dietetic Association* 101(1) (2001).

48. Charles Atkin, "Television Advertising and Socialization Consumer Roles," in *Television and Behavior: Ten Years of Scientific Progress and Implications for the Eighties*, ed. David Pearl (Rockland, MD: National Institute of Mental Health, 1982), pp. 191–200.

49. Dale Kunkel and Donald Roberts, "Young Minds and Marketplace Values: Issues in Children's Television Advertising," *Journal of Social Issues* 47(1) (1991): 57–72.

50. Paul B. Kaplowitz, Eric J. Slora, Richard C. Wasserman, et al., "Earlier Onset of Puberty in Girls: Relation to Increased Body Mass Index and Race," *Pediatrics* 108 (2001): 347–353.

51. Richard P. Nelson, Jeffrey Brown, Wallace Brown et al., "Improving Substance Abuse Prevention, Assessment and Treatment Financing for Children and Adolescents," *Pediatrics* 108 (2001): 1025–1029.

52. Janice Rosenberg, "Brand Loyalty Begins Early; Savvy Marketers 'Surround' Kids to Build Connection," *Advertising Age* (12 February 2001): S2.

53. U.S. Department of Health and Human Services, *The Surgeon General's Call to Action to Prevent and Decrease Overweight and Obesity* (Rockville, MD: U.S. Department of Health and Human Services, Public Health Service, Office of the Surgeon General, 2001).

54. Ann Oldenberg, "New Generation of Teen Shows Turns Up the Heat," *USA Today* (2004): 3d; and Becky Ebenkamp and Laurel Scheffel, "Divide of the Tweens," *Brandweek* 44(26) (2 March 2003): 18.

55. Dean Foust and Brian Grow, "Coke: Wooing the TiVo Generation," *BusinessWeek* (1 March 2004): 77.

56. Sonia Reyes, "Into the Mouths of Babes," *Brandweek* (26 May 2002).

57. Linn, 2004.

6

Big Food, Big Money, Big Children

KATHERINE BATTLE HORGEN

THE OBESITY EPIDEMIC

Despite the booming diet and fitness industries, which in the United States alone generate over $33 billion annually,[1] the prevalence of obesity has grown in every segment of the population.[2] Nearly one third of American adults are classified as obese—up from 23 percent in 1994[3]—and almost two thirds are overweight.[4] While this statistic is alarming in its own right, childhood obesity is increasing at twice the rate of adult obesity.[5] Over 10 percent of two- to five-year-olds (up from 7 percent in 1994),[6] and over 15 percent of children ages six to nineteen, are overweight.[7] An additional 14 percent are on the cusp of becoming overweight.[8] The proportion of overweight six- to nineteen-year-olds has *tripled* since 1980.

Obesity-related deaths total approximately 325,000 per year in the United States and—at the current rate at which the obesity epidemic is growing—will soon surpass tobacco-related deaths.[9] It is estimated that obesity costs the United States nearly $100 billion dollars annually in direct and indirect healthcare costs.[10]

A range of medical conditions that until recently were rarely seen in childhood are now becoming commonplace among obese children. As reported in *Food Fight*, which I co-authored with psychologist Kelly Brownell, one of the most serious consequences of obesity in childhood is "the clustering of risk factors for heart disease known as insulin resistance syndrome, now identified in children as young as five years old. Problems with glucose toler- ance and insulin resistance place severely overweight children at risk for Type 2 diabetes, a disease once seen only in adults. These children risk having diabetic complications, including heart dis- ease, stroke, blindness, limb amputation, and kidney failure, before they reach age 30."[11]

In addition, obese children are more vulnerable to low self- esteem, social exclusion, bullying, and poor physical functioning.[12]

FAST FOOD CULTURE

Most approaches to fighting childhood obesity have focused on weight loss once the problem already is established. An underly- ing assumption in this approach is that genetics and personal responsibility are the main culprits. In fact, genes account for only 25 to 40 percent of body weight, which means that at a minimum, 60 percent of body weight is influenced by the environment.[13] Studies on Samoan children aged five to eleven showed that those in the traditional Samoan lifestyle weighed significantly less than their peers who adopted a more modern lifestyle in American Samoa or Hawaii. Similarly, preschool children in modernized areas of Kuwait weigh more than those in traditional areas of the country.[14]

The fast food industry spends billions of dollars annually to influence children's eating habits and to lobby the U.S. legislature to favor its products. As evidence of the extent to which we have become a "fast food culture," Ronald McDonald is the second most recognizable figure in the world, bested only by Santa Claus.[15] Is it reasonable to expect children to resist the relentless campaigns of an industry whose products are advertised and sold in their schools, and that are associated with beloved media figures, pop stars, and athletes? Ironically, while engulfed by a toxic food envi- ronment, girls in particular feel enormous pressure to be thin, which contributes to obsessive concerns about weight and to eat- ing disorders.[16]

The Three Essential Food Groups: Fat, Salt, and Sugar

When we examine what children are eating these days, it becomes immediately apparent that the fast food industry has succeeded brilliantly in its nonstop efforts to influence children's diets. The proportion of children's diets consisting of "fast food" increased almost 300 percent from 1977 to 1996. Adolescents in particular are consuming large amounts of fried and high-fat foods when eating away from home.[17] Soft drink consumption in children has also skyrocketed.[18] A study of eight- to eighteen-year-olds found that low-nutrient snack foods accounted for over 30 percent of their daily energy intake. As the number of meals consumed in fast food restaurants and restaurant chains continues to soar, calories from fat, salt, and sugar are supplanting valuable nutrients from fresh fruits, vegetables, and milk.[19]

TELEVISION ADVERTISING AND OBESITY IN CHILDREN

On average, American children see 10,000 commercials per year on television alone, the majority of which are for unhealthy foods. Kids see a food ad every five minutes while watching Saturday morning cartoons, and most of these ads are for sugared cereals, candy, fast food, soft drinks, and snack foods.[20] Of fifty-two hours of Saturday morning television analyzed, two thirds of the ads were for fat- and sugar-laden food, but *not one was for fruits or vegetables,*[21] although studies indicate that exposure to fruit commercials and public service announcements do encourage fruit selection.[22]

Children's early knowledge of brands evidences the impact of this advertising barrage. Ninety-four percent of children aged nine to eleven know that Tony the Tiger is associated with cereal, and 81 percent linked frogs to Budweiser Beer.[23] Perhaps even more disturbing, nearly one third of three-year-olds and over 90 percent of six-year-olds associated Joe Camel with cigarettes.[24]

The relationship between TV viewing and obesity was first established in the 1960s when researchers uncovered a direct link between obesity in children aged six to seventeen and the amount of time spent watching TV, even after controlling for other causal factors.[25] More recent research tells us that the number of hours of television watched per week by three- to eight-year-olds is correlated with their caloric intake and their requests—as well as subsequent parent purchases—for foods they see on television.[26] In fact, 75 percent of the discussion between parents and children about a product are fueled by the child demanding something advertised on television.[27] Children aged ten to fifteen who watch more than five hours of TV daily have a four and a half times greater risk for being overweight compared to children watching zero to two hours daily, and reducing TV viewing leads to significant weight reduction.[28]

A 2004 review of over forty studies on the relationship between TV viewing and obesity in children conducted by the Kaiser Family Foundation found that food advertising and marketing to children were the primary mechanisms through which obesity was related to media use.[29] The relationship between TV advertising and obesity is particularly alarming when we consider that American high school graduates have spent more time in front of the TV than in the classroom; and these findings don't even include the considerable efforts to manipulate children's eating habits through the Internet, movies, print media, and advertising in schools.

MEDIA MANIPULATION

As we are about to see, advertisers employ a variety of highly effective techniques to sell products to children, capitalizing on their developmental vulnerabilities.

Advertainment

Research has established that children under age five have difficulty distinguishing between commercials and programming. Even when children do, they generally are unable to recognize the commercials' persuasive intent before they are seven or eight.[30] A study of Australian children aged nine to ten showed that over half believed that Ronald McDonald knew best what children should eat.[31] An even more alarming study of eight-year-olds found that, when asked whom they would most like to accompany them on an outing for a treat, they chose Ronald McDonald and Tony the Tiger before their fathers, teachers, or grandparents.[32] As these examples illustrate, most children eight years old and undertake what they "learn" on TV at face value and are utterly vulnerable to manipulation by advertisers.

Policy changes that led to deregulation of the media in the mid-1980s made program-length advertising feasible. Now in many cases, the program and the advertisement are one, rendering it virtually impossible for children to know that they are being targeted.[33] We see even more insidious trends on the Internet with "advergaming," in which the game invites the child to interact with various fast food and candy products as part of its plot or reward system.[34]

Selling Emotions

Products for children are generally promoted by linking the products with fun or happiness, as opposed to providing information about them. McDonald's may feature Ronald dancing and singing, or cereals may show well-known characters such as Frosted Flakes' playful Tony the Tiger.[35] Other food advertisements directed at children feature violence, conflict, achievement, mood alteration, and trickery.[36]

Selling Media Characters

Marketers frequently link food products to popular media characters. A stroll down the supermarket aisle reveals the PowerPuff Girls on Keebler Sandwich Cookies, Homer Simpson on Kellogg's Corn Pops, and Scooby Doo on Oscar Mayer's Lunchables. Children's meals at Burger King and McDonald's feature Disney characters, as do Kellogg's and General Mills cereals.[37] So, for example, when a popular Disney movie launches, its characters appear in McDonald's Happy Meals and on cereal boxes. Hence, Buzz Lightyear from the popular movie *Toy Story* becomes "Buzz Blasts Cereal."[38] Children may not know what the food is, but they recognize the character and want the product. McDonald's is also a regular feature in children's movies, such as *George of the Jungle* and *Richie Rich*—who has a McDonald's in his home.

Selling Stars

Numerous kid icons including pop stars Britney Spears and Beyonce Knowles (Pepsi) and basketball star Michael Jordan endorse fast food (McDonald's) and junk food. It should be noted that some high-profile young adults such as soccer stars Mia Hamm and Kristine Lilly have elected to take the high road, supporting the Safeway Supermarket's *Eat Like a Champion Program*, which promotes healthy eating to children.[39]

SCHOOLS SELL OUT

Although parents can take responsibility for controlling media use in their own homes, and purchases at the grocery store, they cannot control their children's exposure to advertisements, vending machines packed with soda and candy, and fast food franchises in their children's schools. The public school system has a legal and moral obligation to guide and care for our children. Unfortunately though, budget cuts have obligated many school districts to seek funding through the private sector, and school administrators on tight budgets face difficult temptations to sell their students to the highest bidder.

However, when principals make contracts with corporations whose guiding principle is profit, it becomes nearly impossible for schools to fulfill their mandates. While those in the food industry have argued that placing vending machines filled with junk food in schools allows students to exercise free choice, this logic is akin to advocating that cigarette machines be placed in schools so that children can make other important health decisions. It is unconscionable to promote products known to undermine children's health on school grounds, especially when we consider that obesity is overtaking smoking as the number one killer in the United States. When children associate the moral authority of their principals and teachers with these products, parental authority is severely compromised.[40] Increasingly, parents have begun to speak out against such contracts, and numerous schools have begun to refuse them or let existing contracts expire.[41]

Even toddlers are being seduced by the food industry by linking its products with educational activities. Books for toddlers and preschoolers that feature M&Ms, Reese's Pieces, Skittles, and Oreos teach concepts such as counting. Teachers, parents, and pediatricians have lamented that these books may hook children on junk food at an early age.[42]

Soft Drink Contracts

The Soft Drink Association estimates that 62 percent of school principals have signed "pouring rights" contracts, which give a particular brand exclusive access to sell soft drinks in their school in return for money and equipment. School administrators in Colorado Springs signed a ten-year, multimillion dollar contract with Coca-Cola in 1998, requiring them to sell 70,000 cases of Coke products in one of the first three years of the contract—which would triple the rate of their students' consumption. Worried that they might not meet the quota, the district's executive director of school leadership sent a letter requesting principals to move machines where they were accessible to students all day and asking that teachers allow children to drink Coke in the classroom.[43]

A high school in Augusta, Georgia, held a "Coke in Education Day," featuring analyses of Coke products in chemistry classes and Coke officials lecturing in economics classes. For the grand finale, the entire student body was to dress in red and white shirts to spell "Coke" on the school grounds. One student pulled off his shirt at the last minute to reveal a Pepsi t-shirt and was suspended.[44]

Channel One

One of the most insidious ways in which school districts have made devil's bargains with corporations is through the use of a corporate news program called Channel One. Channel One programs consist of ten minutes of news coverage and two minutes of advertising. Schools that contract with Channel One are given the loan of video equipment necessary to air its broadcasts, but in return, they are obligated to air the programs in their entirety on 90 percent of school days and in 80 percent of the classrooms.[45] Over eight million children, including nearly 40 percent of the nation's teenagers, are a captive audience for two-minute commercials during each school day. A close analysis of the program reveals that actual news filled only 58 percent of the time, while 42 percent was advertising, promotional activities, music, banter, and a news quiz. Also, 69 percent of the forty-five commercials shown during a four-week period were for food products. Advertisers pay nearly $200,000 per thirty-second spot.[46] McDonald's airs special ads encouraging children to enter contests at their local franchises.[47] Other foods advertised on Channel One include M&Ms, Snickers, Pepsi, Mountain Dew, and Twinkies.[48]

The use of Channel One is yet another explicit endorsement of the fast food and soft drink industries by our nation's schools. Tragically, while peddling junk food to children, schools routinely cut physical education programs in favor of "more important" classes, despite evidence that physical activity promotes academic success.[49]

EXISTING REGULATION

Advertising to children is largely unregulated in the United States. In 1990, the Children's Television Act was passed to limit advertising during children's programming to 10.5 minutes each hour on weekends and twelve minutes per hour on weekdays. The Act did not, however, specify how these guidelines would be enforced, and so the Children's Advertising Review Unit (CARU) has assumed the responsibility of reviewing ads directed at children under the age of twelve.[50] However, cooperation with the guidelines is voluntary, and watchdog groups have no legal authority to enforce them. In fact, CARU was created by advertisers to self-police rather than to allow FTC regulation. Members, whose ranks include Frito-Lay, Kraft Foods, Hershey Foods, Nestlé USA, M&M Mars, General Mills, Kellogg Company, and Nabisco Foods, pay a fee to belong.[51]

The Center for Media Education successfully lobbied for the Children's Television Rules in 1996, which mandate that television networks broadcast a minimum of three hours of children's programming daily.[52] The quality and intent of these programs, however, are not regulated. Although both the Children's Television Act and the Children's Television Rules of 1996 are steps in the right direction, America's children remain extremely vulnerable. The American Academy of Pediatrics and the American Psychological Association agree that America's children are being exploited and have called for change.[53]

Other countries have been more aggressive in protecting their children from advertising. In Quebec, Canada, commercials targeted at children under the age of thirteen are disallowed. Norway and Sweden prohibit advertising to children under twelve. Greece bans toy ads until 10 p.m., and Belgium forbids advertising for five minutes before, during, and after children's programming.[54]

DETOXIFYING OUR FAST FOOD ENVIRONMENT

Current Actions

Government Actions

Although the government has proposed healthier environments for children through programs including Healthy People 2010, the Center for Disease Prevention's *Guidelines for Healthy Eating Environments in Schools,* and the Competitive Food Service Rule (passed by Congress in 1985 to prohibit competing sales of food with minimal nutrition during meal times), none of these has prevented the infiltration of school cafeterias and vending machines by the fast food industry.[55]

The U.S. Department of Agriculture has proposed providing free fruits and vegetables and the National School Lunch Program has dietary guidelines, but these options cannot compete with the enticing junk food available on campus. Children deserve and require stronger federal regulation of school food options[56] in order to stem the obesity epidemic that may soon become our nation's number one killer.

Grassroots Interventions

Lawmakers have tried to introduce legislation restricting commercialism and food sales in schools, but thus far restrictions have been applied only on a school-by-school basis. Grassroots interventions by parents have shown success. Seattle parents prevented the city's school board from entering into a corporate partnership and set up a task force to monitor other corporate propositions. Parents in Philadelphia successfully prevented a $43 million Coke contract, and New York parents instigated a class action lawsuit leading to an agreement that schools could sell only healthy snacks during lunch.[57]

Recommendations for Change

While grassroots efforts have had a local impact, our government must take more responsibility to combat the obesity epidemic among our nation's children. The following sections outline recommended actions.

Regulate Advertising Directed at Children

Young children are not capable of interpreting the intent of advertisers or making informed choices about food products being advertised. Food commercials impact their desires, which in turn influence what parents buy. Advertising for foods low in nutrition should be restricted during children's prime television viewing hours and during shows directed at children. Alternatively, legislation might mandate equal time for pro-nutrition and activity ads to counter what is currently available. This tactic was used to counter tobacco advertising, and tobacco advertisers instead decided to pull their ads from television.[58]

Advertising Should Be Banned in Schools

It is unconscionable for schools to sell our children to the highest bidder. Even the most conscientious parent cannot control what a child sees in schools, and advertisers know they can reach otherwise unreachable children there. The ban should include direct advertising on "educational" shows such as Channel One as well as on sports equipment, vending machines, textbooks covers, and promotional materials.

Remove Soft Drink and Snack Vending Machines
and Fast Food Franchises from Schools
Children do not need sugary drinks or low-nutrition snacks at schools. These machines should remain only if filled with water, milk, and healthy snacks. Fast food outlets in school cafeterias also should be ousted.

Parents Must Become Advocates for Their Children
School administrators need to know that parents do not approve of their children being sold to soft drink and fast food companies. Parents have proven instrumental in blocking or discontinuing soft drink "pouring rights" contracts in several states. Pressure from parents is a powerful tool.

Make Exercise a Priority in School
Inactive preschoolers are nearly four times as likely as their active peers to carry more weight.[59] Physical education gets bumped when school budgets and time are crunched, but children suffer from a lack of exercise. Studies link physical activity to improved academic performance. An active school models a healthy lifestyle. Research on weight loss in children has indicated, however, that exercise alone does not substantially reduce weight, but combined with a focus on diet, it can help guard against obesity.[60] This suggests that a multidimensional approach, with a focus on the toxic environment, is necessary.

Promote Media Literacy in Children
While young children to not have the capacity to fully discern or disarm the impact of advertising, programs designed to expose the intent of advertisers can help.

CONCLUSION

Children have been afforded special protection from health threats including tobacco and alcohol, but the food industry has been allowed to target them in a largely unregulated manner. As obesity gains attention as a major public health threat to rival tobacco and alcohol, the spotlight must shift to prevention and public policy rather than attempts to reverse the epidemic as it grows at record pace. Children deserve a healthy food environment and protection from forces that are beyond their understanding at this vulnerable stage in life.

NOTES

1. Food and Nutrition Board, Institute of Medicine, Committee to Develop Criteria for Evaluating the Outcomes of Approaches to Prevent and Treat Obesity. Weighing the options: Criteria for evaluating weight-management programs. Washington, DC: National Academy Press, 1995.

2. Flegal, K. M., Carroll, M., Kuczmarski, R., & Johnson, C. Overweight and obesity in the United States: Prevalence and trends, 1960–1994. *International Journal of Obesity, 22* (1998): 39–47.

3. National Center for Health Statistics. Obesity still on the rise, new data show. Retrieved March 11, 2004. Available at www.cdc.gov/nchs/releases/02news/obesityonrise/htm.

4. Brownell, K. D., & Horgen, K. B. *Food Fight: The Inside Story of America's Obesity Crisis, and What We Can Do About It*. New York: Contemporary Books, 2003. The World Health Organization sets the definition of overweight at a body mass index (BMI) of 25 kg/m squared and obesity at a BMI of 30 kg/m squared. These numbers correspond to about 20 percent and 40 percent above ideal body weight respectively.

5. Ibid., chap. 1.

6. National Center for Health Statistics, Obesity still on the rise.

7. Ogden, C., Flegal, K., Carroll, M., & Johnson, C. Prevalence and trends in overweight among U.S. children and adolescents, 1999–2000. *Journal of the American Medical Association, 288* (2002): 1728–1732.

8. St. Onge, M., Keller, K., & Heymsfield, S. Changes in childhood food consumption patterns: A cause for concern in light of increasing body weights. *American Journal of Clinical Nutrition, 78*(6) (2003): 1068–1073.

9. Allison, D., Fontaine, K., Manson, J., Stevens, J., & Van Itallie, T. Annual deaths attributable to obesity in the United States. *Journal of the American Medical Association, 282* (1999): 1530–1538.

10. Wolf, A., & Colditz, G. Current estimates of the economic cost of obesity in the United States. *Obesity Research, 6*(2) (1998): 173–175.

11. Brownell & Horgen, *Food Fight*.

12. Friedlander, S., Larkin, E., Rosen, C., Palermo, T., & Redline, S. Decreased quality of life associated with obesity in school-aged children. *Archives of Pediatrics and Adolescent Medicine, 157*(12) (2003): 1206.

13. Brownell & Horgen, *Food Fight*, chap. 2.

14. Berkowitz, R., & Stunkard, A. Development of childhood obesity. In T. Wadden and A. Stunkard (Eds.), *Handbook of Obesity Treatment* (pp. 515–531). New York: Guilford Press, 2002.

15. Brownell & Horgen, *Food Fight*, chap. 1.

16. Horgen, K. B., & Brownell, K. D. Confronting the toxic environment: Environmental and public health actions in a world crisis. In T. Wadden and A. Stunkard (Eds.), *Handbook of Obesity Treatment* (pp. 95–106). New York: Guilford Press, 2002.

17. McGinnis, J. The public health burden of a sedentary lifestyle. *Medicine and Science in Sports and Exercise, 24* (Suppl.) (1992): S196–S200.

18. St. Onge, M., Keller, K., & Heymsfield, S. Changes in childhood food consumption patterns: A cause for concern in light of increasing body weights. *American Journal of Clinical Nutrition, 78*(6) (2003): 1068–1073.

19. Brownell & Horgen, *Food Fight*, chap. 2.

20. Ibid.

21. Kotz, K., & Story, M. Food advertisements during children's Saturday morning television programming: Are they consistent with dietary recommendations? *Journal of the American Dietetic Association, 94* (November 1994): 1296–1300.

22. Gorn, G., & Goldberg, M. Behavioral evidence of the effects of televised food messages on children. *Journal of Consumer Research, 9*(2) (1982): 200–205.

23. Leiber, L. Commercial and character slogan recall by children aged 9–11 years: Budweiser versus Bugs Bunny. Center on Alcohol Advertising, Trauma Foundation, 1996.

24. Fischer P., Schwartz, M., Richards, J., Goldstein, A., & Rojas, T. Brand logo recognition by children aged 3 to 6. Mickey Mouse and Old Joe Camel. *Journal of the American Medical Association, 266* (1991): 3145–3148.

25. Horgen, K., Choate, M., & Brownell, K. Television food advertising: Targeting children in a toxic environment. In D. Singer & J. Singer (Eds.), *Handbook of Children and the Media* (pp. 447–461). Thousand Oaks: Sage Publications, 2001.

26. Taras, H., Sallis, J., Patterson, T., Nader, P., & Nelson, J. Television's influence on children's diet and physical activity. *Journal of Developmental and Behavioral Pediatrics, 10*(4) (1989): 176–180.

27. Kunkel, D. Children and television advertising. In D. Singer & J. Singer (Eds.), *Handbook of Children and the Media* (pp. 375–393). Thousand Oaks: Sage Publications, 2001.

28. Berkowitz & Stunkard, Development of childhood obesity.

29. Kaiser Family Foundation. Kaiser Family Foundation releases new report on role of media in childhood obesity (February 24, 2004). Retrieved April 5, 2004. Available at www.kff.org/entmedia022404nr.cfm.

30. Kunkel, Children and television advertising.

31. Food Commission. Advertising to children: UK worst in Europe. *Food Magazine* (January–March 1997).

32. Horgen, Choate, & Brownell, Television food advertising.

33. Kunkel, Children and television advertising.

34. Linn, S. The commercialization of childhood. In S. Olfman (Ed.), *Childhood Lost: How American Culture Is Failing Our Kids* (chap. 5 of this volume). Westport: Praeger, 2005.

35. Kunkel, D. Children and television advertising; and Barcus, F. The nature of television advertising to children. In E. Palmer and A. Dorr (Eds.), *Children and the Faces of Television* (pp. 273–285). New York: Academic Press, 1980.

36. Horgen, Choate, & Brownell, Television food advertising.

37. Brownell & Horgen, *Food Fight*, p. 111.

38. Ibid., p. 110.

39. Ibid.

40. Study says commercialism rampant in public schools. *Education Reporter: The Newspaper of Education Rights, 178* (November 2000). Retrieved March 3, 2004. Available at www.eagleforum.org/education/2000/nov00/commercialism.shtml.

41. Brownell & Horgen, *Food Fight*, chap. 7.

42. Study says commercialism rampant in public schools. *Education Reporter*.

43. Brownell & Horgen, *Food Fight*, chap. 7.

44. Beck, J. Teen suspended from school for wearing Pepsi t-shirt on Coke Day. *Chicago Tribune* (April 1, 1998). Retrieved August 3, 2001. Available at www.flipside.org/volq/apr98/pc4-16htm.

45. Consumers Union. Evaluations. In *Captive Kids: A Report on Commercial Pressures on Kids in School*. Washington, DC: Consumers Union, 1993, p. 3. Available at www.consumersunion.org/other/captivekids/evaluations.

46. Marketing to students: Corporations launch assault on schools. *Education Reporter: The Newspaper of Education Rights, 168* (January 2000). Retrieved March 3, 2004. Available at www.eagleforum.org/educate/2000/jan00/marketing.html.

47. Channel one wants kids to SUPERSIZE those fries. Retrieved March 3, 2004. Available at www.obligation.org/co3bsupersizethem.html.

48. Would you like to Supersize that? Channel One launches new junk food campaign. Retrieved March 3, 2004. Available at www.obligation.org/co3bsupersizeit.html.

49. Brownell & Horgen, *Food Fight*, chap. 2.

50. Horgen, Choate, & Brownell, Television food advertising.

51. Ibid.

52. Scott-Hill, K. Industry standards and practices: Compliance with the Children's Television Act. In D. Singer & J. Singer (Eds.), *Handbook of Children and the Media* (pp. 605–620). Thousand Oaks: Sage Publications, 2001.

53. Brownell & Horgen, *Food Fight*.

54. Ibid.

55. Ibid., p. 153.

56. Ibid.

57. Ibid.

58. Ibid.

59. Berkowitz & Stunkard, Development of childhood obesity.

60. Goldfield, G., Raynor, H., & Epstein, L. Treatment of pediatric obesity. In T. Wadden and A. Stunkard (Eds.), *Handbook of Obesity Treatment* (pp. 532–555). New York: Guilford Press, 2002.

7

So Sexy, So Soon: The Sexualization of Childhood

Diane E. Levin

CHANGING TIMES

The feature story in the May 2004 issue of the *New York Times Magazine* was called "Friends, Friends with Benefits and the Benefits of the Local Mall."[1] One hundred suburban teenagers were interviewed for the article. They described a world of casual sexual encounters devoid of emotions or relationships. "Hooking up" and "friends with benefits" are part of the new slang to describe casual sex with friends. The author of the story, Benoit Denizet-Lewis, reported that "the teenagers talked about hookups as matter-of-factly as they might discuss what's on the cafeteria lunch menu."[2] Sixteen-year-old Brian put it this way: "Being in a real relationship just complicates everything. When you're friends with *benefits*, you go over, hook up, then play video games or something. It rocks."[3] Formal dating relationships were frowned upon. In the words of Irene, a high school senior, "It would be so weird if a guy came up to me and said, 'Irene, I'd like to take you out on a date.' I'd probably laugh at him. It would be sweet, but it would be so weird."[4]

Three days after the *New York Times* story appeared, the *Boston Globe* published an op-ed piece by Scot Lehigh, who bemoaned the realities of the casual and unencumbered sexual behavior revealed by the teenagers. "It's truly sad to read of a high-school generation too detached to date, too indifferent for romance, too distant for commitment. ... You can't help but hope that today's teenagers will come to understand that to rob sex of romance, to divorce it from emotion, is to deny themselves exactly what makes it special."[5]

Besides describing and bemoaning a "surprising" change in adolescent sexual behavior, attitudes, and relationships, neither article paid any attention to the root cause of these changes. Nor did they connect this issue to other related concerns about the overall health, development, and well-being of today's youth such as the growing number of children and teens who regularly view cyberporn,[6] an upsurge in teen dating violence,[7] and eating disorders.[8]

In order to address concerns about adolescents' sexual behavior, we need to start with a better understanding of the factors that are shaping their ideas about gender, sexuality, and interpersonal relationships. We also need to understand how the "casual sex epidemic" relates to other aspects of their lives. An essential starting point for developing this understanding is through an examination of the vastly expanded role of media and commercial culture in children's lives over the past three decades.

New Sexual Issues in Childhood

As I read the *New York Times* article, I was reminded of accounts that I had been hearing with increasing frequency about the changing content of sexual issues that are being raised by young children today. Here are a few particularly salient examples:

"Professional Wrestling Girls with Big Boobies"
Kara, a kindergarten teacher, showed me an entry that her student James had recently made in his "daily diary." It was a drawing of a woman with long hair and big bright red lips with the letters *WWWWWWF* scrawled beside it. When Kara asked him to formulate a caption for the picture, he asked her to write *a professional wrestling girl with big boobies*. "At first I thought he was trying to be 'fresh,' to cause trouble," Kara told me, "but I caught myself before I reacted too harshly and asked James what he knew about 'wrestling girls.' He replied with his eyes open wide, 'I saw her on TV last night with my dad. That's how she looked!' I was pretty taken aback that his parents let him watch such a program [rated TV-14]. But it's what he's seeing that really worries me. I wonder if he made his drawing because he needed someone to talk to about it?"

"Skinny Bodies Are Sexy"

A couple of years ago, Shirley, the mother of seven-year-old Brenda, reported an incident that distressed her greatly. On and off for several weeks Brenda had been asking Shirley how you "go on a diet." This had escalated into Brenda stating that she *was* going on a diet. A couple of days later, Shirley found Brenda crying in the bathtub. When she asked her what was wrong, Brenda responded, "I'm fat. I want to be sexy like Joanie, pretty like Joanie [the very thin, seemingly very popular girl in Brenda's class]!" Shirley assured me that her daughter had a normal seven-year-old girl's body. However, she didn't think it was age-appropriate for her little girl to be thinking about being "sexy" and wanting to diet. Shirley began wondering what kinds of experiences outside of her family were contributing to this problem. She felt anxious and unsure about how best to respond in the short run. Also, she had heard news stories about preteen girls' precocious sexual behavior and eating disorders, and worried about what the psychological and physical consequences might be for Brenda in the long run.

"What's a Blowjob?"

Recently, Margie told me that her seven-year-old daughter, Eva, had asked, "Mom, what's a blowjob?" Her first reaction was to tell Eva that it wasn't something for children, and end it there. Instead, she asked, "Where did you hear about blowjobs?" Eva replied that she had heard about them at school. Margie asked, "What did you hear about it?" Eva responded, "It's sex." Margie told me that she worked hard to protect Eva from exposure to violence and sex in the media. But now that Eva was with many children who were not as protected, she felt that she was rapidly losing control. While she expected that she would talk to Eva about issues such as oral sex during the adolescent or even the pre-adolescent years, she was alarmed when it had come up at age seven! Furthermore, she felt very uncertain about what was appropriate to tell Eva.

"Learning about Sex from the Internet"

Karen, who is highly experienced at teaching sex education to fifth- and sixth-graders, called me to express concern about something that had come up in a discussion with a group of male students. She had been talking about sex as an expression of deep affection between partners in a relationship. One of her students, Gabe, challenged her by saying, "Well you don't need to *like* the person. I saw sex on the Internet. My cousin showed me. They just do it 'cause it's fun, they like it." A couple of boys seemed surprised, but a few others said that they had seen sex on the Internet, too. Karen felt that she had entered new territory in terms of how to respond to the children and how to approach their parents about it. But she was glad that the boys raised the issue because clearly it had been very much on their minds.

Each of the above stories provides a snapshot of young children struggling to work out ideas about things that they saw in the media or heard from friends about sex and gender. Current research and public discourse about sexual behavior and development rarely focus on children before the age of nine or ten. Yet clearly, exposure to sexual content in childhood will influence adolescent behavior.[9] The lessons that the youth in the *New York Times* article learned when they were young laid the foundation for their current sexual attitudes and behavior. What were those lessons? Where did they come from? What can we learn from them to help us raise children with healthy gender and sexual identities in the midst of the increasing sexualization of childhood?

MESSAGES ABOUT SEX AND GENDER IN OUR CULTURE

Children's ideas about gender, sex, and sexuality develop gradually and are greatly influenced by information that their environments provide. Increasingly, children's environments are dominated by unregulated electronic media.[10] A 2003 Kaiser Family Foundation report found that children aged zero to six averaged approximately two hours of "screen time" a day and that 30 percent of children aged three and under and 43 percent of children four to six had a television set in their bedroom. According to the authors, "This study documented a potentially revolutionary phenomenon in American society: the immersion of our very youngest children, from a few months to a few years old, in the world of electronic and interactive media."[11]

As children are glued to the screen, they are exposed to a very large quotient of sexual material. According to a Kaiser Family Foundation survey, during the 1999–2000 television season, 68 percent of programming contained information of a sexual nature, up from 56 percent in 1997.[12] In a similar survey, 75 percent of traditional TV "family hour" programs were found to have sexual content, compared with 43 percent twenty years earlier.[13] While studies have confirmed that children learn about sex from the media, more research is needed to fully document and understand the impact of such exposure.[14]

Although much of the graphic sexual content in the media is rated as appropriate for adolescents and adults, children are nonetheless viewing these programs much like five-year-old James, who watches professional wrestling on TV with his father. Telling James that the sex and violence on the show are "just pretend," as many adults do, is not meaningful to young children who see real people doing real things. Other programs with sexual content that children routinely watch include soap operas, talk shows, and MTV.

A particularly alarming source of sexual content is highly accessible Internet pornography, which almost any child who does homework using Internet sources can access. Yet, on June 30, 2004, the Supreme court rejected Congress's *Child Online Protection Act* designed to curb children's access to sexually explicit material on the Internet.[15]

Children are also exposed to sexualized toys, many of which are linked to TV shows, video games, and movies. Some of these "toys" foster associations between sex and violence. For example, Sable, a professional-wrestling action figure, has large breasts and wears tight black leather pants, an unzipped bra top, and spiky red heels. She comes with a whip. Photos of other professional wrestling action figures you can buy are on the back of Sable's box—including Billy Gunn, who has lipstick marks on his boxer shorts, and Al Snow, who is holding the severed head of a woman.[16] According to Sable's manufacturers, she is a suitable toy for children "ages four and up," whereas the professional wrestling TV programs that she is linked with are rated TV-14. Creating toys based on TV programs rated for teens, and movies rated R, implicitly assumes that young children are watching these shows. Programming and toys that are marketed to boys, like professional wrestling programs and their action figures, teach boys that males should always be physically powerful and ready to fight, and that sex involves aggressive domination of beautiful women, who serve as objects for male pleasure.

Girls are receiving different but equally shallow messages about femaleness and sexuality from toys and the media. Girls are taught that they should have skinny bodies and that they need to be consumers of clothing, makeup, and accessories in order to look "pretty," "grown-up," and "sexy."[17] We see this message expressed through *Barbie Lingerie*, who comes dressed in sheer black lingerie and stockings. The packaging of the popular, sexy *Bratz* dolls contains the message "The girls with a passion for fashion." *Boston Globe* parenting reporter Barbara Meltz concluded, "There is only one [Bratz] story line: girl as sex object."[18] Sexualized images of femaleness are reinforced through the appearance and behavior of female characters on TV, in video games, and in movies— even those explicitly made for children. For instance, Disney's Pocahontas has more cleavage and fewer clothes and is much sexier than Cinderella ever was. The music and videos of pop stars like Britney Spears are a regular feature of most young girls' lives beginning in preschool. A grandmother of a four-year-old girl laments,

> Jenna, my four-year-old granddaughter, and I were in a store buying shoes for the new school year. The radio was playing and she said to the sales clerk, "Is that the Spice Girls singing?" He shook his head "No," and asked if she liked the Spice Girls. She nodded her head. He asked, "What's your favorite song?" Jenna looked at him coyly and said, "Let Me Be Your Lover!" When he asked if she knew the words to the song, she began to sing the song—including all the "gyrations" of her little body. I wanted to sink into a hole and cry![19]

Increasingly, young girls are encouraged to act in sexual ways in their daily lives. For instance, beauty pageants, like the ones in which JonBenet Ramsey participated, channel young girls into precocious sexual appearance and behavior. I recently heard an account of five- to eight-year-old girls in Texas who were training as cheerleaders. They dress in clothing usually worn by much older cheerleaders. Here's an example of one of their chants:

> Like totally, for sure,
>
> I just got a manicure.
>
> The sun up there is bleaching out my gorgeous hair.
>
> 16, 24, I don't know the silly score.
>
> Go, go! Fight, fight!
>
> Gee I hope I look all right!

The highly publicized account of Janet Jackson's exposed breast during the half-time show at the Super Bowl in 2004 served as a useful lightning rod for public concern about sexual content in the media. However, Justin Timberlake's gesture of ripping off part of her top against her will—a sexually aggressive gesture—was far more offensive than her naked breast and yet rarely mentioned. The anger and blame directed at Janet rather than Justin speaks to deeply held cultural biases that are then amplified by the media.

THE IMPACT OF TELEVISION DEREGULATION ON THE SEXUALIZATION OF CHILDHOOD

In 1984, the Federal Communications Commission deregulated children's television, making it possible to market television programs and toys together for the first time. The television and toy industries quickly joined forces to create whole lines of toys and other products, such as bedsheets, pajamas, and breakfast cereals, which were linked to children's programs.

Increased Gender Stereotyping

Soon after the deregulation of television, I began hearing concerns voiced by parents and teachers about incidents with children involving gender stereotyping. Many of the stories, like Brenda in the bathtub above, involved girls focused on body image and appearance. Increasingly, girls were expressing the desire to be thin, pretty, sweet, and nice. At the same time, early childhood educators who had been in the field for a long time began reporting that they were seeing increased gender divisions in children's classroom play.

As I began to explore why this might be the case, I found that in the wake of deregulation, children's television programs had become highly gender-divided and gender-stereotyped. *My Little Pony* was one of the most popular TV programs for girls in the eighties. The program's best-selling toy line included such items as combs, makeup, and a vanity table. Media deregulation contributed to a major setback in efforts during the 1960s and 1970s to reduce gender stereotyping in childhood culture and expand children's definitions of what it meant to be a boy or girl.

Increased Sexual Content

In 1996, a survey by Children Now and the Kaiser Family Foundation found that 43 percent of parents of eight- to twelve-year-olds were at least as worried or more worried about sexual content on TV than they were about violent content.[20] Parents and professionals alike are increasingly concerned that they are losing control over how children are introduced to ideas about sex and sexuality. Yet, this issue is drawing far less attention, criticism, or controversy than violence in the popular culture does. For example, in stark contrast to extensive research on the impact of media violence, there is almost no research to date that has explored how the increasingly sexualized media and popular culture are affecting children. One possible explanation is that talking about sex is much more complicated and less clear-cut than talking about violence. We are all in relative agreement that "violence is bad" and that it is desirable for children to use non-violent approaches to solve their conflicts, and we have direct ways to convey and teach this message. By contrast, the messages we hope to convey about sex and sexuality are complex and age-dependent.

DERAILED PSYCHOSEXUAL DEVELOPMENT

Children's psychosexual awareness and understanding are gradually constructed over time. As infants, they explore their bodies, and they experience the emotional and sensory pleasures of embraces and kisses, and the satisfaction of being deeply attached to a parent or other caregiver. At around eighteen months they learn to refer to themselves as boys or girls, and they slowly begin working out the meanings of these labels. Learning is influenced by their developmental maturity and by the experiences and information their environment provides.[21] If there is a consistently healthy match between experiences and information provided by their environment and their level of development, then they will likely become capable of mature and meaningful social and sexual relationships in adulthood.

However, as the stories I recounted earlier illustrate, these days there is a mismatch between young children's psychosexual maturity and the sexual information that they are routinely exposed to. Not only is the content too graphic, but portrayals of highly stereotyped maleness and femaleness, male sexual domination of women, and women as sex objects are not ones that most parents would wish children of any age to be exposed to.

How Children Think Affects What They Learn

Children between the ages of three and six are typically drawn to content that is visible and concrete.[22] They often use play and art as vehicles for understanding their world. We see this kind of thinking at work when James focuses on the big red lips and "big boobies" (undoubtedly a term he learned from someone older than himself) of the "wrestling girl" in his drawing. James's drawing is a vehicle with which to explore what he witnessed on television and one that helps him make contact with his teacher. We also see Brenda focusing on concrete aspects of her experience when she equates Joanie's thinness with "sexiness." The media feeds into and reinforces children's one-dimensional concrete thinking with its increasingly shallow focus on appearance, as seen in the recent deluge of "makeover" shows.

With their focus on the concrete, young children also have a hard time understanding the motives, intentions, and feelings underlying sexual behavior. When Eva asked her mother about "blowjobs," this characteristic of her thinking would lead her to focus on the sexual act and not on what her mother might say about the nature of the relationship that would result in this behavior. We see this aspect of thinking at work when Brenda focuses on how "fat" her body looks compared to that of Joanie, the thin, popular girl in her class. Brenda does not look at other factors that might contribute to friendship and popularity; she considers only appearance. This kind of thinking predisposes young children to think that how they look (and not their behavior or ideas) determines what people think of them and how they treat them. While Brenda's and Eva's thought processes are normal, we have to wonder about the normality of a culture that obligates seven-year-olds to think at all about "sexiness" and "blowjobs." Clearly, these precocious lessons on sex and gender are contributing to the rise in dieting and eating disorders among preteen and adolescent girls.[23]

Another common feature of young children's thinking is that they often attend to only one thing at a time. When Brenda thinks about being sexy, she focuses on one attribute: Joanie's thinness. When Kara asks James "what he knows about wrestling girls," he responds with one piece of information: "I saw it on TV with my dad." Often the one thing a child attends to is himself or herself. This is connected to young children's egocentrism—their failure to think about the impact of what they do on someone else. Similarly, when Jenna imitated the suggestive words and sexy gyrations of a Spice Girls song for the shoe salesman, she seemed totally oblivious about what her grandmother or others around her might think (or whether other children in her environment did such things). Because young children attend to one thing at a time, their thinking is often more like a slide than a movie. That is, they tend to deal with one static moment or a series of non-logically connected static moments. They do not focus on logical causality or relationships between events. This limits children's ability to understand the sexual behaviors they are viewing. It can also make it hard for them to sort out *what is pretend and what is real*.

By contrast, when Gabe talks about pornography with his fifth-grade teacher, Karen, he reveals his growing ability to process two ideas at once (his and Karen's) and think about intentions that he cannot see (the nature of the relationship in which sex occurs), and he tries to make logical causal connections. Still, we must feel outrage that Gabe had to process this "information" at the tender age of ten, and that his teachers and parents must now work so hard to provide him with a healthier understanding of mature sexuality.

THE HARM CAUSED BY BEING SO SEXY SO SOON

When children are young, we should be laying the foundation for later healthy sexual relationships. We do this by providing children with models of caring and affectionate relationships. We can also answer questions about such issues as physical differences between males and females or "where babies come from." However, today's children are bombarded with large doses of graphic sexual content that they cannot process and that are often frightening. While children struggle to make sense of mature sexual content, they are robbed of valuable time for age-appropriate developmental tasks, and they may begin to engage in precocious sexual behavior.

Young children are routinely exposed to images of sexual behavior devoid of emotions, attachments, or consequences. They are learning that sex is the defining activity in relationships, to the exclusion of love and friendship. They are learning that sex is often linked to violence. Also, they are learning to associate physical appearance and buying the right accessories with being successful as a person. Such lessons will shape their gender identity, sexual attitudes, values, and their capacity for relationships.

We can see the long-term effects of these lessons in the casual sexual behavior and attitudes among the youth in the *New York Times* article. An escalation in eating disorders among preadolescent and adolescent girls is almost certainly related to images in the media and popular culture that equate thinness with sexiness and popularity. It has become common for girls to start "dieting clubs" in fifth grade. Seven-year-old Brenda is a prime candidate for such a club! There have also been several reports about the widespread practice of oral sex among middle school students.[24]

A Toll on Families and Parents, Too

Parents also pay a high price for the sexualization of childhood. In a 2002 survey by an organization called Public Agenda, it was found that 76 percent of parents felt it was a lot harder to raise children today than it was when they were growing up. When asked what was the biggest challenge they faced with their children, 47 percent reported that it was trying to protect them from negative societal influences. Certainly one of those influences is the sexualization of childhood in the mainstream culture.[25]

Parents see their children drawn into the sexual content that surrounds them, but talking with children about sex often feels harder and more complex than talking about other complex issues such as poverty, violence, or illness. Many adults struggle to talk openly and comfortably about sex and sexuality with other adults, let alone with children, and the task becomes even more daunting in the current context. As we saw in the examples throughout this chapter, when parents see the impact of today's culture on their children (and children often see and know more than we are able to admit) and try to respond or intervene, they worry about doing or saying the wrong thing. It is easy to say things that make children feel guilty or bad, or to cut off the discussion and thereby encourage them to stop seeking their advice altogether. Parents may also begin to deny the potential harm of their children's exposure to graphic sexual content because it has become so ubiquitous in our culture, and they are so helpless to stem the tide.

Parents are often told by the wider society (and especially by the industry that markets to children) that *it is their job* to decide what is appropriate for their children and to protect them from what they feel is not appropriate. While never easy, this task was less difficult for parents in the past when the prevailing cultural messages were more compatible with the values and goals they held for their children. Today, parents need to fight the prevailing culture at every turn with younger and younger children. Even the best-prepared and most conscientious parents find it impossible to stem the onslaught of negative media messages.[26]

A CALL TO ACTION

By allowing children to be exposed to information about sex and sexuality that undermines their healthy sexual development, society is failing its children and their families. For too long the increasing sexualization of childhood has not been given the attention it desperately needs. Until we address this problem as a society and work to regain control over it from those who are motivated solely by financial gain, children, families, and ultimately all of society will pay the price.

First Amendment and free speech arguments are often used to protect industry moguls' and Internet pornographers' right to put anything they choose on the screen, even when that material negatively affects children. The arguments used generally ignore the long history in the United States of creating special policies that protect children from harm's way—for example, through laws against child abuse and neglect. It is time for all of us to work together to create policies and practices that will help children develop the foundation they need to become adults who are capable of forming positive, caring sexual relationships.

WHAT CAN WE DO IN THE MEANTIME?

While there are no "magic bullet" solutions, there are many positive steps that we can take to promote healthier sexual development in the current climate.

- Limit exposure to sexual imagery and content in the media and popular culture.[27]

- Establish safe channels for talking about sexual development with children when they are young. Trusted adults have a vital role to play in helping children sort out what they see and hear (no matter how uncomfortable it may make us feel), by answering questions and helping them feel safe asking them. But to open up to adults, children need to know that nothing that they bring up for discussion about what they hear or do is off limits. The more comfortable children feel about raising issues and asking about sexual content when they are young, the better able they will be to use adults to help them process the escalating content they are exposed to as they get older.

- When children are exposed to the inevitable sexual images and messages, expect them to try to work them out in their play, art, and conversations. Pay attention to children's play and art. Talk to them about it. Providing open-ended (versus highly-structured) play materials—such as blocks, baby dolls, generic dress-up clothes, miniature people, a doctor's kit and doll house, markers, and paper—can all support children's efforts.

- Try not to blame children or make them feel guilty or ashamed when they do or say something that feels inappropriate. Too often children are blamed and punished when they act on what makes perfect sense given what surrounds them. Try to take the child's point of view and see the world through his or her eyes. This is a vital starting point for figuring out what led to the "inappropriate" behavior and deciding how to respond. Help children find appropriate and realistic alternative ways to support their efforts to understand as well as alternative ways to get the information and help they need.

- When talking to children about sexual issues, take your lead from what the children do and say and what you know about them as individuals.[28] Base your responses on the age, prior experiences, specific needs, and unique concerns of individual children. Just as many of the adults did in the anecdotes throughout this chapter, try to start by finding out what children know. Before jumping in with the "right" answer, you might ask, "What have you heard about that?" What the child says can guide what you say next.

- Answer questions and clear up misconceptions that worry or confuse. You don't need to provide the full story. Just tell children in an age-appropriate way what they need to hear to allay their worry or confusion. Don't worry about giving "right answers" or if children have ideas that don't agree with yours. Clear up misconceptions when doing so seems helpful and appropriate. Try to calmly voice your feelings and concerns, and reassure children about their safety.

- Teach alternative lessons to the messages in the popular culture that undermine healthy sexual development and behavior. What this means will vary with age and experience of the children. Make sure children are exposed to positive and caring relationships between adults at home, at school, and even in the media. Then they will have a foundation for gradually connecting ideas about sex to their understanding of positive adult relationships. Help them experience and express positive physical affection with appropriate people in their lives. Convey clear, age-appropriate guidelines about what is and is not appropriate.

- To the extent possible, try to engage in give-and-take discussions with children when working on all of the guidelines suggested here. Give-and-take conversation can help us decide how to respond and how much information a child actually needs. We can also use situations when sexual content comes up in the media or elsewhere as opportunities to discuss with children what they think about what they saw as well as sharing our own opinions.

- Share your values and concerns with extended family members, teachers, and other parents. The discussions that result can help you build a community of adults who share your values and who will respect rather than undermine your efforts with your child.

- Involve schools in efforts to promote healthy sexual development. In addition to parents' efforts, an important part of this task rests with the schools. Children need age-appropriate sex education programs in schools that help them build ideas about meaningful sexuality and address their real issues and concerns. The outspoken efforts of certain segments of society to preach sexual abstinence until marriage (and without the benefit of meaningful sex education), while at the same time enabling media and corporations to market sex to children more or less as they choose, are untenable and irresponsible.

- Help to create a society that is more supportive of children's healthy gender and sexual development by working to limit the power of corporations to market sex to children.[29] On a positive note, while few major efforts exist today to specifically address the sexualization of childhood, more and more individuals and groups are working at all levels to stop the commercial takeover of childhood. Several organizations have developed strategies and materials that can help you with your efforts. These organizations and their Website addresses are listed below.

ORGANIZATIONS THAT ARE WORKING TO STOP THE COMMERCIAL EXPLOITATION OF CHILDHOOD

The Alliance for Childhood promotes policies and practices that support children's healthy development, learning, and play. www. allianceforchildhood.net.

The American Psychological Association has prepared a comprehensive position statement on the negative impact of marketing to children that calls for restrictions on marketing to children. www.apa. org/releases/childrenads.pdf.

Commercial Alert advocates for legislation, policies, and practices that will stop harmful marketing practices. www.commercialalert.org.

The Motherhood Project is working to create a grassroots movement that will help mothers (and fathers) reclaim their rightful power to raise their children free of corporate exploitation. www. watchoutforchildren.org.

Campaign for a Commercial Free Childhood (CCFC) is a coalition of many organizations working to reduce marketing to children. www. commercialexploitation.org.

Teachers Resisting Unhealthy Children's Entertainment (TRUCE) is a group of educators that prepares materials for parents about effective ways to resist the commercial culture and promote positive play, learning, and social relationships. www.truceteachers.org.

NOTES

1. Benoit Denizet-Lewis, "Friends, Friends with Benefits and the Benefits of the Local Mall," *New York Times Magazine*, May 30, 2004, pp. 30–35, 54, 56, 58.

2. Ibid., p. 33.

3. Ibid., p. 32.

4. Ibid., p. 33.

5. Scot Lehigh, "The Casual Emptiness of Teenage Sex," *Boston Globe*, June 2, 2004, p. A11.

6. For instance, see Dick Thornburgh & Herbert Lin (Eds.), *Youth, Pornography and the Internet* (Washington, DC: National Academy Press, 2002). It was sponsored by the Computer Science and Telecommunications Board of the National Research Council. "The Cyberporn Generation," *People Magazine*, April 26, 2004. Whether this legislation will become a vehicle for limiting children's access to the Internet is now in the courts. On June 30, 2004, the Supreme Court upheld a Philadelphia District Court order that blocked the implementation of COPA on First Amendment grounds.

7. Jay Silverman, Anita Raj, & Karen Clements, "Dating Violence and Associated Sexual Risk and Pregnancy among Adolescent Girls in the United States," *Pediatrics*, 114(2), August, 2004, pp. e220–e225.

8. American Academy of Pediatrics, "Policy Statement: Identifying and Treating Eating Disorders," *Pediatrics*, 111(1), January, 2003, pp. 204–211.

9. Researchers who study violence and children have concluded from a much larger body of research that patterns of aggression at age eight are highly correlated with adult aggressive behavior. For instance, see Leonard Eron, Jacquelyn Gentry, and Peggy Schlegel (Eds.), *Reason to Hope: A Psychosocial Perspective on Violence and Youth* (Washington, DC: American Psychological Association, 1994). The authors conclude that to reduce adult aggression, it is vital to work with children when they are young. While we do not have a similar body of research on the relationship of early sexual development to later sexual behavior to draw the same definitive conclusions, child development experts generally accept the importance of the first eight years in laying the foundations for later behavior.

10. Ed Donnerstein & Stacy Smith, "Sex in the Media: Theory, Influences, and Solutions," in *The Handbook of Children and the Media*, Dorothy G. & Jerome L. Singer (Eds.). (Thousand Oaks, CA: Sage, 2001),289–307.

11. Victoria Rideout, Elizabeth Vandewater, & Ellen Wartella, *Zero to Six: Electronic Media in the Lives of Infants, Toddlers and Preschoolers*. The Kaiser Family Foundation, Fall, 2003, p. 12.

12. *Sex on TV: Executive Summary, A Biennial Report of the Kaiser Family Foundation*, 2001, p. 2.

13. *Sex, Kids and the Family Hour: A Three-Part Study of Sexual Content on Television*. Report from Children Now and the Kaiser Family Foundation, 1996.

14. Donnerstein & Smith, "Sex in the Media."

15. L. Greenhouse, "Court Blocks Law Regulating Internet Access to Pornography." *New York Times*, June 30, 2004.

16. The action figure is "Sable Bomb" Series 2 from World Wrestling Federation, made by Jakks Pacific, Inc., 1998. Its age recommendation is "for ages four and up."

17. For more detailed explanations of the connections among sexualization, consuming, and corporate interests, see Nancy Carlsson-Paige & Diane E. Levin, "Whatever Happened to Annie Oakley: Girls, Sexism, and War Play" in *Who's Calling the Shots? How to Respond Effectively to Children's Fascination with War Play and War Toys* (Gabriola Island, BC, CAN: New Society Publishers, 1990); and Jean Kilbourne, *Deadly Persuasion: Why Women and Girls Must Fight the Addictive Power of Advertising* (New York: Free Press, 1999).

18. Barbara Meltz, "Super Sexy Fashion Dolls Are Asking for Trouble," *The Boston Globe*, December 11, 2003, pp. H1 & H4.

19. Stories like these prompted the *Boston Globe* column by Barbara Meltz, "Dodging the Britney Spears Bandwagon," August 17, 2000, pp. F1 & F3; and *Good Morning America* to do a feature called "Too Sexy Too Soon" in April, 2001 about the influence of such singers on children.

20. Children Now and the Kaiser Family Foundation, *Sex, Kids and the Family Hour*.

21. For a more detailed account of how children's ideas about gender are shaped by the information and images that surround them, see Carlsson-Paige & Levin, "Whatever Happened to Annie Oakley"; Mary Pipher, *Reviving Ophelia: Saving the Selves of Adolescent Girls* (New York: Ballantine Books, 2001); and William Pollack, *Real Boys: Rescuing Our Sons from the Myths of Boyhood* (New York: Random House, 1998).

22. These characteristics of young children's thinking outlined here are adapted from what Jean Piaget called the "preoperational stage of development." See Jean Piaget, *The Language and Thought of the Child* (New York: Routledge & Kegan Paul, 1926).

23. For instance, see Susan Linn, *Consuming Kids: The Hostile Takeover of Childhood* (New York: The New Press, 2004); and Pipher, *Reviving Ophelia*.

24. Laura Sessions Stepp, "Unsettling New Fad Alarms Parents: Middle School Oral Sex," *Washington Post*, July 8, 1999, p. A1.

25. Steve Farkas, Jean Johnson, & Ann Duffett, *A Lot Easier Said Than Done: Parents Talk about Raising Children in Today's America*, New York: Public Agenda, October 2002.

26. For instance, see Sylvia A. Hewlett & Cornel West, *The War on Parents: What We Can Do for America's Beleaguered Moms and Dads* (New York: Houghton Mifflin, 1998).

27. For concrete help doing this, see Diane E. Levin, *Remote Control Childhood? Combating the Hazards of Media Culture* (Washington, D.C.: National Association for the Education of Young Children, 1998).

28. For help shaping responses to the age, needs, and questions of specific children, see Kent Chrisman & Conna Couchenour, *Healthy Sexual Development: A Guide for Early Childhood Educators and Families* (Washington, D.C.: National Association for the Education of Young Children, 2002).

29. There are a growing number of organizations working to accomplish this. Many of them can be found on the Website of the Coalition to Stop Commercial Exploitation of Children, www.commercialexploitation.org.

8

Techno-Environmental Assaults on Childhood in America

VARDA BURSTYN AND GARY SAMPSON

Increasingly over the past decade, scholars, educators, and parents have become deeply disturbed by the myriad ways in which both American culture and contemporary socioeconomic realities are undermining childhood—whether by undermining children's ability to develop their minds, psyches, and spirits directly, or by compromising the ability of parents and schools to give children what they need for such development to unfold. Yet another urgent dimension to this cultural and socioeconomic picture is the techno-environmental assault on childhood. *Techno* refers to the deployment of industrial technologies developed to bring us the "miracles of modern living" that are at the root of the problem of undermining childhood; and *environmental* is used because the byproducts of these technologies diffuse into the biosphere—the air, the water, the soil—and are then directly assimilated by children or are picked up and "bioaccumulated" in living organisms such as the crops and animals we and our children eat.

We contend that without the basic physiological integrity of the growing child's body—from gestation through adolescence—emotional and mental development are fundamentally compromised and cannot be diagnosed or remedied by purely cultural or pharmacological forms of intervention. Many people, particularly scholars and educators, are aware that environmental toxins can have an impact on children. But very few people know the quantity or quality of the dangers to which children are exposed. Even fewer people understand the *cumulative* and *synergistic* nature of such problems.

The immune system is able to handle only so much. Think of it as a rain barrel that works to contain water, but only as long as it doesn't overflow or leak. The more environmental problems a child's immune system must handle, the more likely it is that the child will develop pathological symptoms—that its barrel will over-flow or spring holes. A healthy child with a healthy immune system will be able to handle more; a child whose immunity was already compromised in gestation or infancy or later in childhood will be able to handle less. Genetics play a role, but in the majority of cases, nothing like the role that the great promoters of the geneticization of illness and psychology would have us believe. Finally, because the body experiences all stressors in similar biochemical ways, children who are socially and emotionally stressed will have a harder time dealing with physical stress, because their rain barrel is already brimming over, and vice versa. The grim realities of poverty place less-privileged children in the highest risk categories of all.

The technologies and pollutants we discuss below are bad for everyone, yes; but they have particularly devastating effects on chil-dren. This is the rule of thumb: *children are, by far, the most vulnerable to environmental hazards.* Pound for pound, children eat more food, drink more water, and breathe more air than adults do. Because they are smaller and closer to the ground, because they play out-doors more and don't practice the same level of hygiene as adults, their exposure to all environmental pollutants is greater than that of adults. In addition, their bodies are still works in progress, incom-plete and more susceptible to developmental disruptions.

Considering how fundamental many of the substances we will be discussing are to the existing industrial economy, and to the huge companies whose billions of dollars of profit are vested in them, it should come as no surprise that the charges of serious health damage laid against these pollutants have been contested on every front. Finally, to set the stage, we want to draw your atten-tion to the views and actions of the current federal administration. In February 2004, the Union of Concerned Scientists (UCS) released a report that documented what many of us feared over the last few years: in effect, the Bush Administration has rejected the methods by which we normally measure environmental dangers and seek solutions to them—scientific testing, evaluation, extrapolation, epidemiology, and biostatistics.[1] The UCS reports at length on serious incidents involving the suppression of scientific evidence and the appointment of unqualified persons with gross conflicts of interest to regulatory positions in government.[2] The combined result of these problems is to make it impossible for the United States, as a nation, to come to grips with pressing environmental problems, despite many knowledgeable and dedicated people within the Food and Drug Administration (FDA), the Environmental Protection Agency (EPA), and the Department of Agriculture.

Although by no means an exhaustive list, in this chapter we discuss four of the most damaging types of techno-environmental dangers—or byproducts of the manufacturing and agricultural industries—facing our children today. These include persistent organic pollutants such as pesticides and pseudo-estrogens; agricultural hormones in the food chain, including recombinant bovine growth hormone (BGH); antibiotics in the food chain; and heavy metals such as mercury and lead.

PERSISTENT ORGANIC POLLUTANTS

We will begin with a brief overview of the toxins known as persistent organic pollutants, or POPs. Since the 1950s we have introduced more than 100,000 man-made chemicals into the biosphere. At the turn of the twenty-first century, 400 million tons of 70,000 different chemicals were being manufactured annually on a global basis and were being absorbed—or not—in a variety of ways by the environment.[3] We are speaking here of industrial chemicals such as polychlorinated biphenyls (PCBs) and hexachlorobenzene; by-products such as dioxins and furans; and a host of pesticides such as aldrin, chlordane, DDT, and endrin, among many, many others. These toxic substances are now present in our air, water, soil, food, household products, and work environments. Children take in more of these substances, pound for pound, than adults.

The Great Lakes and St. Lawrence River regions of North America, especially places like Sarnia and Detroit with their huge petrochemical processing plants, carry an especially heavy burden of these chemicals on this continent. People who live near the sites of production exhibit much higher rates of cancer, and this has been documented for decades. But the other diabolical feature of POPs is that they migrate: from plastic pacifiers and toys to the babies who use them, and from areas of past or present industrialization to all parts of the world.[4] Plumes of wind carry airborne particles hundreds, indeed thousands of miles from their place of origin. Hence, poisons from the industrial heartland affect bald eagles on the Florida coast, where wind adds them to the high concentrations of POPs the birds ingest when they eat fish that live in pesticide-laced lakes. POPs bio-accumulate in ever-larger concentrations in the tissues of fish, birds, and mammals that humans consume as food. Humans are highest on the food chain. The concentrations of toxic substances in Inuit women's breast milk—women who are as far as it is possible to be from industrial production sites—are as high or higher as those of many women in the Great Lakes areas.

Organic pollutants from pesticides, plastics, and other chemical-dependent industries *persist* in the environment even after some of them (e.g., DDT) have been removed from the market and considerable environmental clean-ups have been achieved. Because they persist, they are seriously eroding, in the words of the 1996 path-breaking book *Our Stolen Future*, our "fertility, intelligence, and survival."[5] While almost all existing public health standards set for the levels of such pollutants have been based on concern about cancer among adults, many studies by distinguished scientists and epidemiologists since the 1990s have suggested or concluded that the gravest damage these chemicals do is related not to this disease, but to the disruption of the developing endocrine and neurological systems in children.

Herbicides and Pesticides

Herbicides and pesticides are enormous reservoirs of POPs. On April 24, 2004, the Ontario College of Family Physicians released a comprehensive report on the chronic effects of pesticide exposure at home and at work. The report was a meta-analysis of hundreds of reputable studies worldwide. Despite decades of protest and denial from the chemical industry, this comprehensive and careful study established a link between common household pesticides and fetal defects, neurological damage, and cancers strong enough that they called on citizens to *avoid the chemicals in any form* and called on governments *to ban their use in all households* and even municipal settings. The report named brain cancer, prostate cancer, kidney cancer, pancreatic cancer, and leukemia among many other acute illnesses linked to pesticide use. As well, there were consistent links between parents' exposure to certain agricultural pesticides at their jobs and effects on growing fetuses, ranging from various forms of developmental damage to death. The *Globe and Mail*, Canada's leading newspaper, reported on the findings of the study as follows:

> after examining 12,000 studies conducted from 1990 to 2003 around the world, and winnowing that down to the most sound 250, the researchers said there is no evidence that some pesticides are less dangerous than others, just that they have different effects on health that take different periods to show up. They said they are preparing brochures for patients and education material for family doctors to fill them in on the findings. The risks of pesticide use, concluded the Family Physicians, can come even from residue on food, ant spray and the tick collar on the family cat.[6]

The Canadian Cancer Society, the Learning Disabilities Association of Canada, the Registered Nurses Association of Canada, and the Ontario Public Health Association have called for these bans as well.

Pseudo Sex Hormones

We will now turn our focus to POPs in the form of chemicals that cause hormonal disruption that have come to be known, variously, as "pseudo-hormones" or hormonal acting agents (HAAs). One key thing must be understood about hormones: their biochemical composition and effects are similar throughout the animal kingdom. Estrogen is estrogen, and testosterone is testosterone, from locusts and boll weevils all the way up to humans. If you use a chemical to disrupt the reproductive abilities of an insect—say a tent caterpillar or a cockroach—that chemical, in sufficient quantity, is going to have similar effects on us. [7]

Without knowing it, just by using products in the course of our normal everyday lives, we are exposing ourselves and the environment to hormone-disrupting chemicals. These products include soaps, cleaning materials, plastic wrappers, toys, PVC siding, paints and varnishes, garden pesticides and herbicides, and electric and automotive machines.[8] We ingest these chemicals as they migrate from their points of production through the air and into our water, soil, and food. We absorb the chemicals when we make direct contact as we use them. The chemicals that disrupt the development of our sexual glands have been called pseudo-estrogens and anti-androgens. These chemicals mimic the biochemistry of our own hormones, and our hormone receptors lock onto them and assimilate them into our bodies as though they were the real things. What this means is that we are accumulating much higher levels of hormone-like substances than we were ever meant to have.

The research on animals is conclusive. Male animals such as frogs, birds, crocodiles, and fish exposed to the most common endocrine disrupters show signs of hermaphroditism; tiny penises incapable of mating; damaged testicles and low sperm count, motility, and health; enlarged breasts (in mammals); and the like. Female animals also display symptoms of too much estrogen, including premature sexual maturation and disrupted fertility, leading to a series of reproductive and health problems.

In humans, tragically, the greatest concentration of POPs is in the umbilical cord and breast milk of mothers. Indeed, an adult woman can effectively detoxify herself by carrying a baby to term and breastfeeding for a few months, as the POPs will migrate from her body to that of her child. In this way, tiny fetuses and babies take on adult loads of toxicity. Hence it is no surprise that their delicate reproductive tracts are often affected.[9] In recent years, alarms have been raised about the apparently precipitous drop in the onset of puberty among American girls. Many have been developing breast buds and pubic hair as early as five and six years of age, some even earlier. In POP-saturated areas of India, authorities have noted girls who have developed these characteristics as early as three years of age. We'll see soon what other factors are bound to affect delicate young reproductive systems. But the presence of pseudo-hormones is certainly a crucial factor. Exposure to excessive estrogens, pseudo or otherwise, seriously predisposes women to breast cancer, which is of epidemic proportions. It is also associated with fibroid tumors, endometriosis, and disrupted ovulation, all of which are implicated in problems with fertility. Further, as we will see, sex hormones affect neuro- and immunological functions, and damage there is also evident.

For males, the story is also very disturbing. Male babies and young boys are exposed to pseudo-estrogens and to androgen-blockers—chemicals that undermine the function of male hormones. Many of the chemicals involved are based on chlorine—the basis of almost half the world's chemical industries—and these are thought to disrupt key sexual developmental stages in the fetus and baby. There have been many studies that strongly suggest that the human sperm count has been falling in industrialized locations by as much as 50 percent over the last fifty years.[10] As with most of the pathologies we are writing about, we tend to think that there are multiple causes involved. But the exposure to gender-bending chemicals seems to us to merit the most serious consideration as a prime factor.

Recently, scientists have been looking at these chemicals as possible risk factors in the obesity epidemic in the United States. Currently, 59 million Americans are obese, and 300,000 are dying each year from related causes, making this disorder the second-leading cause of death in the United States, after smoking. At a February 2004 symposium titled *Obesity: Developmental Origins and Environmental Influences*, co-sponsored by the National Institute of Environmental Health Sciences (NIEHS) and the Duke University Integrated Toxicology Program, presenters discussed data that "support the hypothesis that in utero or neonatal exposures to environmental chemicals, notably endocrine disruptors, play a role in the etiology of obesity."[11] Estrogens regulate the size of adipocytes (fat cells) in adult humans and animals. Hence Retha Newbold, a developmental biologist with the NIEHS Environmental Toxicology Program, says, "[T]here is compelling evidence that exposure to endocrine disruptors during critical phases of cell differentiation may have long-lasting consequences. These exposures likely alter mechanisms involved in weight homeostasis. We're still trying to determine if it's a direct effect on the adipose cells and how they differentiate or proliferate, or whether it's a disruption of the endocrine feedback loops."[12]

Other Endocrine and Neurological Effects of POPs

The endocrine system, including the sex glands and hormones they produce, affects every other system and organ in the body. We know now that sex hormones affect the development of the fetal brain—hence, there is a neurological impact when sex hormones are disrupted. In addition, however, scientists have shown that some chemicals directly disrupt the development and functioning of other glands as well. Evidence of withering of the thymus gland, known as the master gland of the immune system, on exposure to PCBs has been found in lab animals and animals in the wild.[13] Harm to the lymph system has been found, too.[14] For some time now, scientists have drawn a lot of attention to thyroid function. The thyroid plays a crucial role in fetal, neo-natal, and childhood neurological and psychological development, and, of course, in the regulation of metabolism.

The neurological damage created by POPs' thyroid disruption has been directly linked to a variety of learning and attention deficit disorders, to a decreased ability to withstand stress among children, and to a lowering of average intelligence by 5–6 percent.[15] Some experts have begun to suggest that despite the other benefits of breastfeeding, women in heavily industrialized regions or in regions where POPs are deposited should forego it for the developmental health of their children.[16] The scientific evidence linking many of these chemicals to a variety of harms has existed for some time among specialists, and in the late 1990s finally began to receive official attention. The United Nations organized a conference in 1998 to devise a treaty to ban the twelve worst offenders ("the dirty dozen"), a task that remains uncompleted.

The thyroid gland is also crucial to regulating the metabolism of energy, food, and fat. When the thyroid gland is functioning at suboptimal levels, people feel tired and have difficulty exercising and meeting work commitments; they are more prone to a variety of infections; and, what is better known, they are also more prone to becoming seriously overweight. We know that American children have problems in all of these areas. We don't at all discount the cultural factors that have been cited in the etiology of this problem. A mammoth fast food industry, too much screen culture, not enough exercise, a sport culture that includes only the high performers and excludes the low performers, not enough physical activity and education in school—all these are important without question. But it would be very unwise to stop with this list and ignore the way in which children's bodies are being affected by toxins in the environment.

AGRICULTURAL HORMONES IN THE FOOD CHAIN

In addition to the "pseudo-hormones" inadvertently created by industrial production, every day most of us, simply by consuming meat and dairy products, are ingesting substances purposely created to simulate real hormones.

Recombinant Bovine Growth Hormone

A special danger for children is the use of recombinant bovine growth hormone (rBGH or rBST)—a product of the Monsanto chemical company. The milk industry uses it to increase milk output by as much as 25 percent, according to Monsanto claims. Between

5 and 30 percent of the cows in the United States are injected with it. The Food and Drug Administration approved the hormone for use in 1994, but Canada and Europe have not. Many advocacy groups—for example, the Consumers Union and the Cancer Prevention Coalition—oppose the use of bovine growth hormone.

In addition to the increased risk of cancer in humans, numerous studies have shown that this hormone undermines the health of cows and increases disease agents in the milk, including bacteria, viruses, and pus. Indeed, this was the reason officially cited by Canada's Health and Safety Branch for refusing to approve its use in 1999. In Europe, the use of bovine growth hormone is banned, and the European Union's Scientific Veterinary Measures has stated that all six hormones used in the United States could pose a risk of cancer. Further they state, and we quote, "children are most at risk."[17]

Because hormones tend to have the same biochemical makeup throughout the animal kingdom, one consequence of bovine growth hormone in cattle is growth in humans. We return now to the obesity epidemic among Americans, both adults and children. As serious as the problem may be in adults, it is worse when it begins in childhood because of the predisposition to adult onset diabetes, heart disease, and arthritis—indeed a host of miseries and premature deaths—that comes along with childhood obesity. And there is strong anecdotal evidence to suggest that this bovine growth hormone may play a significant part in premature puberty for girls, as well.

Other Hormones in the Food Chain

There are other hormones in the food chain, too. In fact, more than 90 percent of U.S. cows are given one or more of six FDA-approved hormones, including anabolic steroids (derived from or mimicking estrogen and testosterone). Cows and humans produce three of these hormones naturally; the others are purely synthetic. The National Toxicology Program and the National Institutes of Health consider two of them probable carcinogens.[18] The USDA does no testing for natural hormones and only sporadic testing for synthetically produced hormones in beef. This is highly unfortunate because Swiss inspectors, for example, have detected diethylstilbestrolin (DES) in two different shipments of American beef. DES is an infamous fertility-destroying, cancer-causing, antimiscarriage drug long banned for human use in the United States, and its import in any form has been banned in Europe. DES's worst effects were on fetuses, and without question its worst effects in the food chain will be on the very young—whether in the womb or already born.[19]

It is almost unbelievable, but there have been virtually no American studies of the long-term effects of using hormones in beef cattle—a practice that has been going on for twenty years. Producers, particularly the large industrial concerns, have no interest in looking for problems, and regulators haven't told them to look. The good news is that hormones aren't approved for use in chickens or pigs—though antibiotics have been, as we shall see.

Finally, new evidence is emerging that our groundwater is increasingly contaminated with a variety of pharmaceutical substances, including hormones from agricultural animals and from human hormone replacement therapy—until recently, the most successful pharmaceutical products ever made. Now that the synthetic estrogen and progesterone replacement hormones have been linked to increased predispositions to breast cancer and heart disease in women, their use is beginning to slacken. But we still have to contend with the larger problem of hormone pollution in the environment.

Let's stop for a moment in this bleak landscape to deliver a little good news: the Burgerville chain—a Northwest-based fast food chain—announced in February 2004 that it would eliminate generic ground beef from its burgers and instead make them from range-fed, hormone-free cattle raised on Oregon ranches.[20] The switch means Burgerville will have to pay at least 30 percent more for its beef, and for the time being, this means a costlier hamburger. But it is worth it to parents, and very good news, because it will reward organic ranchers, and ranchers as a sector need to get the message that they will do well—indeed better—economically by growing healthy, drug-free animals.

ANTIBIOTICS IN THE FOOD CHAIN

We now turn our attention to pharmaceutical pollution: specifically the massive use of antibiotics in raising farm animals. Massive and continuous in-feed use of antibiotics in agriculture began in the early 1950s. Today antibiotics are used in the raising of pigs, chickens, cattle, and in aquaculture. Many people have increased their fish consumption, thinking they have found a drug-free alternative to beef, pork, and chicken; but unless the fish is caught in the wild, this is an illusion. Farmed fish, unless organically raised, are loaded up with antibiotics as well.

There have been several serious results from this widespread use of antibiotics. The best known—though not well-enough known, apparently, to stop the practice in the United States—has been a large increase in the development of bacteria that are highly resistant to antibiotics in both animals and humans. The problem is that when antibiotics are used wrongly or abused, they have the effect of increasing the strength and virulence of bacteria. Many people have heard of the so-called superbugs—virulent *E. coli* in manure-contaminated water or in hamburgers, vancomycin-resistant enterococcus (VRE), and salmonella. But the list is longer. There are resistant staphylococcus and streptococcus bacteria and indeed mycobacteria, which are very trenchant fungal/bacterial hybrids, on the rise. Many of these superbugs can spread via the food chain, and increased international travel allows them to ride along on airplanes just like people do. One virtually unknown source of these drug-resistant bugs is the air around and significantly downwind of factory farms where antibiotics are in use. The reason that this is unknown is that the evidence for it has been suppressed. One particularly dramatic and well-documented case of suppression of scientific evidence reported by the Union of Concerned Scientists involved Dr. James Zahn, a research microbiologist at the USDA. Zahn asserted that he was prohibited on no fewer than eleven occasions from publicizing his research on the potential hazards to human health posed by airborne bacteria resulting from farm wastes.

Zahn's research had uncovered significant levels of antibiotic-resistant bacteria in the air near hog confinement operations in Iowa and Missouri. But, as Zahn recounts, he was repeatedly barred by his superiors from presenting his research at scientific conferences in 2002. Zahn had accidentally stumbled on the issue of airborne antibiotic resistance while researching a related topic and, prior to the start of the Bush Administration, was initially encouraged by his supervisors to pursue the work. But he says that with the change in administration, he soon came to feel that his research was being suppressed because it was perceived to be politically unpalatable.

Antibiotic-resistant bugs are an enormous problem in other sites as well. Notoriously, hospitals are extremely dangerous places, especially for the young and the elderly who are there because of other problems that have placed a load on their immune systems. Antibiotic-resistant strep and staph infections lurking in hospitals that have not invested sufficient money in cleaning (this has been shown to be the key factor in fighting these infections) kill ever-larger numbers of people.[21] Tuberculosis is making a comeback. Especially vulnerable are poor children. Of course, while tuberculosis is rising most dramatically in prisons and low-income neighborhoods, it travels out of these locales and puts everyone at risk. This illustrates a basic population health axiom: the health of the lowest socioeconomic stratum of society affects the health of the highest, so equity and redistributive measures to reduce the gap between the rich and the poor are health measures *par excellence*.

Most of our older stores of antibiotics work poorly for these so-called superbugs, and long courses and high doses are often prescribed; or perhaps one of the very few "new" antibiotics may be prescribed. Or, in ever-greater numbers, no antibiotic is effective. If a person's immune system cannot fight the bug on its own, death results. We have been seeing very large numbers of such deaths in the past few decades.[22]

Even when antibiotic treatment appears to work in the short run, coming as it does on top of long-term exposure to antibiotics in the food chain as well as physician overuse of antibiotics for other purposes, in many cases it may have a cascade of serious consequences: the health and integrity of the mucus membranes of the body, especially those of the gut, are compromised. The gut is crucial to a healthy immune system. Antibiotics destroy the healthy bacterial flora of the gut, permit unhealthy fungi and bacteria flora to proliferate. This sets up what will, in untold numbers of children, be a lifelong struggle with a variety of auto-immune disorders ranging from trenchant fungal infections (thrush and vaginal yeast infections are epidemic) and food allergies to lupus and multiple sclerosis, as well as colitis, inflammatory bowel disease, and the like. Further, when the gut is compromised, a person's ability to deal with the other chemical assaults in the environment—the POPs we have mentioned already, and the food additives, sugars, and fats so present in the American diet—is undermined. Some very powerful negative synergies are launched or accelerated.

Why are antibiotics being used in this way in agriculture, even when the evidence of their harmful effects has been in for well over twenty years? Primarily because of the power of two industries— pharmaceuticals and agribusiness. Current industrial (factory farming) practices raise animals in conditions that undermine their health and promote disease. Hence, the rhetoric goes, we need loads of antibiotics to keep these animals going. This has become an important and highly controversial issue for both health and animal-welfare reformers in recent years. Guidelines being developed at the World Health Organization strongly suggest there is little economic benefit to be gained from the widespread use of in-feed antibiotics, and many harmful consequences.[23] Yet the practice persists. The two industries—often fused into the same corporate structures—have incredible weight and power. They buy politicians and public officials, and they saturate farming publications with their advertising.

Once again, let us relieve the bleak landscape with a piece of better, if not yet great, news: in a move similar to Burgerville's, the much-larger McDonald's Corporation announced in June 2003 a *phasing out* of the use of antibiotics from its global supply chain. The move is part of a set of "guiding principles for sustainable use" by McDonald's direct suppliers. The policy results from negotiations between the management of McDonald's and a group of stakeholders called the Antibiotics Coalition. However, a shareowner resolution co-filed by Trillium Asset Management (the oldest and largest independent investment advisor devoted exclusively to socially responsible investing) asking shareholder approval to apply the new standards it set on animal welfare in the United States and the United Kingdom to all of its global operations and supply chain failed, receiving only 4.8 percent of the general shareholders' vote. What is good is that McDonald's move does affect 2.5 billion pounds of chicken, beef, and pork purchased annually. What is bad is that the billions of pounds of these meats that are produced in other jurisdictions are unaffected. As Trillium's Senior Social Research Analyst, Steve Lippman, pointed out, McDonald's by its very existence is predicated on getting people to eat higher on the food chain. Beef in particular is inherently unsustainable as a staple. Lippman also denounced the McDonald's advertising campaigns "that get kids to be obese." Lippman concluded that, therefore, "who cares if they have 100 percent recycled paper wrappers or whatever." Indeed.

MERCURY, LEAD, AND OTHER HEAVY METALS

Many heavy metals are present in toxic levels in our environment. The list includes mercury, lead, cadmium, aluminum, arsenic, copper, and many others. We have chosen to concentrate on three that are present in the largest concentrations and are known to do grave damage.

Mercury

Mercury is one of the most dangerous chemical pollutants found in the environment and belongs to a dangerous class of chemicals known as persistent, bio-accumulative toxins (PBTs). This means that once mercury is released into the environment, it never goes away. It may combine with other compounds and assume different chemical forms, but it never breaks down into harmless byproducts. Mercury attacks the central nervous system and hurts the ability to learn, remember, and pay attention. In large-enough concentrations, it may also damage many other tissues and organ systems in the body, including those in the gut. In addition to the direct neurological damage it does, it can also directly affect the immune system itself.

The fetus is the most vulnerable to the effects of mercury. Recent research has shown that the umbilical cord can have an average mercury concentration almost twice that of the bloodstream.[24] In February 2004, the EPA put the number of children at risk for developmental disorders at birth at *more than one in six*, a rate equivalent to 630,000 of the 4 million babies born each year in the United States. As reported in the *New York Times*, the Centers for Disease Control and Prevention estimates that one woman in twelve of childbearing age has a mercury blood level in the danger range. But blood levels only poorly reflect true levels, since the body tends to sequester mercury in tissues, so the number must be much higher. The EPA has estimated that as many as 3 million American children have elevated levels of mercury in their blood, and about 7 million women and children regularly eat fish that is tainted with unsafe levels of mercury. The situation is so critical that Consumers Union (publisher of *Consumer Reports* magazine) recommends that a forty-four-pound child eat not more than one six-ounce can of white tuna or two cans of light tuna per week.[25]

The main source of ingested mercury appears to be contaminated fish that ingest mercury. Mercury in the water comes from the emissions of power plants that burn coal and other fossil fuels and subsequently falls from the sky in rain or snow, then travels in water runoff and accumulates in virtually all bodies of water. Once in the water, mercury changes into methylmercury—a bioavailable and toxic material—and is absorbed by fish as they feed on aquatic organisms. Through bio-accumulation, mercury is then passed up the marine food chain. Figures released by the FDA in 2003 showed that mercury contamination in four important species of fish had increased to levels higher than those used to establish its health advisory guidelines. These species are canned albacore tuna, grouper, sea bass, and bluefish. Canned albacore, known as white tuna, had mercury levels twice as high as previous FDA estimates for canned tuna and three times the levels in light tuna. Incidentally, the FDA data was not volunteered. The Environmental Working Group (EWG) obtained it through the Freedom of Information Act.

A second major source of mercury—and one that is virtually unknown to the vast majority of people—comes from automobile ignition switches. Between 1974 and 2003, an estimated 217 million switches were installed in American cars and contained up to 493,000 pounds of mercury. Over 50 percent of this mercury has already been released into the environment during end-of-life-processing. In the last three years, over 54,000 pounds of mercury have been released into the environment from these switches. More than eleven tons of mercury are still put into new cars each year. In January 2001, the Clean Car Campaign issued a report called "Toxics in Vehicles: Mercury" and called for the establishment of a mercury recovery program by automakers.[26] We suggest that an alternative to mercury be found, and soon.

Mercury is also present in thermometers, fluorescent light bulbs, many batteries, light switches, and many "silver" (more accurately, silver-mercury amalgam) dental fillings. In Sweden, such fillings have been banned. Despite the self-protective denials of the American Dental Association, which is terrified of an avalanche of lawsuits, many enlightened dentists will no longer place such fillings. Mercury is a component of thimerosal, a compound widely used as a preservative and antiseptic. In the guise of thimerosal, mercury shows up in some eyedrops, nasal sprays, contact lens cleaners, and even childhood and flu vaccines, where its purpose is to keep the medicine uninfected by bacteria. But, as we are learning, if a substance is lethal to one form of life, it is bound to be toxic to other forms as well—including us.

In the last ten years, a number of researchers have suggested that mercury is a major culprit in the dramatic increase in reported instances of autism in children. Autism is an extremely serious disorder, a true life-disrupting disability that creates terrible problems for the children who have it and extraordinary financial, practical, and emotional challenges for their families. Mercury's implication in autism is controversial, both because autism is a complex disorder or set of disorders that are not yet fully understood, and because mercury-using and mercury-producing industries fund scientists and organizations to contest findings of harm with their own counterclaims.[27]

The FDA under President George W. Bush suppressed its own report detailing the hazards of mercury toxicity, particularly to pregnant women and children, until an anonymous official finally leaked it to the *Wall Street Journal* on February 23, 2004. Had this leak not occurred, the report may never have surfaced. Even more recently, the Union of Concerned Scientists reported that the new rules the EPA finally proposed for regulating power plants' mercury emissions were discovered to have no fewer than twelve paragraphs lifted, sometimes verbatim, from a legal document prepared by industry lawyers, a flagrant violation of FDA norms in which regulations are to be drafted by staff.[28]

Thankfully, some Congressmen are attempting to halt the most dangerous forms of air pollution, which include mercury. The Clean Power Act and the Clean Smokestacks Act, reintroduced into the House of Representatives in February 2004, would require polluting power plants to reduce emissions of nitrogen oxide, sulfur dioxide, carbon dioxide, and mercury in a manner that is "feasible"—a problematic term, unfortunately. This legislation supports the 1990 Clean Air Act and would provide some protection from the Administration's new, so-called "Clear Skies Initiative." The term *clear skies* is truly disinformation because the initiative would allow at least 36 percent more nitrogen, 50 percent more sulfur dioxide, and *three times* the amount of mercury allowed under current regulations. Calculations based on EPA analysis show that the Clear Skies Initiative will result in 54,000 deaths over the next sixteen years from power plant pollution that would be avoided if the current law were simply enforced. EPA experts say that new technology could reduce mercury pollution by 90 percent or more, but the Clear Skies Initiative would permit power plants to delay implementation of the new technology through the year 2018. Legislation following the president's plan was introduced to the House and Senate in February also.

On a more positive note, the National Wildlife Federation reports that public health agencies in forty-three states have issued formal advisories warning people against eating certain fish because of mercury contamination. In 2003 in California, the state attorney general filed suit against five grocery chains for failing to properly warn consumers about the risk of mercury in fish.[29]

Lead and Arsenic

While we're speaking of heavy metals, let us not forget our old friends lead and arsenic. According to the Natural Resources Defense Council, lead is now recognized as the single most significant environmental health threat to American children. The good news is that the average blood-lead level in the United States has fallen by more than 80 percent since 1976. This is mainly due to the ban on using leaded gasoline, leaded paint, and lead-soldered food cans. The bad news is that we now know that blood-lead levels once thought to be safe are really quite hazardous—especially to children. Children readily absorb lead from their intestinal tracts. Playing in the dust and engaging in hand-to-mouth behavior facilitate exposure to lead as well as many other contaminants.[30]

The effects of lead poisoning are chronic and debilitating. Severe exposure (blood-lead levels greater than 80 µg/dL) can cause comas, convulsions, or death. More common levels of exposure (around 10 µg/dL) may not cause distinctive or acute symptoms, but rather decrease stature or growth, hearing acuity, and the ability to maintain steady posture. Such blood-lead levels have also been associated with decreased intelligence and impaired neurobehavioral development.

A major source of lead poisoning has been the paint used in schools. If a school was built before 1978, it is likely to contain paint having a lead content in excess of 0.06 percent. Paint produced after 1992 should be lead-free. Paint that is peeling or chipping poses a safety hazard because eating even one lead-paint chip can poison a child. As lead paint deteriorates it can release lead dust, and removing it from school walls can sometimes release higher levels of lead than leaving it in place. Simply painting over an older lead-based surface is not an effective way of protecting children, either. Proper removal and disposal are and will continue to be expensive and time-consuming processes. But consider the alternatives.

The other serious, but still not fully assessed, source of lead in the United States is from deteriorating water pipes; at present, the United States has 700,000 miles of aging pipes, some more than a hundred years old, many made of lead. For example, in January 2004, the *Washington Post* revealed that lead levels in Washington, DC had been exceeding the allowable norm for the first time since the late 1980s, when monitoring started. "It's shocking," said Charles Eason, a resident of Georgetown, where the water registered *thirty-six times* the EPA's lead limit. "It's a particular risk for young people, and I have a 4-year-old grandson in my house regularly."[31] The District does not offer a screening program for adults or for children six and older, so most parents couldn't even find out if their children had been harmed. A detailed description of this situation cannot be repeated here, but we urge readers to consult the lengthy *Washington Post* articles on the subject.

Arsenic is a naturally occurring substance that can be deadly in large doses in the short term and a dangerous carcinogen in small doses in the long term. It is found in insecticides, herbicides, paints, dyes, rat poison, and wood preservatives. It is used in mining. Wood treated with arsenic-based preservatives can cause chronic arsenic poisoning. Arsenic easily rubs off such wood, and at levels found in lumber obtained from popular outlets could be expected to cause cancer in one out of 500 children playing on equipment made from such wood. Arsenic remains the only known human carcinogen still approved for use as a pesticide (though this begs the standards and definitions of carcinogens. For example, pesticides commonly used to kill mosquitoes break down into carcinogenic components).[32]

CONCLUSIONS AND REFLECTIONS

From this review of industrial byproducts that constitute techno-environmental hazards, we can draw a number of conclusions. The first is that whatever we do to nature—whatever chemicals we put into the environment, whatever hormonal manipulation we attempt on animals, whatever effluents and drugs we dump in our soil, water, or air— comes back to affect us. We live in a closed system. As we used to say in the 1960s, there is no "away." But there is "blowback," and this blowback differentially affects and harms children. Thus, fighting for an agenda of environmental remediation and democratic, environmentally sound technological control is the *sine qua non* of achieving a way of life that assures childhood health, normal development, and the integrity of coming generations.

We must face the empirical verdict that materials foreign to nature will cause problems in nature. From there we need to understand that, on the one hand, we must clean up the toxins that industry has generated and, on the other, begin a massive campaign to substitute old technologies and methods with those that are benign.

All this amounts to an understanding, and a declaration, that we are going to rapidly bring to an end the heroic period of techno-industrialism that is based on the idea that the biosphere is infinitely

malleable and we can do anything we want to it without consequence for us. This may seem like an obvious conclusion, but in
fact, it has not been understood or adopted by the vast majority of
the world's industries or governments or, indeed, populations.
Today's White House ranks among those regimes in the industrialized world that are most ignorant of this premise and most hostile
to taking the necessary steps to address it.

We must also admit that while there are many separate and
frightening problems that have already been identified, the *unstudied
negative synergies of these problems are even more disturbing*. For it is
often in the *accumulation* of problems that children's systems are
overloaded and break down, and parents' abilities to support their
children are overwhelmed. Further, the presence of these synergies
puts a serious limit on what we might call "individual solutions."
This is especially true for less-privileged families, who are also those
most at risk for environmental harms—although at least some of
these harms spread across the socio-economic scale. This is not to say
that parents and educators cannot take important steps to protect
children—they can, and they must. Rather it is to underline that in
many cases, collective action to address problems, and, indeed, to
create social services to help damaged children and exhausted parents, is necessary for meaningful results.

To move forward on these points and to protect our children, we
also urgently need to restore science to its rightful place in policymaking and address the destructive practices of appointing industry leaders to regulatory positions.[33] This will undoubtedly require
a "regime change" in the United States, which in turn requires cultural and political shifts in how we understand the place and importance of technological and environmental issues—as central, not
peripheral; as urgent, not postponable. In line with this, we must
pursue a larger agenda that seeks to recreate a public sector capable
of protecting the common weal, including the environment and
children; and which is capable of controlling the environmentally
and socially murderous behavior of major corporations.

We use the word *murderous* advisedly. A wonderful documentary film entitled *The Corporation*, based on the book of the same
name by Joel Bakan, has been cleaning up awards at documentary
film festivals this spring and making the rounds of repertory
cinemas.[34] It is a smash hit with a simple thesis, brilliantly supported:
if corporations were persons—which they are, in law, and in fact
they have rights far surpassing those of mere human persons—
what kind of people would they be? Using psychiatric manuals and

internationally accepted guidelines, the filmmakers suggest that corporations are clinically equivalent to psychopaths: constitutionally incapable of perceiving any interest other than their own short-term gain, and willing and able to pursue deadly strategies to gain advantage for themselves. Economists have more polite ways of saying the same thing—speaking of people and the environment as "externalities" that are not corporate responsibilities. Corporate public relations have a doublethink rhetoric that tells us that this behavior is actually good for us and our kids.

In any case, the implications are clear: unless corporations are compelled to be good citizens, in their drive for profits they will bring all of us down. Good corporate citizenship in this context means a wholesale "greening" of technology. A full green economic strategy is far beyond the scope of this paper. But we can advance one basic guiding approach that can be adapted in almost infinite ways: costs and profits are the *raison d'être* of corporations. If public policy subsidizes healthy technologies and products, and creates negative incentives for harmful ones—the opposite of the situation that now obtains—change can be remarkably rapid and effective. If plastic bottles and harmful cleaning agents are heavily taxed, likewise coal emissions and mercury car starters, corporate directives will quickly replace these with other products. If we took away tax breaks to Monsanto and gave them to organic farmers, and if we taxed meat raised with bovine growth hormone but featured (by law) organic produce in restaurants along our interstate highways, we would see the agrochemical-biotech companies developing safe agricultural methods and products faster than you could say "sustainable agriculture." Again, this approach requires cultural and political will, as well as technological and environmental understanding—and those are up to the citizens of this country to exercise.

The amount of learning and the investment of time, emotional commitment, and funds required for individual families to address the harms we have written about are very considerable, even when children are healthy. With children who have been harmed and have chronic problems, that investment rises qualitatively, to a point that is often profoundly stressful and destructive of family health in its own right. As such, collective and government supports and actions are also essential.

We have listed a number of specific actions for each of our four "techno-environmental assaults," for parents and educators on the one hand and for communities and governments on the other, in an appendix at the end of this chapter. Keep in mind that we can only briefly sketch certain measures, but a great deal of information is more generally available and can be traced through our reference list as well as other sources. Our Toxic World, by allergist and pediatrician Doris J. Rapp, is an excellent compendium of toxic dangers, the symptoms they produce, and many different approaches to treatment.

As Joe Hill famously said of his own death: Don't mourn. Organize! Elect politicians and officials who understand the issues and the availability of alternatives. Never separate environmental issues from economic or health issues and say, "We'll deal with those later." Instead, put environmental issues at the top of the political agenda and at the center of economic strategizing. Make school boards leaders in the fight to save our environment, and hence our children. Make sure that public policy always factors environmental and health costs into public accounting, tax, and other economic policy,[35] and that it rejects the approach that looks at them as "externalities"—the approach of business schools and traditional economics, which are single-handedly responsible for mass delusions about environmental harms and necessities. Finally, work to create public programs and services that acknowledge the impact on our children and on our families of already existing environmental problems, so that parents can have the resources to both care for families and be responsible citizens rebuilding a living planet.

APPENDIX: RECOMMENDATIONS FOR PARENTS, EDUCATORS, COMMUNITIES, AND GOVERNMENTS

Endocrine Disrupters/Hormone Acting Agents, Neurological Disrupters, and Heavy Metals

Parents and Educators

For parents, to the extent possible—and this is often not a very flexible factor—choose a place to live that does not have a heavy load of pesticides, other petroleum by-products, and heavy metals. Eat organic when possible. When you can't, eat "low on the food chain"—as larger animals tend to bio-accumulate toxins. Use environmentally friendly household cleaners, paints, and products, thus protecting your family and adding your own financial disincentive to the makers of toxic products. Do not let your children play with PVC plastic toys, and don't give them to your infants. Don't use PVC siding or windows in your house. Do not use pesticides. There are environmentally friendly solutions that don't require chemicals, even if they are more time-consuming. In general, with these issues as with all the others addressed here, use your power as a consumer to vote for products and technologies that are human- and environment friendly. Do not, to the extent you are able, contribute to the deadly economy. Greenpeace often makes available lists of environment-friendly consumer products; and several books are available, such as *Clean House, Clean Planet* (see note 8 for more information).

Don't let the dentist place silver-mercury fillings into your children's teeth. Insist on porcelain or composite fillings. If you have sick children, you will need to find out whether they have been poisoned by chemicals and/or heavy metals. The majority of family physicians and pediatricians don't know very much about this yet, but holistic practitioners, whether medical doctors, naturopaths, and/or nutritionists, lists of whom are available by locale on the Internet, do. There are de-toxification treatments that can be pursued, ranging from special diets to forms of pharmaceutical chelation, to pull heavy metals from the body. Many forms of neurological damage can be greatly relieved by the avoidance and purge of toxins on the one hand, and special nutritional supplementation to help rebuild the brain and nervous system on the other.

For educators, make all of the above a part of the health and environmental education children receive. As with all the issues we have addressed, work to make your school and school boards leading agents of environmental education and change. Get together parents and schools and make a list of your most important merchants. Demand organic food and environmentally friendly products; educate your community and ask them to buy those products—think globally, act locally, as the old green saying goes.

Communities/Governments

POPs and endocrine disruption are environmental and technological problems that respect no regional, state, or national borders. While working class people are much more at risk for direct exposures, the patterns of migration of POPs, and their presence in so many products, mean that everyone is vulnerable. If there are local deposits of persistent organic pollutants, they have to be cleaned up. This has become harder in recent years, because there is so little public money for such cleanups. The Superfund program stopped "making the polluter pay" in 1995, and, at the federal level, this has made cleanups less frequent and less effective. Hence direct action to remediate must often pass through indirect action—elections and political pressure—to ensure politicians and officials capable of prioritizing and acting on these problems.

Like other persistent organic pollutants that, once released into the environment, go on doing harm forever, mercury pollution needs to be cleaned up and eliminated at the source. We need to correct problems at dirty power plants, redesign mercury-containing consumer products, including car switches, and carefully monitor our fish stocks. At the national level in the United States, responsibility for regulating mercury is shared by two federal agencies: the Food and Drug Administration (FDA) and the Environmental Protection Agency (EPA). The FDA is charged with regulating commercially sold fish and seafood. The EPA monitors concentrations in the environment and regulates releases of mercury to surface water and air. FDA and EPA guidelines can be read on the Web at www.fda.gov and www.epa.gov.

Likewise, as a nation, we must develop the technical, social, and political means to test for other heavy metals, such as lead, arsenic, and cadmium, and find ways to eliminate these at toxic levels in the same manner that we approach mercury.

Hormone and Antibiotic Pollution in Food

Parents and Educators

The first point is to be aware of and to understand the problems and challenges involved. While we urge parents to educate themselves on the issues we have detailed, we also believe that school boards need to assimilate the information on the problems with our food supply into curriculum for kids, into the food and drink they provide, and into support programs for parents; and to proactively promote this knowledge.

Clearly, the best way to preserve children from the poisonous products in the food chain is to make sure that they ingest as few of them as possible. Once again, shopping and eating organic is the best possible strategy. When dealing with hormones and antibiotics in the food chain, as long as you are buying products that originate in the United States (for example, New Zealand lamb does not contain antibiotics or hormones), only organic meats and dairy will give you food that is not contaminated with these pollutants. One extremely important measure to take is to fight antibiotics with good bacteria—with "probiotics." We are speaking here of

high-quality acidophilus and bifidus bacteria, available at drug-
stores and health food stores—to be taken during and after every
course of antibiotics, and to be incorporated into the daily diet of
any children with chronic health, especially digestive, problems.

Teachers and school boards, take note, too! Schools should offer
only healthy foods. In addition to the well-known admonition to
get schools to throw soft drinks and fast foods out of school cafeterias, schools should be places where children get healthy food—and
that means meat, fish, and poultry free of chemical, hormonal, and
pharmaceutical pollution. If we made the preparation of fresh,
organic meals mandatory in schools, we would create a huge market for organic foods. Agribusiness would go green as it scrambled
to take advantage of it.

For parents with sick children: find holistic physicians, nutritionists, and naturopaths who can diagnose food-related disorders,
who can help design therapeutic diets, and who understand that it
is essential to find alternatives to antibiotics and other heavy
pharmaceuticals whenever possible, because these have negative
long-term consequences on the immune system.

Communities and Governments

Population health is profoundly dependent on the food we eat. If
we want healthy children, we will have to find a way to provide
them with healthy food and clean water. So it is time to clean up
agriculture and food processing via appropriate public policy, public agencies, and enforcement. A few guidelines here: antibiotics
should be reserved only for individual illness in animals, never for
mass in-feed use. Animals should be raised in conditions that do
not require the use of these substances. The same goes for hormones, which should be banned outright for agricultural use. If
such processes point to a reorganization of agriculture and a return
to smaller, more people- and animal-friendly farms, then public
policy, turning on economic incentives and disincentives and
enforcement agencies with teeth, should be enacted to make them
so. In fact, given the extraordinary levels of so many different kinds
of pollutants because of industrial agriculture, we need, as a society, to go back to the drawing board and redesign how we feed
ourselves, so that we are not poisoning ourselves at the same time.

The biosphere cannot sustain us if we do not protect its integrity. We have learned that many of our older technologies and
products have infernal consequences. But we are an ingenious

species, and there are many among us who have *already* devised new technologies and products capable of putting a stop to the damage we're doing, and, at least in large measure, eventually remediating it. From wind turbines and solar panels, to herbal anti-infectives and probiotics, to scientifically enhanced methods of organic farming, to filtration systems that use plants to produce pure drinking water without depositing one ounce of sewage in our waterways, we can do things to help our biosphere to survive and to protect our children and their children after them. *The technology—the appropriate technology—to make fundamental improvements in all the areas we have written about here, and more, already exists.* There is hope. To the extent possible, we urge individual families and schools to adopt helpful and appropriate technologies and products. But we also know that many of the big solutions—or the ability to take advantage of such solutions—are largely determined at the community, governmental, and societal levels.

NOTES

1. See Union of Concerned Scientists, *Scientific Integrity in Policymaking: An Investigation into the Bush Administration's Misuse of Science*, February 2004. Cambridge, MA. Roger G. Kennedy, a former director of the National Park Service, said, "Tinkering with scientific information, either striking it from reports or altering it, is becoming a pattern of behavior. It represents the politicizing of a scientific process, which at once manifests a disdain for professional scientists working for our government and a willingness to be less than candid with the American people."

2. Ibid.

3. Theo Colborn, Dianne Dumanoski, and John Peterson Myers, *Our Stolen Future: Are We Threatening Our Fertility, Intelligence and Survival? A Scientific Detective Story*, Dutton, New York, 1996. See also Lois Marie Gibbs, *Dying from Dioxin: A Citizen's Guide to Reclaiming Our Health and Rebuilding Democracy*, Black Rose Books, Montreal, 1997.

4. For studies reporting that "much of the precipitation in Europe contains such high levels of dissolved pesticides that it would be illegal to supply it as drinking water." Also, for links between pesticides and rising cancer rates, see Fred Pearce and Debora Mackenzie, "It's raining pesticides," *New Scientist*, April 3, 1999.

5. Colborn et al., *Our Stolen Future*.

6. Alanna, Mitchell, "Pesticides too harmful to use in any form, doctors warn." *The Globe and Mail*, April 24, 2004. June 10, 2004. Available

from www.theglobeandmail.com/servlet/ArticleNews/TPStory/LAC/20040402/PESTICIDES/TPHealth/.

7. For a discussion of sperm damage, see Colborn et al., *Our Stolen Future*, pp. 68–86. There have been many reports of deformed and hermaphroditic fish and frogs in the Great Lakes region. In January 1999, it was reported that "female mollusks in a Lisbon lagoon are developing male characteristics apparently caused by pollution." *The Gazette*, January 16, 1999, J8. See also "Canadian study ties birth defect to solvents," *Reuters/Yahoo News*, March 24, 1999.

8. For a comprehensive, easy-to-read and -understand list of the toxic ingredients in most commercial household cleaning products, as well as for easy to use, inexpensive, benign alternatives, see Logan, Karen, *Clean House, Clean Planet*, Pocket Books/Simon and Schuster, New York, 1997.

9. Colborn et al., *Our Stolen Future*.

10. See Swann, S. H., E. P. Elkin, and L. Fenster, "Have sperm densities declined? A reanalysis of global trend data," *Environmental Health Perspectives* 105: 1228–1232; and also "Big fall in sperm counts revealed in UK," *NewScientist.com News Service*, January 5, 2004. June 10, 2004. Available from www.newscientist.com/news/print.jsp?id=ns99994529.

11. "Chemical Obesity," *Environmental Health Perspectives* 112(6), May 2004 (online).

12. The meeting also considered other environmental factors in causing obesity, and the meeting presentations are available online at www.niehs.nih.gov/multimedia/qt/dert/obesity/agenda.htm.

13. Commission on Life Sciences (CLS), *Hormonally Active Agents in the Environment*, National Academies Press, 1999, p. 188.

14. Ibid.

15. "Thyroid function, PCBs, and brain damage." June 10, 2004. Available from www.foxriverwatch.com/thyroid_humans_PCBs_1.html.

16. Colborn et al., *Our Stolen Future*.

17. Leavitt, Kathryn Perrotti, "Hormones in our food," *CHEC's Health-House*. June 1, 2004. Available from www.google.ca/search?q=cache:J8VMXLPOnyOJ:www.checnet.org/healthhouse/education/articles-detail.asp%3FMain_ID%3D127+european+union+veterinary+measures+risk+of+cancer&hl=en.

18. National Institute of Environmental Health Sciences, *New Federal Report on Carcinogens Lists Estrogen Therapy, Ultraviolet, Wood Dust*, December 11, 2002. June 10, 2004. Available from www.niehs.nig.gov/oc/news/10thre.htm.

19. Stemming from a set of very different cultural pressures and a different branch of pharmaceutical production, ingested and injected hormones such as anabolic steroids and testosterone have also become a health hazard to young people, largely but not only teenaged boys. In the mid 1990s, 1,084,000 Americans (0.5 percent of the population) admitted to having used anabolic steroids, and that rate was double for the

eighteen-to-thirty-four age group. There is good impressionistic evidence to suggest that such use has increased, not decreased, as these drugs have moved progressively from the high-performance sports arena to the local gym. Whereas women take these drugs to increase athletic performance only, more and more teenaged boys and young men take them for cosmetic purposes as well. Possession of anabolic steroids and prescription testosterone is illegal for non-medical uses, but there is a thriving black market and clearly a steady supply made by companies who are well aware of the illicit use to which their products are being put. Anabolic steroids function to increase muscle mass and help rapid recovery from training in the short run. Testosterone, now common in the treatment of AIDS patients, helps to resist muscle withering and boost energy. But the long-term effects of abuse of these hormones are often shrunken testicles, reduced sperm count, impotence, baldness, development of breasts in men (and hirsutism and deepening of the voice in women), difficulty or pain in urinating, and an enlarged prostate.

20. Brettman, Allan, and Cole, Michelle. "Beefing up its local appeal," *The Oregonian*, February 22, 2004. April 10, 2004. Available from www. thefoodalliance.org/Oregonian2.22.04.htm.

21. "Controlling hospital infection," *BBCNews*, January 21, 2002. May 10, 2004. Available from news.bbc.co.uk/l/hi/health/1773721.stm.

22. "New survey shows one-third of Americans use antibiotics inappropriately," *PRNewswire*, November 21, 2002. June 10, 2004. Available from www.elekta.com/controlcenter.nsf/va_LookupResources/ newsfeedToday/$file/00070014.htm. In the UK deaths from certain resistant germs are up from 51 in 1993 to 800 in 2002: "Superbugs MRSA (methicillin-resistant staphylococcus) deaths up 1400 percent in a decade," *Medical News Today*, February 26, 2004. June 6, 2004. Available from www. medicalnewstoday.com/index.php?newsid=6167.

23. Kauffman, Marc. "WHO urges end to use of antibiotics for animals' growth." *Washington Post*, August 13, 2003. May 10, 2004. Available from www.washingtonpost.com/ac2/wp-dyn?pagename=article&node=&co ntentID=A51996-2003Aug12&notFound=true.

24. Dalgard, Christine, et al. "Mercury in the umbilical cord: implications for risk assessment for Minamata disease." *Environmental Health Perspectives*. June–July 1994, June 10, 2004. Available from ehp.hiehs.nig. gov/members/1994/102-6-7/dalgard-full.html. See also Natural Resources Council of Maine, *Taking on Toxics in Maine, a Guide to Eliminating Mercury in Maine*. April 14, 2004. Available from www.maineenvironment.org/toxics/Mercury_Brochure_Menace.htm.

25. Bender, Michael T. "FDA tests show mercury in white tuna 3 times higher than can light, says mercury policy project," *U.S. Newswire*, September 12, 2003. June 10, 2004. Available from releases.usnewswire.com/ GetRelease.asp?id=120-12092003; "Is the government too lax in advice on

tuna consumption?" *ConsumerReports.org.* June 10, 2004. Available from www.consumerreports.org/main/detailv4.jsp?CONTENT%3c%3.

26. University of Tennessee Center for Clean Products and Clean Technologies: Ecology Center, *Toxics in Vehicles: Mercury,* January 2001. June 10, 2004. Available from www.cleancarcampaign.org/pdfs/toxicinvehicles_mercury.pdf.

27. We have not included opposing views in this article, but couldn't resist this one. The Cato Institute's Steven Milloy published a piece in January 2004 that cited a study done in the Seychelles Islands. According to Milloy, the study contained "a surprising finding in the results of the examination of children at 66 months of age . . . several [intelligence] tests scores improved as either pre- or postnatal mercury levels increased." Surprise. Mercury is good for you!

28. For the full report on the threat to rational scientific inquiry in the United States, see Union of Concerned Scientists, *Scientific Integrity in Policymaking: An Investigation into the Bush Administration's Misuse of Science,* March 2004. June 10, 2004. Available from www.ucsusa.org/global_environmental/rsi/page.cfm?pageID=1322.

29. "California sues five grocers over mercury warnings," *Reuters/Yahoo Science Wire,* Friday, January 17, 2003. In Sacramento, CA, the state attorney general filed suit against five grocery chains including supermarket giants Kroger Co. and Albertson's Inc. for failing to properly warn consumers about the risk of mercury in fish. Attorney General Bill Lockyer's lawsuit in state court seeks to force the grocers, who also include Safeway Inc., Whole Foods Inc., and Trader Joe's, to warn customers that tuna, swordfish, and shark sold in their markets contain the metallic element linked to cancer and birth defects. Lockyer alleges the markets have violated Proposition 65, a California ballot initiative approved in 1986 that requires businesses to provide "clear and reasonable" warnings before exposing people to known carcinogens and reproductive toxins. "Public health agencies have advised pregnant women not to eat swordfish and shark because those fish contain relatively high levels of mercury," the attorney-general said, explaining the reasoning behind the suit.

30. Lopes, Marilyn. *Lead Exposure in the Home,* National Network for Child Care. June 10, 2004. Available from www.nncc.org/Health/lead.home.html.

31. Nakamjure, David, "Water in D.C. Exceeds EPA Lead Limit," *Washington Post,* January 31, 2004, page A01. Available from www.washingtonpost.com/wp-dyn/articles/A64766-2004Jan30.html.

32. Cathy Vaskill of the Family Medicine Centre at Queen's University in Kingston and one of the authors of the Ontario College of Family Physicians report cited above, noted that the pesticides used in Toronto's 200,000 storm sewers to kill mosquito larvae emit a product as they break down that is a retinoid, a family of chemicals known to cause limb deformities in fetuses. That chemical then washes into Lake Ontario and in turn into the drinking water of the greater Toronto area.

33. In February 2004, the Union of Concerned Scientists summed up the situation as follows: "There is a well-established pattern of suppression and distortion of scientific findings by high-ranking Bush administration political appointees across numerous federal agencies. These actions have consequences for human health, public safety, and community well-being. [Cited] incidents involve air pollutants, heat-trapping emissions, reproductive health, drug resistant bacteria, endangered species, forest health, and military intelligence. There is strong documentation of a wide-ranging effort to manipulate the government's scientific advisory system to prevent the appearance of advice that might run counter to the administration's political agenda. These actions include: appointing underqualified individuals to important advisory roles including childhood lead poisoning prevention and reproductive health; applying political litmus tests that have no bearing on a nominee's expertise or advisory role; appointing a non-scientist to a senior position in the president's scientific advisory staff; and dismissing highly qualified scientific advisors. There is evidence that the administration often imposes restrictions on what government scientists can say or write about "sensitive" topics. In this context, sensitive applies to issues that might provoke opposition from the administration's political and ideological supporters. There is significant evidence that the scope and scale of the manipulation, suppression, and misrepresentation of science by the Bush administration is unprecedented." *Scientific Integrity in Policymaking: An Investigation into the Bush Administration's Misuse of Science*, Union of Concerned Scientists, February 2004, Cambridge, MA.

34. *The Corporation*, a film directed by Mark Akbar, Jennifer Abbot, and Joel Bakan, released February 2004; and Bakan, Joel, *The Corporation*, Penguin Canada, 2004.

35. "Policies relevant to fundamental causes of disease form a major part of the national agenda, whether this involves the minimum wage, housing for homeless people, capital-gains taxes, parenting leave, head start programs, or other initiatives of this type. Such policy initiatives often lie outside the realm of influence and expertise of health policy experts. Yet if fundamental causes are potent determinants of the disease, the potential health impact of these broad policies needs to be thoroughly understood," said Bruce G. Link and Jo Phelan in "Social Conditions as Fundamental Causes of Disease," *Journal of Health and Social Behaviour*, extra issues, 1995, pp. 80–84. These crucial points are all the more true with respect to environmental issues.

9

"No Child Left": What Are Schools for in a Democratic Society?

Peter Sacks

In recent years, policymakers have been engaged in a massive and unprecedented social experiment on American schoolchildren. This experiment in public school accountability was launched upon the implausible notion that learning and teaching could be precisely and unambiguously measured with standardized tests, and that such tests would prod children and schools to perform their best. The costs of this experiment have been staggering, not only in terms of the taxpayer outlays to support these new huge testing and accountability bureaucracies, but also in terms of what we lose as a democratic society. What are we giving up as a nation for the sake of this exceedingly narrow definition of school accountability and academic success?

Americans are relinquishing democratic control over their public schools to a new generation of rather cynical politicians and technocrats who have defined education in the most self-serving and narrow of terms. The wizards of the accountability machine have fostered the dubious proposition that technological fixes alone, with more standards, more standardized tests, and harsher sanctions attached to these tests will fuel lasting gains in academic achievement for all children and lead to a more prosperous and productive citizenry.

The grand experiment on American schools and schoolchildren has transformed the very meaning of what it is to be an educated person in our society. Yet, hardly a word is uttered in the public sphere about the implications of this experiment on the nature and purpose of public schools in a democratic society.

What are schools for? Do schools exist to train "products" to be used as "inputs" for the exclusive use and benefit of private enterprise, as many policymakers and business leaders would have Americans believe? Or, could I dare to propose that the overarching purpose of our schools is to awaken and nurture young minds to a love of learning that lasts a lifetime, and help young people take that love of learning wherever it might lead them in a free and open society?

I recall my high school English teacher, Mr. Robert Kohn, at a Seattle-area high school I attended in the early 1970s. Mr. Kohn taught from virtually no syllabus. The state required him to teach no standard curriculum. Certainly, neither he nor his bosses were required to have students sit for a standardized test to determine whether we were competent in English or whether Mr. Kohn was a good teacher. He gave me books to read. He suggested I think about the books; and he asked me to write about what I thought. Mr. Kohn gave me room to think, to flounder, and to take creative risks. Frankly, I can't imagine learning *anything* worthwhile or memorable had Mr. Kohn been forced by the state to teach me the junk knowledge and junk facts necessary for me to pass some state-mandated, standardized exam. I can't imagine great teachers like Mr. Kohn even wanting to teach in the mechanistic, test-driven schools that students encounter these days.

There's a certain Wizard of Oz quality to the new approaches to education reform, which are so heavily reliant on testing and measurement of children and the surveillance and control of public schools—all enforced by the state under the guise of supposed fairness, equity, and scientific validity. The show is impressive. It's got all the bells and whistles and the blustery rhetoric about "world class" standards, leaving no child behind, and removing kids "trapped in failing schools." But when you look behind the curtain, you see that it's all show. The accountability wizard has no clothes. Americans, it would seem, can be a bit pliable when it comes to the showy quick fix, the technological magic bullet. Politicians understand this, and they've exploited these tendencies in their new approaches to school reform. Americans have permitted these wizards to get away with the foolish proposition that educational outcomes can be precisely measured, without the slightest ambiguity, much like a firm's profit and loss statement.

Indeed, Americans have been suckered into a foolish game, in which teachers and schools aim all instruction to the content of overly simplistic and artificial standardized tests. The public has been lured into believing that such a game is the same as genuine teaching and learning.

"TRAPPED IN FAILING SCHOOLS"

The most recent iteration of government pushing standardized mental tests to sort schoolchildren and measure schools is the federal No Child Left Behind Act. Congress, Democrats included, overwhelmingly approved President George W. Bush's education agenda in 2001, imposing unprecedented testing and school accountability mandates to be enforced by the budgetary and rule-making power of the federal government. Surely, No Child Left Behind (NCLB), as it has been euphemistically labeled by federal authorities, is among the most sweeping federal interventions in the nation's classrooms in recent history.

On top of the states' existing blizzard of testing and accountability measures, such as the increasingly widespread high school graduation exit exams, the NCLB law requires states to impose annual testing of all schoolchildren from grades three through eight, in both reading and math, in order for schools serving low-income students to qualify for federal assistance. Schools that fail to meet annual growth targets for test scores are embroidered with the proverbial scarlet A, branding them "failing schools." Parents of children "trapped in failing schools" are invited to transfer their children to supposedly better schools, which of course are the ones with more impressive performance on state-issued exams.

Whether a school is a good school or a bad school is pretty much a question of black and white for President Bush, as evidenced during his visit to the Read-Patillo Elementary School in Florida to push NCLB. The president, while touting Florida's school rating system, which assigns letter grades to schools based on test performance, described the Read-Patillo school this way:

> This school increased its rating from a C in 1998 on the Florida testing to an A. And that's important for parents to know. And that's an important fact for teachers to know, and your principal to know. It's a fact—an important fact for the school board members to know. It's an important fact for the community to know. It must make you feel proud to know you've got a school which has defied the so-called odds, and now you're an A. It's important to know you've got an

A in your midst. It's also important to know whether your school is not an A. It gives you a chance to ask the question, wait a minute. There's one school in Volusia County I know is an A, how come ours isn't an A? It's important to be in a position where you're able to say, it matters how we rank, because no child should be left behind.[1]

Of course, based on these unassailable "facts," countless schools in Mr. Bush's scheme will be labeled failures, subject to all manner of federal sanctions and interventions. The president seemed undisturbed by the Orwellian doublespeak when he also said during his visit, "I'm a big advocate of local control of schools."[2]

Since NCLB was enacted, the train wreck predicted by many scholars and critics of the law has come to pass. The way the law is working out is the predictable result of a scheme conceived from the political and economic motivations of a few rather than the desire to truly improve opportunities for all children to learn.

Consider the NCLB's mandate of so-called "Annual Yearly Progress." The law requires that, starting from a baseline year of 2001–2002, all schools receiving federal Title I money for poor children must move 100 percent of their students into a so-called "proficient" category in reading and math by the year 2014. Accordingly, schools must meet annual growth targets for test scores, not just as a whole, but also for different ethnic subgroups. All of this is to be measured according to a state's test of choice with the approval of the federal government.

In the overly simplistic world of political rhetoric, the NCLB scheme for rating, rewarding, and punishing schools sounds reasonable. According to the tests, a school can be easily identified as an A or B or C school, as either a success or failure, and the public is better off for knowing these "facts," as Mr. Bush claimed. Unfortunately, reality has proven that the NCLB law is so technically onerous and ill-conceived that states have found it impossible to comply unless they cheat or fudge their numbers, borrowing the creative accounting techniques of Enron and WorldCom. Nevertheless, the law's proponents insist that the tests will tell parents, taxpayers, and policymakers virtually all they need to know about teacher performance, the leadership skills of principals, and the educational achievements of schoolchildren.

But Bush's reductionistic approach to school improvement is littered with minefields, and the president fell into his own trap when he visited Vandenburg Elementary School in Southfield,

Michigan, to promote NCLB. According to *NEA Today*, Bush said, "This is a successful school. ... This school doesn't quit on kids, and that's why it's heralded for its excellence." But, not long afterwards, that same wonderful school showed up on Michigan's watch list for low-performing schools, as indicated by its relatively poor standardized test performance.[3]

Indeed, when the federal government says "annual yearly progress," it means it quite literally. If a school like Vandenburg fails to meet test-score targets two years running, it then becomes subject to an escalating series of sanctions that are a delight to the Bush Administration's neoconservative supporters, including everything from school-choice programs, subcontracting for services, replacing staff and administrators, mandating new curricula, state takeover, and installing private managers of public schools.

Most politicians and business leaders who support such test-driven approaches to school improvement rarely talk about the arcane technical details of standardized testing, nor will most news organizations endeavor to explain these details to their readerships. But, the fact is, the testing technology that policymakers are relying on to make these most serious judgments about schools simply isn't that good. A recent report by the Center on Education Policy (CEP) summed up the dirty little secret of high-stakes testing policy, which many scholars and testing experts have known from the start of the high-stakes testing movement. "The state of the art in testing is not yet reliable or consistent enough for year to year changes in scores to always be an accurate reflection of progress," according to the CEP. "Studies suggest that as much as 70 percent of the year-to-year fluctuations are due to outside factors" that are beyond the ability of schools themselves to even manage.[4]

For a number of reasons related to the technical quality of the tests themselves, learning gains at a given school may not be reflected in the test scores, resulting in scores of good schools like Vandenburg falling through the cracks. Worse, these measurement errors become increasingly larger going from aggregate state scores down to the school level, where the school performance data can get skewed by a whole host of extraneous factors that have nothing to do with teaching and learning. Due to this intrinsic volatility of test scores from year to year, a "substantial number of schools will be incorrectly identified as needing improvement" under the NCLB rules, according to scholars at the National Center for Research on Evaluation, Standards, and Testing (CRESST) at the University of California–Los Angeles.[5]

Consider, too, the meaning of *proficient*. Like Alice in Wonderland, the word means whatever different states want it to mean. In Texas, according to CRESST's research, the standard for math or reading proficiency is considerably less stringent than in say, Maryland, where very recently, only 30 percent of students scored at or above the proficient level on the state's test. Under Texas's more modest standards, schools are indeed on track to meet the annual yearly progress goals of 100 percent proficiency by 2014, according to CRESST. Yet, Maryland actually had the better-performing students when measured by the highly regarded National Assessment of Educational Progress (NAEP).[6]

Furthermore, the NCLB law will treat schools differently depending on whether they serve wealthy or poor communities. Consider the following example of two schools, each required to meet the intermediate goal of 50 percent proficiency in reading and math by the year 2003. School A in inner-city Los Angeles started from a 2001–2002 baseline of 30 percent proficiency; thus it was required to quickly accelerate by adding twenty percentile points over two years to meet the 50 percent proficiency target. But School B in Beverly Hills, which *started* at a baseline of 75 percent proficiency, could have actually suffered *declines* in its percentage of math and reading proficiency and still met the state's intermediate targets under NCLB. According to testing expert Robert Linn, "The NCLB adequate yearly progress requirements represent enormous, if not overwhelming, challenges to schools, districts, and states."[7]

What is the moral of this story? To meet federal muster, a state might well decide to dumb down its standards. In the end, the NCLB law will treat different schools and schoolchildren differently, depending on how the state one happens to live in defines "proficiency" and how rich they are.

SAME AS IT EVER WAS

The new breed of high-stakes testing enterprises, embodied in NCLB and state accountability testing, promises to further stratify an already deeply divided nation along race, class, and ethnic lines, rewarding affluence and privilege while punishing poor, working-class, and minority children. Throughout the nation's history of high-stakes educational testing, the losers have always been children of the poor, the working class, and the undereducated. Government-mandated use of these mental tests has always served to exclude, erect barriers, and protect the privileges of the few. Recall the U.S.

government's use of IQ tests to sort World War I army recruits. The testing experts of the time, such as Carl Brigham, who would go on to invent the Scholastic Aptitude Test (SAT), told us that recent immigrants such as Jews, Italians, and Poles were feeble-minded "idiots"[8] and how very "scientific" and "objective" was this Darwinian competition. If one were a social engineer intent on creating the perfect inequality machine, then these new test-based accountability systems would be that socially engineered marvel one would invent.

Consider who passes state "exit" exams, now required for a high school diploma in more than half the states. Consider who fails, who drops out, and who gets prematurely shoved out of school as a result of these new barriers. Failure rates on the exit exams as well as dropout rates are horrific for some minority groups. Texas is especially noteworthy because its approach to school reform was the model for President Bush's No Child Left Behind Law. In fact, that state's early adventures with high-stakes testing had been dubbed the "Texas Miracle," an allusion to how the state's newly adopted school reform and accountability system in the early 1990s supposedly sparked a surge in student achievement and narrowed performance gaps between whites and minorities.

The Houston school district, where education secretary Rod Paige had been superintendent, was considered one of the big stars of the Texas Miracle. But a recent *New York Times* investigation showed that Houston schools had a big-time Enron problem of their own with their phony accounting of student dropouts. In order to make its test scores and dropout rates look better than they were, officials simply got rid of students who were likely to fail the state's exit exam. While Houston schools were reporting an official dropout rate of just 1.5 percent, a state audit found that an additional 5,500 students had been forced out of school in one year when they should have been counted as dropouts.[9]

It gets worse. In one of the most comprehensive studies to date measuring the extent to which states' so-called accountability programs have pushed kids out of school, Walt Haney and his colleagues at Boston College have looked at what happens to students in the critical period between ninth grade and high school graduation. The researchers discovered that hundreds of thousands of students have, in essence, disappeared from public schools, most likely the result of states' imposition of high school exit exams. For example, in 1987 in South Carolina, 65 percent of ninth graders went on to graduate from high school. But by the year 2000 with its graduation exam fully in place, just 51 percent of ninth graders made it to graduation. In New York, also among the worst states on this measure, 66 percent of ninth graders went on to graduate in the late 1980s, prior to the state's regents exams being required for all students. But more recently, just 58 percent of New York ninth graders made it to graduation. Across the nation, some 444,000 ninth graders—about 11 percent of all ninth graders—left school before reaching the tenth grade—an attrition rate that is more than double what it had been in the mid-1980s.[10] "It appears that the pressures of high-stakes tests are generating educational strategies that deform, rather than reform the system for the customers of our public education system—the children," says Haney.[11]

After nearly two decades of such "reforms" at the state level following the 1983 diatribe against America's schools known as *A Nation at Risk*, the evidence seems overwhelming that the accountability movement, particularly the No Child Left Behind Act, has at best been counterproductive to the aims of education, and at worst a cynical ploy to privatize a large segment of the nation's public schools by setting up schools as expensive failures.

In Maine, for example, officials have estimated that by the ninth year in the annual yearly progress tabulation under NCLB, 100 percent of Maine schools will be labeled as failing. Maine Education Association President Rob Walker said recently, "In the Lewiston Middle School where I teach, there are ten severely disabled students who are non-readers. We can give them the Maine Educational Assessment test for eighth graders and include their grades with the other 103 students and watch our average test score plummet to failing levels, or we can humanely excuse them and fail for not having 95 percent of the students taking the test." He adds, "This clearly is an attempt to set up so many unrealistic standards for student performance that we cannot meet them. And, once a school fails it is subject to sanctions that divert funding and control from the public to the private sector."[12]

Indeed, the National Conference of State Legislatures estimates that 70 percent of all schools in the country will be labeled failing under the NCLB law. The American Association of School Administrators is even more pessimistic. Says the organization's public policy director: "If states follow the strict letter of the law, every school in the country will be considered 'low-performing' within five years."[13]

The dominant message most Americans hear on a daily basis is that our schools are in a perpetual state of near-calamity. But even more fundamentally, the prevailing zeitgeist is driven by an antigovernment, free-market ideology holding that government enterprises do nothing that supposed "free markets" cannot do better. Like an Orwellian political propaganda machine, some very powerful institutions, influential politicians and think tanks, and the immense authority of the office of the U.S. president have fostered the view that our education system is broken and that free-market solutions to the school "crisis" will be the magic-bullet solution. The "debate"—if you can call it that—has been so rendered that one is either for high standards or against them. One is either for high achievement for all or instead for mediocrity and injustice.

Nowadays, policymakers will tell you with a straight face that more tests and sharper sanctions attached to those tests will actually benefit the very poor, working class, and minority children who have historically been most seriously harmed by such methods. Thus, the accountability wizards have quite cleverly diverted public attention from the root causes of educational inequality, which stem from a gaping divide between haves and have-nots in American society.

CLASS RULES

Not so long ago, the nation's perspective on these questions was far different than now. Amid the idealism of the 1960s, both scholars and leaders recognized the overwhelming importance of social class regarding questions of educational equality, and the nation seemed poised to take an entirely different path from the one we have taken.

Consider the 1966 Coleman Report, *Equality of Educational Opportunity*, the far-reaching study Congress had called for in the 1964 Civil Rights Act, headed by the prominent sociologist James S. Coleman. In a subsequent follow-up to the study by a Harvard faculty study group, Daniel P. Moynihan and Frederick Mosteller described the Coleman Report as "the most powerful empirical critique of the myths (the unquestioned assumptions, the socially received beliefs) of American education ever produced."[14]

The Coleman Report's startling finding was that schoolchildren's social and economic standing—the stuff they bring to school—trumped just about all else in accounting for their educational achievements and prospects. The unavoidable policy implication, equally radical, was that good schools could go only so far in raising the achievement levels of disadvantaged black children, and that attacking the problem with policies that improved the social and economic conditions of individuals and families would be more effective than policies that targeted only schools.

In one way or another, that basic finding has been re-discovered and reiterated in the literature ever since. In his re-analysis of the Coleman data—as part of the Harvard faculty reassessment published in 1972—the sociologist Christopher Jencks noted, "In the short run it remains true that our most pressing political problem is the achievement gap between Harlem and Scarsdale. But in the long run it seems our primary problem is not the disparity between Harlem and Scarsdale but the disparity between the top and the bottom of the class in both Harlem and Scarsdale."[15]

Nearly thirty years later, as reported in *The Black-White Test Score Gap*, edited by Jencks and Meredith Phillips, the authors concluded that fully two thirds of the school achievement gap between whites and blacks could be explained when the researchers accounted for the full range of social and economic conditions of individuals. These included the intergenerational resources that grandparents pass on to heirs—social and economic capital that goes beyond the more conventional measures defined strictly by parent education and income.[16]

Time and time again, the research establishes similar patterns, and virtually all of it has been ignored by the most recent generation of policymakers. Instead of a policy agenda driven by the implications of the Coleman Report and subsequent findings that have continued to confirm the centrality of family poverty, parent education levels, and other factors related to one's social and economic class, Americans instead got *A Nation at Risk*, that "other" government report published in 1983.[17]

Risk, it now seems apparent in retrospect, buried the Coleman Report once and for all. It firmly entrenched the notion among state and federal policymakers, conservatives and liberals, from Bush I through Bush II, that targeting schools and sanctioning the ones that don't perform up to par on standardized tests, rather than helping families and individuals improve their social and economic conditions, was to be the focus of virtually all educational policymaking henceforth.

Instead of addressing root causes, policymakers in the last generation have discovered the political expediency of waging ideological war on easy targets such as teachers, schools, and even children themselves. But how much can schools alone really accomplish? According to the Donahue Institute at the University of

Massachusetts, just six economic and social variables, including family income, poverty rate, and educational attainment of parents, accounted for fully 85 percent of the variance in test scores among that state's school districts. This means that teachers, administrators, staffing levels, and all other factors that go into the mix of school quality explained no more than 15 percent of the differences in school test scores at the district level.[18]

Are there exceptions to this? Proponents of free-market solutions to school improvement would maintain that there are so many exceptions to the overwhelming forces of economics and social class that such exceptions turn "conventional wisdom" on its head. Indeed, "No excuses" is their marketing slogan. But, time and again, upon closer scrutiny, these exceptions turn out to be no more than short-term spikes in test scores, deviating only temporarily from long-term averages—attributable to the far more fundamental factors of poverty and class.[19]

Still, Bush's NCLB law and the new approaches to school "reform" insist that educational outcomes are the entire responsibility of the schools. There is virtually no recognition of the differences, for example, between two children entering kindergarten—one who comes in knowing her letters and numbers and the other who doesn't know how to properly hold a book. Let me be clear: that non-school factors account for much of the differences in school test scores is not to suggest that all children cannot learn or that good schools and good teachers do not make a huge difference in children's lives and their educational achievements. But the propaganda machine's official failure to even recognize the underlying inequities is simply foolish public policy, and it allows us Americans to stick our collective heads in the sand.

THE CORPORATE MODEL OF SCHOOLS

Meanwhile, the agenda-setters have persuaded the public that public schools have little value but to serve corporate interests and to model their operations after corporate enterprises. The entire scheme is erected upon a pie-in-the-sky proposition: turning public education into a pseudo-marketplace in which schools compete on the basis of test scores for their "customers" (i.e., parents and their children) will improve educational quality across the board.

The prevailing policy tools presume school improvement is limited only by the degree to which policymakers can bribe or punish schools and children on the basis of their performance on standardized tests. Teachers, principals, and even parents who dare question these suppositions are treated as irresponsible citizens who are willing to give up on underachieving children by going soft on high standards for all.

Under the corporate model of education, schools are businesses and children are "products," who are trained to serve the labor needs of American industry. At an alarming rate, the teaching force is being de-skilled, as teachers are transformed from professional practitioners to mere cogs of state and federal education agencies—regulatory bodies that define good teaching as repetitive and mindless drills aimed at raising test scores. Children in this corporate vision of public education are to be measured, sorted, and processed on the basis of standardized test results. Do schools scraping for every available penny have much choice? For example, the J. A. and Kathryn Albertson Foundation, the philanthropic arm of a giant supermarket chain, says it will hand out "cash awards" to financially strapped schools in Idaho based on improvements in standardized test scores.[20] The Albertson Foundation finds itself in good corporate company. Joel I. Klein, the former Bertelsmann, Inc. CEO and now chancellor of the New York City schools, wants to give hefty bonuses to superintendents of up to $40,000 a year largely on the basis of standardized test performance. The way Klein talks about the proposal, it seems as if he had little choice owing to the widely accepted rules of the free market. "It's the way most systems of accountability and reward work in America," he told a *New York Times* reporter.[21]

To the economist or CEO, nothing could be simpler than to reward and punish superintendents and teachers on the basis of simple productivity measures, like test scores. But the lessons of the recent research literature on the effects of high-stakes testing in schools are quite clear, and they should give pause to policymakers when contemplating these test-laden incentive systems.

Schools operating in high-stakes environments sometimes can rapidly engineer impressive gains in test scores by installing intensive test-preparation programs narrowly focused on drilling for a specific exam, and children end up being the real losers of such gaming strategies. Among the unintended consequences of these narrowly focused test-prep programs is that test score gains don't transfer into real and lasting learning, because the test-specific gains typically cannot be detected in other assessments of achievement.

Teaching is turned into practice tests, worksheets, short-term recall, and regurgitation of isolated, atomistic facts—and damn all else that might be interesting and engaging for young minds. Forget art, forget in-depth work on projects, forget learning to apply all those facts to real world problems. Forget anything that won't be on the test and can't be formatted in terms of a standardized test item. Often, test scores will go up, sometimes by staggering amounts in short periods of time. But we have to ask, what do the gains really mean when the results are so distorted by teaching to test schemes and other forms of brinksmanship?

In the not-too-distant past, most educators and administrators deplored the practice of teaching to tests and excessive test coaching because such methods were antithetical to the notion of genuine learning for understanding. Many of our best educators still deplore the practice. But teaching to tests is not just encouraged, it's institutionalized: students at schools that underperform on the standardized tests are targeted for even more intensive test-preparation and coaching, as a matter of law in many states. Thus, as in Houston, school systems forced to operate in these high-stakes environments often have an "Enron" problem, cooking the books to make their standardized test performance look better than it actually is.

The scientific evidence calling into question the efficacy of high-stakes testing on student learning runs headlong into the entrenched belief among many politicians that test scores are some absolute and infallible measure of student performance, like measuring temperature or height. But, in fact, test scores are rather imprecise measures, plagued by statistical noise that creates the illusion of performance gains or declines.

When test scores go up from year to year, we have to ask what factors contributed how much to the various changes. How much of the yearly change is due to persistent social and economic factors, like parent wealth and education? How much of the change is due to measurement errors that are inherent in standardized tests, or due to simple variation in the sample of students tested from year to year? In essence, we want to know how much any given improvement in test scores can actually be attributed to teachers and schools. Otherwise, we're flying completely blind when it comes to knowing what is working and what is not working to help children learn better.

What is the real impact of imposing high-stakes tests on student achievement, after filtering out the statistical and extraneous noise? The evidence can't be very comforting for the proponents of these exams. For example, a national study by a University of Chicago researcher found that high school graduation exams had essentially no effect on student math and reading achievement in twelfth grade.[22] That result was bolstered by a researcher at Washington State University looking at that state's high-stakes test known as the WASL (Washington Assessment of Student Learning). In fact, the study found that, despite the considerable expenditure of taxpayer resources, WASL had no detectable effect on yearly changes in student achievement. "The experience in the state of Washington apparently shows that setting [annual yearly progress targets] may not only be an assessment fallacy, but a gross misapplication of adapting the banking practice of applying compound interest calculations to human cognition," writes the study's author, Donald C. Orlich. "Is education reform anything you can get away with?"[23]

What is more, a recent study completed at the University of Arizona looked at gains on a given state exam and compared the apparent gains against other independent measures of academic achievement, such as the SAT, ACT, and the NAEP. They found that the gains on the state exams could not be independently verified, leading the study's authors to conclude that the state gains were at best illusory and at worst phony, the result of excessive teaching-to-test schemes. The authors conclude,

> High-stakes testing policies are not now and may never be policies that will accomplish what they intend. Could the hundreds of millions of dollars and the billions of person hours spent in these programs be used more wisely? Furthermore, if failure in attaining the goals for which the policy was created results in disproportionate negative effects on the life chances of America's poor and minority students, as it appears to do, then a high-stakes testing policy is more than a benign error in political judgment.[24]

"THE AIMS OF EDUCATION"

When endless amounts of measurement, surveillance, officially sanctioned bribery and punishments, and other tools of the modern school accountability movement rule public education, lots of people "win." Some get their bonus checks, or at least keep their jobs. Politicians trot out their dog and pony shows dramatizing big turnarounds at even the poorest schools, and they take the credit for their courage and commitment to so-called "world class" standards.

That is, everyone wins except schoolchildren themselves, who wind up as pawns in a political game and as guinea pigs in a grand social experiment. The children who lose the most are always the poor, the working class, the blacks, the Hispanics, and recent immigrants. They are the perennial poor performers, whose schools are constantly bombarded with the threat of seizure by the state. Meanwhile, the children of the affluent, as always, are treated to the most enriched learning experiences, immune from the crisis mentality that pervades schools for the unprivileged.

Ultimately, this cult of measurement, the imposition of standardized knowledge by the state, and the standardized means of measuring knowledge also enforced by the state, pose a grave threat to democratic values in America. In post-millennium America, the very idea of teaching and schooling as a human-centered, humanistic endeavor is being expunged from our collective language.

We ought to be concerned when educational bureaucracies, through high-stakes testing enterprises, are setting the terms and definitions of knowledge itself. What is knowledge? Who defines it? Who is allowed to go outside the officially permitted boundaries of that predetermined knowledge established by state or even federal authorities? The prevailing systems of school accountability promote closed-ended learning and knowledge systems; in fact, these outcomes are mandated: nothing is considered worthwhile to learn unless the state has approved it worthy. If certain knowledge, however valuable for the real world, isn't on the test or easily formatted as a multiple-choice test item, then it is deemed not worthy to teach and not worthy to learn.

Americans should be concerned about the tendency of these high-stakes accountability systems to quash individual expression, points of view, creativity, open-ended inquiry, and different modes of thinking that don't easily fit into to a standardized box. What happens to a free society when the adult world informs a whole generation of young people that, in no uncertain terms, learning, genuine accomplishment, and test performance are deemed to be one and the same? Is this the stuff of a free society, one that fosters creativity, independence, critical inquiry, and the joy of discovery? Or is it the stuff of a regimented society? Are we unwittingly creating a generation of young people who will grow up to be standard-issue students, standard-issue consumers, and standard-issue workers?

A little book called *The Aims of Education*, published in 1929 by the esteemed mathematician Alfred North Whitehead, ought to be required reading for the modern accountability wizards. What would Whitehead have made of these standardized, bureaucracy-laden accountability systems that are supposed to demonstrate whether children are learning or not? I think he would be appalled. In his lead essay, Whitehead targets what he calls "inert" ideas and the tendency of educational institutions to define success in terms of the degree to which they force-feed inert ideas to students as passive receptacles of information. He is the enemy of boredom and rote, the imparting of atomistic facts without broader appreciation for the whole. He is the enemy of superficiality, the teaching of too many subjects, none in sufficient depth for a learner's deeper understanding.

Back to my initial question. What are schools for anyway? Whitehead answers it this way: "There is only one subject-matter for education, and that is Life in all its manifestations. Instead of a single unity, we offer children—algebra, from which nothing follows; science, from which nothing follows; history, from which nothing follows; a couple of languages, never mastered; and most dreary of all, Literature, represented by plays of Shakespeare, with philological notes and short analysis of plot and character to be in substance committed to memory." Whitehead's stated purpose is none other than to "eradicate the fatal disconnection of subjects which kills the vitality of our modern curriculum." As for what Whitehead calls the "common external examination system," he says such testing is "fatal" to the aims of education. "We do not denounce it because we are cranks, and like denouncing established things," he writes. "We are not so childish. ... The reason is that we are dealing with human minds, and not with dead matter."[25]

Those words seem so simple and true, and yet so far from our present reality. Perhaps, unfortunately, Americans have gotten the education system and the school reform they deserve. Perhaps the cult of measurement and the politicization of schools through endless testing and endless bureaucratic meddling is the perfect system for a largely apathetic public that pays a lot of lip service to the value of schools and education, but oftentimes seems more engaged in Bachelorettes and Apprentices.

In the end, the only way to see the Wizard for what he is is to look behind the curtain.

NOTES

1. Bush, George W. (2002, Oct. 17). Remarks by the president on education, Read-Patillo Elementary School, New Smyrna Beach, Fla. Retrieved May 10, 2004 at www.whitehouse.gov/news/releases/2002/10/print/20021017-5.html.

2. Ibid.

3. Jehlen, Alain. (March 2003). "High Stakes Questions," *NEA Today*, pp. 8–11.

4. Stark, D., Rentner, N. C., Fagan, T., Gayler, K., Hamilton, M., Jennings, J., et al. (January 3, 2003). *From the Capital to the Classroom*. Center on Education Policy. Retrieved from CEP Website on May 10, 2004, at www.ctredpol.org/pubs/nclb_press_release_jan2003.html.

5. Baker, E., Linn, R., Herman, J. (Spring 2002) No Child Left Behind. *The CRESST Line*, Center for Research on Evaluation, Standards & Student Testing, UCLA, pp. 1–5.

6. Ibid.

7. Linn, R. (Winter 2003). *Requirements for Measuring Annual Yearly Progress*, Policy Brief 6, Center for Research on Evaluation, Standards & Student Testing at UCLA, pp. 1–5.

8. Sacks, P. (2001). *Standardized Minds: The High Price of America's Testing Culture and What We Can Do to Change It*. Cambridge, MA: Perseus Publishing, pp. 27–32.

9. Schemo, D. (July 11, 2003). "Questions on Data Cloud Luster of Houston Schools," *The New York Times*, p. A1.

10. Haney, W., Madaus, G., Abrams, L., Wheelock, A., et al. (January 2003). *The Education Pipeline in the United States, 1970–2000*. National Board on Educational Testing and Public Policy, Boston College. Retrieved January 20, 2003 at www.bc.edu/research/nbetpp/reports.html.

11. National Board on Educational Testing and Public Policy, Boston College. (January 20, 2003). *Where Have All the Students Gone?* Press release dated Jan. 18, 2003. Retrieved January 20, 2003 at www.bc.edu/research/nbetpp/statements/nbr3_press.pdf.

12. Harvie, K. (February 2003). "ESEA." *Maine Educator*. Vol. 63, Number 6, p. 1.

13. Prah, P. (December 9, 2002). *New Rules May Guarantee F's For Many Schools*. Stateline.org. Retrieved May 1, 2004, at www.stateline.org/stateline/?pa=story&sa=showStoryInfo&id=275753.

14. Mosteller, F., Moynihan, D. P. (1972). A Pathbreaking Report. In F. Mosteller and D. P. Moynihan (Eds.), *On Equality of Educational Opportunity* (pp. 3–66). New York: Vintage.

15. Ibid.; and Jencks, C. S. (1972). The Coleman Report and the Conventional Wisdom (pp. 69–115).

16. Phillips, M., Brooks-Gunn, J., Duncan, G. (1998). "Family Background, Parenting Practices, and the Black-White Test Score Gap." In C. Jencks and M. Phillips (Eds.), *The Black-White Test Score Gap* (pp. 103–145). Washington, DC: Brookings Institution Press.

17. United States Department of Education, The National Commission on Excellence in Education. (1983). *A Nation at Risk: The Imperative for Educational Reform*. Retrieved May 1, 2004 at www.ed.gov/pubs/NatAtRisk/title.html.

18. University of Massachusetts Donahue Institute. (March 2000). Effective School Districts in Massachusetts: A Study of Student Performance on the 1999 MCAS Assessments. Retrieved May 1, 2004 at www.donahue.umassp.edu/docs/?item_id=3524.

19. Sacks, P. (2001). Standardized Minds: The High Price of America's Testing Culture and What We Can Do to Change It. Cambridge, MA: Perseus Publishing (pp. 143–151).

20. Atienza, H. (October 11, 2002). Albertson Foundation Offers Rewards to Schools. *Idaho Statesman*. Local p. 1.

21. Goodnough, A. (September 25, 2002). "New York Superintendents to Get Bonuses if Test Scores Rise." *The New York Times*, p. A1.

22. Jacob, B. A. (2001). "Getting Tough? The Impact of Mandatory High School Graduation Exams on Student Achievement and Dropout Rates." *Educational Evaluation and Policy Analysis 23*(2), 99–122.

23. Orlich, D. C. (June 12, 2003). "An Examination of the Longitudinal Effect of the Washington Assessment of Student Learning (WASL) on Student Achievement." *Education Policy Analysis Archives 11*(18). Retrieved May 10, 2004, from epaa.asu.edu/epaa/v11n18/.

24. Amrein, A. L., Berliner, D. C. (March 28, 2002). High-Stakes Testing, Uncertainty, and Student Learning. *Education Policy Analysis Archives 10*(18). Retrieved May 10, 2004, from epaa.asu.edu/epaa/v10n18/.

25. Whitehead, A. N. (1929). *The Aims of Education*. New York: Free Press (pp. 1–14).

10

Where Do the Children Play?

SHARNA OLFMAN

Well I think it's fine building Jumbo planes,

or taking a ride on a cosmic train,

switch on summer from a slot machine,

yes get what you want to, if you want,

cause you can get anything.

I know we've come a long way,

we're changing day to day.

But tell me,

where do the children play?

Cat Stevens[1]

Cat Stevens wrote these lyrics in 1970 for an eerily prescient song called *Where Do the Children Play*. The song predicted that as technologies transformed and infiltrated our lives, play would begin to disappear from the landscape of childhood. Indeed, creative, open-ended play is rapidly vanishing from our homes, outdoor spaces, and schools. Today instead, children consume forty hours of media each week (mostly on screens), surpassing the time given to every activity but sleep.[2] As media moguls compete for their market share,

these entertainments are increasingly rapid-paced, violent, and sexualized, jolting children out of their age-appropriate activities and
encroaching not only on the time available to play, but on their very
capacity for deeply imaginative play. As economic and cultural
constraints force parents to work longer days and weeks, the "block
parents" who once kept neighborhood play within safe boundaries
are relics of an earlier era. Whereas a generation ago, parents insisted
that their children go *outside* to play, increasingly, parents rely on
"electronic babysitters" to keep kids *inside*, or alternatively in structured after-school programs. With the intense escalation of standardized testing and curricula in the public school system, many
preschools and most kindergartens are emphasizing structured
academic work in lieu of play. While the current mantra among
education reformers is *No Child Left Behind*, as Peter Sacks suggests
in chapter nine, it may be more apt to rephrase it as *No Child Left*.[3]

Upon rereading several classic children's novels to my own children recently, I was struck by a common feature among them. The
children who populate *Little Women, Secret Garden, All of a Kind Family, The Railway Children*, and *National Velvet*, to name a few, *play
make-believe games well into mid-adolescence*. This is in stark contrast to
the contemporary American play scene in which Barbies are passé
by preschool, five-year-olds are playing with edgy, streetwise Bratz
dolls while grooving to Britney, and pre-teens have long since
moved on to electronic games, TV shows, movies, and music with
ultra-violent and explicitly sexual content. Ironically, as children
abandon their time-honored habits, many adults are enjoying a "second childhood." Witness the mushrooming of mindless adult entertainment on TV and the Internet, the second coming of Las Vegas,
and voter apathy during a time of national and international turmoil. A survey released in July 2004 by the National Endowment for
the Arts reported that the amount of time American adults across all
socioeconomic and ethnic groups spent reading had plummeted.[4]

What, if any, are the consequences of the loss of play in children's
lives? Is it really so problematic for children to adopt the outward
trappings of adulthood in their dress, activities, and talk? Should
we care about the loss of innocence and make-believe when so
many dire matters—war, terrorism, environmental decay, poverty—
weigh heavily on our collective consciousness? Perhaps—as those
who have spearheaded the most recent set of educational reforms
believe—it is wise to direct children's attention rapidly away from
play and toward the body of facts deemed necessary to be competent citizens in our technologically advanced society.

In this chapter, I will argue that not only is the demise of play a cause for profound concern, but part and parcel of the myriad other stressors in children's lives discussed throughout this book.

Thousands of studies spanning four decades have established incontrovertibly that creative play is a catalyst for social, emotional, moral, motoric, perceptual, intellectual, linguistic, and neurological development. Many of our greatest thinkers locate their capacity for original and profound thought in their imaginative abilities, first developed through creative play in early childhood.[5] Recollections of child Holocaust survivors reveal that even in the degraded and desperate circumstances of the concentration camps, play sustained them. Across socioeconomic, ethnic, and cultural divides, play is a constant in childhood.[6] It is a central feature in the lives of all young primates and most young mammals, underscoring its lengthy evolutionary history and adaptive value.[7] Research has established a strong correlation between the period of greatest playfulness and the time when brain connections are most actively made.[8]

ACADEMIC SUCCESS IS PREDICATED ON PLAY

According to Erik Erikson's theory of psychosocial stages, the central challenge for young children is the development of *initiative* through fantasy play. Children the world over engage in vivid fantasy play between the ages of three and five. These activities are not mere diversions, but vital exercises that spark creative potential. When we force children to foreclose on the stage of initiative, and then prematurely push them into the stage of *industry*, we may indeed succeed in getting some children to read, write, and complete math equations precociously. But we may also be creating a cohort of children who lack spontaneity, creativity, and a love of learning.[9] As Stanley Greenspan's compelling research demonstrates, emotional awareness is not merely a form of intelligence, but rather a cornerstone of *all* aspects of intellectual development.[10] Children who are not emotionally engaged with the material they are learning and by the teachers who instruct them cannot grow intellectually. Teachers who facilitate healthy play in the early childhood classroom provide an ideal means of integrating social, emotional, and intellectual growth in a stage-appropriate way. In the wake of the No Child Left Behind Act, however, there is a growing disconnect between what education majors learn about optimal child development and what they are told to do in the classroom, which increasingly, is to follow prescribed curricula and to sideline play in preparation for standardized testing.

School reforms did not just drop out of the sky. Over the past few decades, American children have not been performing well in international tests comparing children's math, reading, and science competency. I too believe that our public school system should undergo reform. However, the creation of *standards* and *account-ability* must be grounded in principles of child development and humane pedagogy. If the mandate of the public school system is to support children's capacity to become thoughtful, caring, creative citizens capable of exercising independent judgment and free will, then treating age-appropriate, play-based curricula as expendable diversions in preschool and kindergarten is not the answer.

Perhaps, though, it is a quintessentially American answer, in a culture where "faster is better." There is a well-known anecdote about Jean Piaget—the famous Swiss cognitive psychologist—that he did not like to speak to American audiences because after he had described the natural pattern of children's development, Americans would invariably ask, "Yes, but how can we get them to do things faster?"

Piaget taught us that development unfolds over time in recognizable stages that nonetheless allows for considerable individual variation.[11] In each of these stages, a child's understanding of her world is qualitatively different, and in the preschool and kindergarten years, children think and learn optimally through play. We embrace stage theories that pertain to our children's physical development: they must be able to sit before they can stand, stand before they can walk, and so on. At the same time, we understand that the child who enters puberty at sixteen as opposed to twelve is nonetheless normal, and may tower over us five years hence. However, we have no such patience with respect to cognitive abilities. Woe to the American child who reads and writes at seven, rather than five! She will almost certainly be subject to at least one diagnostic label, even though seven is the normative age for beginning reading instruction in a majority of European countries. (More on this point below.)

If this seems to be an idealistic or romantic notion—that four-, five-, and six-year-olds should be learning through play, let's consider the following research, which gives us a window into the choices that countries whose children are faring particularly well in international comparisons are making. It was, after all, these international comparisons that catalyzed our most recent educational reforms. In a highly respected international survey conducted last year by the Organization of Economic Cooperation and Development (OECD),

Finland came in first in literacy and placed in the top five in math and science among thirty-one industrialized nations. The rankings were based on reading, math, and science tests given to a sample of fifteen-year-olds attending both public and private schools. U.S. students placed in the middle of the pack.[12]

Finland's recipe for success? Children there start learning to read in grade one at seven years of age, on the theory that play is the most effective learning tool in the early years and that it sets the stage for a lifelong love of learning. Preschool for six-year-olds in Finland is optional. At first, the seven-year-olds lag behind their peers in other countries in reading, but they catch up almost immediately and then excel. Also, from grades one through nine, after every forty-five-minute lesson, students are let loose outside for fifteen minutes so they can burn off steam with physical or musical activities. Art, music, physical education, woodwork, and crafts—subjects that are increasingly deemed expendable in U.S. public schools—are required subjects throughout the grades. (How much Ritalin might be spared if all American schoolchildren had the freedom to "burn off steam" every forty-five minutes and participate in physical education, art, music, and crafts on a regular basis?) Although there is a standard national curriculum, teachers in Finland are held in very high regard and have considerable authority to devise and revise curricula suitable to individual students.

While the United States continues to slash play from its preschool and kindergarten curricula, several European nations, including those in the United Kingdom, are reforming their school systems in ways that echo Finland's choices: increasing the age at which children begin formal academic subjects, utilizing play-based curricula in the early years, and eliminating standardized testing in the early grades. The catalyst for these changes is a growing, research-based recognition of the success of developmentally appropriate curricula that do not arbitrarily divide children's cognitive, social, and emotional needs.[13]

In December 2000, the British House of Commons Education Select Committee issued a report stating that there was "no conclusive evidence that children gained from being taught the 3Rs before the age of six." Furthermore, creative play and small class size were deemed *essential* in early childhood education. The report expressed the following concerns about early academics:

> The current focus on targets for older children in reading and writing inevitably tends to limit the vision and confidence of early childhood educators. Such downward pressure risks undermining children's

motivation and their disposition to learn, thus lowering rather than raising levels of achievement in the long term.... Inappropriate formalized assessment of children at an early age currently results in too many children being labeled as failures, when the failure in fact, lies with the system.[14]

Research submitted to the committee from the British Association for Early Childhood Education underscored this point of view:

> Comparisons with other countries suggest there is no benefit in starting formal instruction before six. The majority of other European countries admit children to school at six or seven following a three year period of pre-school education which focuses on social and physical development. Yet standards in literacy and numeracy are generally higher in those countries than in the UK, despite our earlier starting age.[15]

It is unfathomable that the United States is moving its approach to education further and further away from that of the very countries whose academic achievements it strives to emulate, and in a manner that ignores decades of child development research.

THE NATURE OF PLAY

Having established that play is advantageous to development in the early years, we will now turn our attention to *how* creative play translates into developmental and academic gain. While many kinds of play and many play experts compete for our attention, I will focus on *make-believe* play—also referred to as dramatic, sociodramatic, creative, and imaginative play—as seen through the theoretical lenses of Lev Vygotsky and Jeffrey Kane.

Vygotsky was a Russian psychologist whose work on cognitive development from the twenties finally found its way to the United States in the seventies with an immediate and profound impact on the disciplines of child development and education. According to Vygotsky, "In play it is as though [the child] is a head taller than himself" as he learns to symbolize objects and events, delay gratification, practice self-regulation, assimilate adult roles, exercise imagination, practice motor skills, and develop emotional, social and verbal literacy.[16]

Vygotsky's observations are most relevant to sociodramatic play—when two or more children construct and act out play scenes together. In contrast to the relative freedom of solitary play, in social play, children must work out a shared set of rules and symbols. They must come to an agreement that the blanket represents their home, the block structure is a stove and that Sally will be the "daddy." They must work out a shared understanding about what a "daddy" or a "mommy" is and does, and how the actors embodying these roles may or may not interact with one another. In order to remain welcome in the play group, they must subordinate their ideas and impulses to the shared ideas of the group. Paradoxically, while we idealize make-believe play as a liberation from the constraints of reality, in fact, social play leads the child to discover through direct experience why rules of conduct exist, why impulse control is necessary, and what the functions and roles of the different adults who populate their world are. In playing out their scenarios, children must "abstract" the defining features of "mommies" and "babies" and "bakers" and "husbands," as well as the rules that guide social discourse. Children do not always utilize roles that exist in reality. Their play might just as easily be about superheroes and fairies. In these instances, children are likely exploring and developing their emotional lives, their fears, anger, love, and longing.[17]

The work of Jeffrey Kane, an educational philosopher at Long Island University, has special relevance to what play experts have termed "dramatic play," meaning solitary make-believe play.[18] Our media-drenched culture rarely provides children with quiet, unscheduled time, alone, in natural settings. As we explore Kane's ideas, we will come to see that this is a profound loss indeed. In a chapter that he contributed to the anthology *All Work and No Play... : How Educational Reforms are Harming Our Preschoolers*, he questions the value of disembodied facts that are learned rather than discovered: what we term "abstract knowledge." He reminds us that when children play at being mother, a kitten, or the wind for that matter, they do not merely mimic their role models, but they *become* them in their play. Through the exercise of their imaginative capacities, and the full use of their bodies and senses, they experience directly what it feels like, and means, to be a mother or a kitten or the wind. This type of play provides young children with lessons that are infinitely deeper and more age-appropriate than the fact sheets or Internet "field trips" they might encounter in an academic preschool.

While preschool children who formally study the properties of, say, butterflies, might spout an impressive array of scientific facts, the child who has the gift of time to observe the dance of a butterfly in its natural environment, and to imagine herself as that butterfly in her play, will have a much richer learning experience. How might this close encounter with a single butterfly in its natural habitat be a superior lesson to an hour spent in a classroom memorizing the names and identifying features of twenty different butterflies? Or observing the same twenty butterflies mounted on a wall at a museum? The child, left alone to gaze and wonder at and then embody the butterfly in her play, trusts the discoveries of her senses and her bodily experiences. She begins to understand what it means to be a butterfly in relationship to other natural delights in her environment, and in the process acquires a deep empathy with her subject. Also, she is acquiring the potential to make new scientific or artistic discoveries by developing her imaginative capacities, as opposed to memorizing other people's decontextualized discoveries whose meaning and relevance may elude her.

When asked how she came to discover properties of genes through her research with maize that her colleagues failed to discover, Nobel prize-winning scientist Barbara McClintock spoke of her capacity to imagine herself into the chromosomes she was studying in much the same way that Einstein spoke of his discoveries about time and space. When we have never played in natural settings, when we have never imaginatively lived as a tiger or a rabbit, but have only been taught atomistic facts about mammals in school, or when "Disney" versions of these creatures override our own imaginings, then like Plato's cave dwellers, our knowledge of the animal world will be a shadow knowledge handed to us by others, as opposed to knowledge gained first-hand that is deeply experienced and trusted. Is it any wonder then that so many students forget what they have learned in physics and history the moment their exams have ended? Most likely their knowledge was a surface knowledge, not richly experienced, understood, appreciated, or assimilated into the broader context of life. While conventional lessons may build upon our earlier free-form discoveries, they cannot replace them. I would venture to say that we never outgrow the need for education that is experiential and contextualized. In the absence of a deep empathy for and understanding of our place in nature, we feel few qualms about using science and technological discoveries as vehicles for dominating and mining nature for resources, and for destroying our ecosystem and our health in the process.

LANGUAGE AND LITERACY

I would like to focus briefly on how play facilitates language and literacy in light of the intensity of the current focus on early reading in preschool and kindergarten settings. It is a sad irony that make-believe play, which has so much to contribute to language development and literacy, is viewed by policy makers, educators, and parents as a hindrance rather than a tool. The building blocks of literacy are so much more than letter recognition and phonics. Children must also acquire a rich vocabulary, the ability to understand and follow a narrative, the capacity to empathize with the characters they encounter so as to imagine themselves into the circumstances of their lives, diverse experiences that help them relate to what they are reading, the ability to "see" the characters in their minds' eyes, and the patience and desire to read.

Make-believe play facilitates many of these building blocks. First, sociodramatic play requires children to articulate their ideas to the group, while at the same time they are introduced to new modes of expression and vocabulary that are quickly assimilated because the children are learning in such an engaging context. Second, make-believe play is an exercise in empathy, as children learn what it feels like to be different characters and what those characters' needs and motives are. Third, make-believe requires children to visualize the characters and scenarios that populate their play. The capacity to empathize with and visualize the characters and scenarios in a book, whether it be a work of fiction, history, or biology, is the difference between a reading experience that lies flat on the page and one that is deeply experienced, understood, and assimilated by the reader. Finally, make-believe play teaches children to create and follow a narrative, just as they must do when reading or writing a story. Without these foundational experiences, some children may suffer from a condition that Jane Healy terms "alliteracy." They read fluently but cannot understand or make use of the material they have read, and they take no pleasure in reading.[19]

Recently, while I was walking in the woods with my seven-year-old daughter, she stopped and pointed to some sun-dappled leaves. "Do you see the sparkles in the leaves?" she asked. "Each sparkle is something good that will happen to me when I grow up."

"What a wonderful thought," I replied. "Thank you for telling me."

"Children think these things all the time," she explained. "We just don't tell grown-ups too often because we think they'll tell us that it's silly or that it isn't true."

I would like to add to this already impressive list of benefits that play confers on childhood that when children are given the time and space to "make believe" without being rushed prematurely into the logic of adult thought, it helps them to acquire the optimism that wonderful possibilities, as yet unknown, await them, as well as the confidence to pursue them.

REINVENTING THE WHEEL

It strikes me that every few years, developmental psychologists and early childhood educators must "reinvent the wheel" and launch yet another campaign to prove the importance of play in early childhood and to reinstate it in the educational curriculum. Why is play such an embattled element in children's lives? Why do we not have a more intuitive grasp of the import of an activity that is a universal of childhood and that we share with all of our primate cousins?

Descartes's Legacy

Part of the answer can be located in Descartes's legacy to contemporary western thought. As Stuart Shanker and Jeffrey Kane propose in *All Work and No Play*, "with respect to our current conception of human knowledge, we are the intellectual heirs of the great seventeenth century philosopher, Rene Descartes."[20] Descartes believed that emotions were no more than base instincts and that reason was the opposite of emotional and bodily experience. For Descartes, "[t]he cognitive universe is composed of unquestionable bits of information, absolute and fixed, that are tied together by strict and logical laws."[21]

These schizoid tendencies to split thought from emotion, mind from body, and fact from context, continue to shape twenty-first-century attitudes, undergirding our blind faith in technological innovation and our attraction to mechanistic models of the mind. Indeed, the information processing model of thinking, with the computer as its guiding metaphor, has become the backbone of American educational philosophy.[22] According to the information processing model, thinking involves processing, storing, and downloading information, in much the same fashion as a computer. Within this framework, fact sheets, computer drills, and multiple choice tests are eminently reasonable vehicles for learning and for testing what has been learned. This also explains why so many school districts feel that cutting art, music, and physical education, and increasing class sizes so that they can devote more funds toward wiring their classrooms, are worthwhile trade-offs. Play, direct experience, and mentoring do not have a valued place in this worldview. This may also explain why we are not more fearful of and outraged by the proliferation of screens and screen time in children's lives, and the de facto absence of regulations to guide their content. The fact that children are spending more time viewing screens than doing any other activity but sleeping (and that we haven't made it a national policy to investigate their impact and regulate their content) is deeply disconcerting.

Perhaps Descartes's legacy has become a self-fulfilling prophecy because in our race to embrace and emulate our machines, we appear to have lost sight of our *human* potential. In sharp contrast to a computer, a child possesses a *self*, which imbues her with the desire to give her life meaning, purpose, and a moral compass. A child is motivated to learn by the desire to be grounded in her family, in her community, and in the natural order, and yet at the same time to express herself and place her own personal stamp on the world. Her thinking is infused with emotion, sensory, and bodily-kinesthetic experience, artistry, imagination, and soulfulness. It is through this uniquely *human* prism, in the service of uniquely *human* needs, that she "processes information." It is thus a tragic irony that we idealize the disembodied, emotionless computer and try to teach our children to think according to its operating principles. Unfortunately, however, when mere information is what we seek to instill in or elicit from our students, the content and context of the information at issue become completely secondary to one's ability to access and manipulate it. Real psychological growth ceases, and the educational system encourages a growing cynicism and despair.

Screen Nation

The inordinate amount of time children spend consuming media not only robs them of valuable opportunities that could be devoted to quiet contemplative play and to social play, *it also undermines their ability to play*. In the absence of effective government regulations of the media, corporations vie for children's attention by upping the levels of sexual and violent content (often linking the two), and by constantly increasing the pace of the action. In her book *Failure to Connect*, Jane Healy articulates how both the content and process of

watching and interacting with screens "short circuits" brain development, in ways that undermine the acquisition of impulse control,
imagination, higher-order thinking, and the ability to generate
visual imagery.[23] A vicious cycle is set in motion. The capacities
needed to initiate play are undermined by screen culture, and the
subsequent loss of playtime undermines these same capacities even
further.

Preschool and kindergarten teachers are reporting that for the
first time, they are witnessing a generation of children, many of
whom literally don't know how to "make-believe," who have to be
taught to play. Grade school teachers are finding that some of
their students don't spontaneously visualize the characters they
are reading about—and so reading becomes a colossal bore.[24]
Increasingly, the "play" that children are bringing to the preschool
and kindergarten classroom is a repetitive mimicry of violent
sequences that aired on their televisions or video game screens
the night before, not tempered by the impulse control and judgment necessary to avoid inflicting injury or pain on other "players." If this is what is now construed as play, then small wonder
that parents and educators sometimes lose sight of the value
of play.

Time Crunch

Healthy play is facilitated by adults, not so much to serve as
"play partners," but rather as models of emotionally centered
human beings engaged in activities that become the raw materials
for play. Whether mother or father is raking the lawn, cooking a
meal, or doing a craft, these activities are woven into healthy play.[25]
But increasingly, parents aren't home much with their children. In
the wake of "welfare reform," our government has failed to provide women re-entering the work force with regulated, high-quality, affordable childcare. As the minimum wage continues to
stagnate, the ranks of "working poor" parents continue to swell.
Wage freezes are becoming ubiquitous among the working and
middle classes even as their workweeks lengthen, and so parents
are burning out. When we add the cult of individualism and the
rampant consumerism in the United States, which prompt us to
place our own needs first, the results are fairly predictable. Already-
exhausted parents may elect to abandon their children to screens,
structured activities, or the streets, while they tune in and "tune
out" with the aid of their own screen entertainments.

When my daughter was five, she told me after visiting a conservatory that "flower fairies" had brushed against her legs. "Did the leaves of the plants touch your legs?" I offered. "No, Mommy, they were flower fairies," she reiterated with quiet resolve before drifting off to sleep.

What would my daughter's inner life be like if she had never been visited by "flower fairies"? Despite decades of empirical research on play, there is much that we still do not understand—that we may never fully understand—and yet must respect and honor. Perhaps in children's imaginative play lie the seeds of the wonder that we feel when we gaze at a sunset, or a starry sky whose secrets will never fully be revealed to us, filling us with a deep reverence for the splendors and mysteries of the universe, and our place within it.

Having begun this chapter with a reference to a singer whose lyrics predicted that play might be under threat in the twenty-first century, I will end by giving thanks to Raffi, whose body of work is a gift to the imaginative play of children everywhere and reminds us that we are not alone in our desire to restore play to the forefront of children's lives. His deceptively simple lyrics to the song *Let's Play* invoke the deep evolutionary imperative of child's play.

> Lion cubs and bear cubs,
>
> pups and kittens do it,
>
> baby belugas do it too.
>
> Baby chimps and elephants and sea otters do it.
>
> Play's the thing, a magic ring,
>
> won't you play with me?

Raffi, 2001[26]

NOTES

1. Stevens, C. (1970). "Where Do the Children Play?" in *Tea for the Tillerman*.

2. See Linn, S. (2005). The Commercialization of Childhood. In S. Olman (Ed.), *Childhood Lost: How American Culture Is Failing Our Kids* (chap. 5 in this volume). Westport, CT: Praeger.

3. See Sacks, P. (2005). "No Child Left": What Are Schools for in a Democratic Society? In S. Olman (Ed.), *Childhood Lost: How American Culture Is Failing Our Kids* (chap. 9 in this volume). Westport, CT: Praeger.

4. Solomon, A. (July 2004). The Closing of the American Book, *New York Times*.

5. Berk, L. (2001). *Awakening Children's Minds*. Oxford, New York; Kane, J., & H. Carpenter. (2003). Imagination and the Growth of the

Human Mind. In S. Olfman (Ed.), *All Work and No Play: How Educational Reforms Are Harming Our Preschoolers*. Westport, CT: Praeger.

6. Bruner, J. Jolly, & K. Sylva (Eds.) (1978). *Play: Its Role in Development and Evolution*. New York: Basic Books; Olfman, S. (Ed.) (2003). *All Work and No Play: How Educational Reforms Are Harming Our Preschoolers*. Westport, CT: Praeger.

7. Bruner, J. Jolly, & K. Sylva (Eds.). (1978). *Play: Its Role in Development and Evolution*. New York: Basic Books.

8. Angier, N. (October 20, 1992). The Purpose of Playful Frolics: Training for Adulthood. *New York Times*, pp. C1, C8.

9. Erikson, E. (1985). *Childhood and Society*. New York: W. W. Norton.

10. Greenspan, S. I. (1997). *The Growth of the Mind: And the Endangered Origins of Intelligence*. Cambridge: Perseus Books.

11. Piaget, J. (1950). *The Psychology of Intelligence*. New York: International Universities Press.

12. Alvarez, L. (April 9, 2004). Flocking to Finland, Land of Literate Children. *Suutarila Journal, New York Times*.

13. Clouder, C. (2003). Early Childhood Education: Lessons from Europe. In S. Olfman (Ed.), *All Work and No Play: How Educational Reforms Are Harming Our Preschoolers*. Westport, CT: Praeger.

14. House of Commons (December, 2000). *Education Select Committee Report*.

15. House of Commons (December, 2000). *Education Select Committee Report: First Report: Early Years*, paragraph 2.

16. Vygotsky, L. (1978). Play and its role in the mental development of the child. In J. Bruner, J. Jolly, & K. Sylva (Eds.), *Play: Its Role in Development and Evolution* (pp. 537–554). New York: Basic Books.

17. Berk, L. (2001). *Awakening Children's Minds*. New York: Oxford Press.

18. Kane, J., & H. Carpenter. (2003). Imagination and the Growth of the Human Mind. In Olfman (Ed.), *All Work and No Play*.

19. Healy, J. (1998). *Failure to Connect: How Computers Affect Our Children's Minds—and What We Can Do About It*. New York: Touchstone.

20. Kane & Carpenter, Imagination and the Human Mind; Shanker, S. (2003). The Vital Role of Emotion in Education. In Olfman, *All Work and No Play*.

21. Ibid., p. 127.

22. Olfman, S. (2003). Pathogenic Trends in Early Childhood Education. In Olfman (Ed.), *All Work and No Play*.

23. Healy, *Failure to Connect*.

24. Almon, J. (2003). The Vital Role of Play In Early Childhood Education. In Olfman (Ed.), *All Work and No Play*.

25. Ibid.

26. "Let's Play," from the CD *Let's Play*. Words and music by Raffi, Michael Creber. © 2001 Homeland Publishing, a division of Troubadour Music Inc. All rights reserved. Used by permission.

Index

About the Editor and the Contributors

Sharna Olfman is a clinical psychologist and an associate professor of developmental psychology at Point Park University, where she is also the founding director of the *Childhood and Society Symposium*. Olfman is the editor of the *Childhood in America* book series for Praeger Publishers. She recently published *All Work and No Play: How Educational Reforms Are Harming Our Preschoolers*. Dr. Olfman is a member of the Council on Human Development and a partner in the Alliance for Childhood. She has written on gender development, women's mental health, infant care, and child psychopathology.

Laura E. Berk received her PhD from the University of Chicago and is a distinguished professor of psychology at Illinois State University. She has published widely in the fields of early childhood development and education, focusing on the effects of school environments on children's development, the social origins and functional significance of children's private speech, and the role of make-believe play in the development of self-regulation. Her books include *Private Speech: From Social Interaction to Self-Regulation*; *Scaffolding Children's Learning: Vygotsky and Early Childhood Education*; and *Awakening Children's Minds: How Parents and Teachers Can Make a Difference*. She has also authored three widely distributed textbooks: *Child Development*; *Infants, Children, and Adolescents*; and *Development through the Lifespan*.

Varda Burstyn is an award-winning author and public policy consultant who has written widely on the culture and politics of film, fine art, television, and sport. As a lifelong environmentalist and health activist, she has also written about and worked on documentary films concerned with new ideas in sickness and health, reproductive technologies, and genetic engineering. Her books include *The Rites of Men: Manhood, Politics and the Culture of Sport*, and *Water Inc.*, an environmental thriller about the current water crisis. Her work has appeared in scholarly and popular journals, books, radio, television, and film.

Gloria DeGaetano is the founder and CEO of the Parent Coaching Institute, the nation's first graduate-level parent coach training program, which offers parent coaching services to individuals, agencies, schools, and businesses. A nationally acclaimed educator, author, and speaker, Ms. DeGaetano has over twenty-five years' educational experience as a classroom teacher, reading specialist, school district administrator, university instructor, and national consultant. Her books include *Screen Smarts: A Family Guide to Media Literacy; Stop Teaching Our Kids to Kill: A Call to Action against TV, Movie, and Video Game Violence* (with Lt. Col. Dave Grossman); and *Parenting Well in a Media Age: Keeping Our Kids Human*. Ms. DeGaetano has produced educational videos for several community media literacy coalitions, including *TV and Video: Children at Risk, Media Literacy: An Impact Video for Youth*, and *Maximizing Your Child's Potential: Healthy Brain Development in a Media Age*—the first parent education video about the impact of screen technologies on young brains.

Sylvia Ann Hewlett is director of the gender and public policy program at the School of International and Public Affairs, Columbia University. She is also the founding president of the Center for Work-Life Policy, a nonprofit organization that seeks to develop policies that enhance work-life balance. The first woman to head up the Economic Policy Council, a think tank comprising 125 business and labor leaders, Dr. Hewlett is well known for her expertise on gender and workplace issues. Her books include *When the Bough Breaks* (winner of a Robert F. Kennedy Memorial Book Prize), *Creating A Life* (named by *BusinessWeek* as one of the top ten books of 2002), and *The War against Parents* (co-authored with Cornel West). Her articles have appeared in the *New York Times*, the *Financial Times*, and the *Harvard Business Review*. She has taught at Cambridge, Columbia, and Princeton Universities and held fellowships at the Institute for Public Policy Research in London and the Center for the Study of Values in Public Life at Harvard. She has appeared on *60 Minutes*, *The Today Show*, *Good Morning America*, *Newshour with Jim Lehrer*, *Charlie Rose*, *Newsnight with Aaron Brown*, *NBC Nightly News*, *Oprah*, *The View*, *All Things Considered*, and *Talk of the Nation*, and has been lampooned on *Saturday Night Live*. A Kennedy Scholar and graduate of Cambridge University, Hewlett earned her PhD degree in economics at London University.

Katherine Battle Horgen received her PhD in clinical psychology from Yale University. She consults with the Yale Center for Eating and Weight Disorders and has written extensively on public health approaches to obesity. She is co-author of *Food Fight: The Inside Story of the Food Industry, America's Obesity Crisis, and What We Can Do about It* (with Kelly D. Brownell).

Diane E. Levin is a professor of education at Wheelock College, where she teaches human development and early childhood education and runs the institute called Media Education in a Violent Society. She is an internationally recognized expert on the effects of violence, media, and commercial culture on children. She is the author of six books including *Remote Control Childhood, Combating the Hazards of Media Culture*, and the newly revised *Teaching Young Children in Violent Times: Building a Peaceable Classroom*. She is a founder of Teachers Resisting Unhealthy Children's Entertainment (TRUCE) and Campaign for a Commercial Free Childhood (CCFC).

Susan Linn is the associate director of the Media Center at Judge Baker Children's Center and an instructor in psychiatry at Harvard Medical School. She is the author of *Consuming Kids: The Hostile Takeover of Childhood*. Dr. Linn is a founder of Campaign for a Commercial Free Childhood (CCFC).

Peter Sacks is an author and social critic. His most recent book is *Standardized Minds: The High Price of America's Testing Culture and What We Can Do to Change It*. His essays on education and American culture have appeared in the *Nation*, the *Chronicle of Higher Education*, the *Boston Review*, the *Los Angeles Times*, the *New York Times*, *Change Magazine*, *Education Week*, and many others.

Gary Sampson is a professor emeritus from Portland State University in Portland, Oregon, where he served (at various times) as a reference librarian, chairman of the library reference department, and systems librarian. While at Portland State, Mr. Sampson was instrumental in creating an annual regional conference called Online Northwest, which dealt with Web-based information sources. Before his library career, Mr. Sampson was a newspaper reporter for several years in New Jersey, Ohio, and California.

Meredith F. Small is a writer and professor of anthropology at Cornell University. Trained as a primate behaviorist, she now writes about all areas of anthropology, natural history, and health. Besides numerous publications in academic journals, Dr. Small contributes regularly to *Discover* and *New Scientist*, and she is a commentator on National Public Radio's *All Things Considered*. She is the author of five books, including *What's Love Got to Do with It? The Evolution of Human Mating*; *Our Babies, Ourselves: How Biology and Culture Shape the Way We Parent*, and *Kids*. Dr. Small is currently working on a book about the anthropology of mental health, titled *The Culture of Our Discontent*, in which she contrasts the now-standard medical model of mental illness with the causes and cures of "abnormal" behavior in traditional cultures.

Cornel West is a university professor of religion at Princeton University. Prior to his appointment at Princeton, he was the Alphonse Fletcher University Professor at Harvard University, teaching Afro-American studies and philosophy of religion. Henry Louis Gates Jr., chairman of Harvard's Department of Afro-American Studies, describes West as "one of America's most important public intellectuals, and a formidable scholar by any measure." He has taught at Yale, Union Theological Seminary, and Princeton University, where he was chair of the Department of Afro-American Studies. A well-respected speaker and authority on issues of race and religion, he was part of President Clinton's National Conversation on Race initiative. Recently, he was the W.E.B. Du Bois Lecturer at Harvard. West is a frequent media commentator; appearances have included *Nightline, Good Morning America, The Today Show, CNN Talk, ABC World News Tonight*, and *Charlie Rose*. He is a regular contributor on National Public Radio's *Tavis Smiley Show*. West is the author of numerous articles and books including *Prophetic Fragments, The Cornel West Reader*, the best-seller *Race Matters, The War against Parents* (co-authored with Sylvia Ann Hewlett), and the forthcoming *Democracy Matters*. Dr. West is a magna cum laude graduate of Harvard with an MA and PhD from Princeton.